On Foreign Service

Also from Westphalia Press

westphaliapress.org

The Idea of the Digital University

Bulwarks Against Poverty in America

Treasures of London

Avate Garde Politician

L'Enfant and the Freemasons

Baronial Bedrooms

Making Trouble for Muslims

Philippine Masonic Directory ~ 1918

Paddle Your Own Canoe

Opportunity and Horatio Alger

Careers in the Face of Challenge

Bookplates of the Kings

The Boy Chums Cruising in Florida Waters

Freemasonry in Old Buffalo

Original Cables from the Pearl Harbor Attack

Social Satire and the Modern Novel

The Essence of Harvard

The Genius of Freemasonry

A Definitive Commentary on Bookplates

James Martineau and Rebuilding Theology

No Bird Lacks Feathers

Gems of Song for the Eastern Star

Crime 3.0

Anti-Masonry and the Murder of Morgan

Understanding Art

Spies I Knew

Lodge "Himalayan Brotherhood" No. 459 C.E.

Ancient Masonic Mysteries

Collecting Old Books

Masonic Secret Signs and Passwords

Death Valley in '49

Lariats and Lassos

Mr. Garfield of Ohio

The Wisdom of Thomas Starr King

The French Foreign Legion

War in Syria

Naturism Comes to the United States

New Sources on Women and Freemasonry

Designing, Adapting, Strategizing in Online Education

Gunboat and Gun-runner

Meeting Minutes of Naval Lodge No. 4 F.A.A.M ~ 1812 & 1813

On Foreign Service

or
The Santa Cruz Revolution

by T.T. Jeans

WESTPHALIA PRESS
An imprint of Policy Studies Organization

Westphalia Press
An imprint of Policy Studies Organization
1527 New Hampshire Ave., NW
Washington, D.C. 20036
info@ipsonet.org

ISBN-13: 978-1633910362
ISBN-10: 1633910369

Cover design by Taillefer Long at Illuminated Stories:
www.illuminatedstories.com

Daniel Gutierrez-Sandoval, Executive Director
PSO and Westphalia Press

Devin Proctor, Director of Media and Publications
PSO and Westphalia Press

Updated material and comments on this edition
can be found at the Westphalia Press website:
www.westphaliapress.org

On Foreign Service

BOOKS BY
SURGEON REAR-ADMIRAL
T. T. JEANS, C.M.G., R.N.

A Naval Venture: The Story of a Gunroom in War-time.

Gunboat and Gun-runner: A Tale of the Persian Gulf.

John Graham, Sub-Lieutenant, R.N.: A Tale of the Atlantic Fleet.

On Foreign Service: or, The Santa Cruz Revolution.

Ford, of H.M.S. Vigilant: A Tale of the Chusan Archipelago.

Mr. Midshipman Glover, R.N.: A Tale of the Royal Navy.

BLACKIE AND SON, LIMITED
LONDON, GLASGOW, BOMBAY, AND TORONTO

On Foreign Service

Or, The Santa Cruz Revolution

BY

SURGEON REAR-ADMIRAL

T. T. JEANS, C.M.G., R.N.

Author of "Mr. Midshipman Glover, R.N."
"Ford of H.M.S. Vigilant"

Illustrated by William Rainey, R.I.

BLACKIE AND SON LIMITED
LONDON GLASGOW AND BOMBAY

c 197

"I HAULED IT UP HAND OVER HAND"

Preface

This story is based on experiences, of my own, in various parts of the world, and describes a Revolution in a South American Republic, and the part played by two armoured cruisers whilst protecting British interests.

It describes life aboard a modern man-of-war, and attempts to show how the command of the sea exercises a controlling influence on the issue of land operations.

As the proof sheets have been read by several officers of the Royal Navy and Royal Marines, and many suggestions and corrections made, the naval portion of the story may be taken to give an accurate description of the incidents narrated.

T. T. JEANS,
Surgeon Rear-Admiral, Royal Navy.

Contents

Chap.   Page

I. ORDERED TO SANTA CRUZ -   - 11

II. A REVOLUTION IMMINENT -   - 26

III. THE REVOLUTION BREAKS OUT -   - 48

IV. THE RESCUE OF THE SUB -   - 77

V. GERALD WILSON CAPTURES SAN FERNANDO   - 106

VI. THE *HECTOR* GOES TO SAN FERNANDO   - 136

VII. GENERAL ZORILLA FALLS BACK -   - 157

VIII. ZORILLA LOSES HIS GUNS -   - 178

IX. ZORILLA ATTACKS -   - 198

X. THE FIGHT ROUND THE CASINO -   - 211

XI. SAN FERNANDO ATTACKED FROM THE SEA -   - 235

XII. HOW WE FOUGHT THE FOUR POINT SEVENS   - 251

XIII. BAD NEWS FOR GERALD WILSON   - 267

XIV. *LA BUENA PRESIDENTE* FIGHTS   - 280

XV. THE SANTA CRUZ FLEET AGAIN -   - 301

XVI. THE ATTACK ON SANTA CRUZ -   - 321

XVII. THE EX-POLICEMAN -   - 350

XVIII. THE *HECTOR* GOES HOME -   - 377

Illustrations

		Facing Page
I HAULED IT UP HAND OVER HAND - - *Frontispiece*		
HIS EYES SIMPLY SPAT FIRE - - - - -		72
"IS THAT GERALD WILSON ABOARD?" - - - -		136
I GAVE THE FIRST A BLOW ON THE POINT OF HIS JAW -		184
I DODGED TO THE REAR OF THE FIRST WAGON - -		216
MR. BOSTOCK TAKES COMMAND - - - - - -		256
THE EFFECT OF THE SHELL - - - - - -		288
SCRAMBLING DOWN THE MOUNTAIN SIDE - - - -		336

CHAPTER I

Ordered to Santa Cruz

Written by Sub-Lieutenant William Wilson, R.N.

ONLY eight months ago Ginger Hood and I had been midshipmen aboard the old *Vengeance*, and of course had spent most of our time, in her, trying to get to windward of her sub, pull his leg, and dodge any job of work which came along. Now the boot was on the other leg, for we were sub-lieutenants ourselves—he in the *Hercules*, I in the *Hector*, with gun-rooms of our own to boss, and as we'd only been at the job for a month, you can guess that we hadn't quite settled down yet, and felt jolly much like fish out of water.

The *Hector* and *Hercules* were two big armoured cruisers, as like as two peas, and they had come straight out from England to Gibraltar to work up for their first gunnery practices. For the last ten days they had been lying inside the New Mole waiting for a strong south-easter to blow itself out, and we had taken the opportunity of trying to make our two gun-rooms friendly; for, as a matter of fact, they hated each other like poison, his mids. taking every opportunity of being rude to mine, and mine to his. These rows were always reported to us, and if we hadn't been such chums, I do believe that we, too, should have fallen out. If a *Hercules* mid. came aboard the *Hector* on duty, my chaps would let him wear his legs out on the quarterdeck for hours sooner than ask him down below, and you can guess that they were just as kind aboard the *Hercules* if any of my mids. had to go aboard her. I had sixteen of the beauties in my gun-room to look after, and Ginger had fifteen; if his were more bother to him than mine were to me, I don't wonder he thought that his hair was turning grey. Never did they meet ashore without a free fight or some trouble or another cropping up. The row had started on board the *Cornwall*, where they had all been together as cadets, over some wretched boat-race. The winning crew had used racing oars, which the second boat's crew either hadn't had the *savvy* to get, or didn't find out till too late that they might have used. However it was, there had been a glorious row at the time, and as some of my mids. had pulled in the losing boat and some of Ginger's in the winning one, both gun-rooms still kept the feud going.

Ginger and I thought that the best way to patch up their quarrel was to make them play matches against each other, and this we had done—'soccer,' hockey, and cricket on the dockyard ground, and a 'rugger' game on the North Front.

There wasn't the slightest improvement. I had jawed my chaps till I was tired, and Ginger had jawed his, without the least effect; and now they'd just spoilt what might have been a grand game of hockey by squabbling all the time, claiming fouls, and 'sticks,' and nonsense like that, every other minute.

The game had been so unpleasant that Ginger and I were thankful when it was finished, slipped on our coats and watched our two teams quarrelling and taunting each other as they left the ground in two separate groups.

'Look at the young fools, Billums!' Ginger said angrily. 'Did you ever see anything so perfectly idiotic?'

'Come along up to the Club,' I said savagely. 'We'll have some tea. It makes one feel perfectly hopeless. I'd like to cane the whole crowd of them.'

Up we went together, and found the Captains and a number of the ward-room fellows from the two ships lying back in the wicker chairs on the verandah, basking in the sun and waiting for afternoon tea. As we came up the steps, they sang out to know which gun-room had won.

'*Hercules* won, sir,' I told our Skipper, Captain Grattan. 'Won by four to two.'

'Tut, tut, boy! What's that now? Still one game ahead, ain't you?'

'No, sir, we're all square.'

'Well, beat 'em next time, lad.'

A jolly chap our Skipper was—short and plump and untidy, with a merry twinkle spreading over his funny old face, all wrinkled up with the strain of keeping his eyeglass in place. Everybody knew him as 'Old Tin Eye,' and he was so jolly unaffected that nobody could help liking him.

As we leant our hockey sticks up against the railings and sat down in the corner, we could hear him chaffing Captain Roger Hill, the tall, thin, beautifully dressed Skipper of the *Hercules*, and could jolly well see by the way he fidgeted in his chair that he didn't like it a little bit. Old Tin Eye would call him 'Spats,' and he didn't like it in public, and squirmed lest we inferior mortals should hear of it. I don't suppose he knew that nobody ever did call him anything but 'Spats.' You see, he never went ashore without white canvas spats over his boots, and they were very conspicuous.

Our Fleet Surgeon, Watson—a morose kind of chap —and Molineux, the Fleet Surgeon of the *Hercules*, stopped talking 'shop' to ask Ginger how many goals he'd scored (Ginger was the terror of his team); and Montague, our Gunnery Lieutenant, and Barton, their gunnery-man, left off talking about the coming gun-layers' 'test' to ask us if the gun-rooms had made up their row.

'No such luck, sir,' we said. 'They're worse, if anything.'

Whilst we were having our tea, one of the Club 'boys' brought along the little Gib. paper, and of course our Skipper had first turn.

'Cheer up, Spats, old boy!' he sang out loudly enough for every one to hear—he loved tormenting Captain Roger Hill; 'there's trouble in Santa Cruz again. Old Canilla, the President, has collared half-a-dozen Englishmen belonging to the Yucan Rubber Company, and won't give 'em up. If you've got any shares in it you'd better sell them.'

'Hello,' I sang out to Ginger. 'I've got a brother out there. He's supposed to be rubber-planting, but I'll bet he spends most of his time teaching his natives to bowl leg breaks at him. Hope they haven't collared him—I'm sorry for them if they have.'

We saw the telegrams ourselves later on, but there wasn't any more information. Old Gerald, my brother, didn't belong to the Yucan Company, and we forgot all about it because there was a much more exciting telegram above this one. The United Services had beaten Blackheath by fifteen points to five—a jolly sight more exciting that was, especially as I had played for the U.S. this season before we left England, and knew all the chaps playing on our side.

Well, that night I had the middle watch, and whilst the Angel and Cousin Bob (you don't know who they are yet, but you precious soon will) were making my cocoa, the light at the Europa Signal Station began flashing our number. I telephoned to the fore-bridge to smarten up the signalman, and ask what the dickens he meant by being asleep; and then, just for practice, and for something to do, leant up against the quarterdeck rails and took in the signal. 'Admiral Superintendent to Captain Grattan. Coal lighters will come alongside at day-break. (Full stop.) Both *Hector* and *Hercules* will fill up with coal and water as soon as possible, and will complete with ten days' fresh provisions. (Full stop.)'

A second or two later the signalman came running up with his signal-pad, and, not having the faintest idea what was in the wind, I took it down to the Skipper. I had to shake him before he would wake; and when he sat up in his bunk, found his eyeglass, tucked it into his eye, and read the signal, he chuckled, 'Tut, tut, boy; we're off somewhere—finish gunnery. Won't old Montague be sick of life? Show it to the Commander, and repeat it to old "Spats"—I mean Captain Roger Hill.'

As I was tapping at the Commander's door, Cousin Bob and the Angel came along, and I knew they were up to some dodge, for I could see them grinning in the light of the gangway lantern.

'Couldn't you let us off watch, as we've got to coal early to-morrow? Your cocoa's just inside the battery door,' they asked me as I went in.

The Commander was out of bed like a redshank,

read the signal, and gave me his orders for the morning. 'Can I let Temple and Sparks turn in, sir, as we're coaling early?'

'Confound them! I suppose they'd better, the young rascals. Turn the light off as you go out, and for heaven's sake make that lumbering ox of a sentry outside my cabin take his boots off.'

I looked round to find the two mids., but they'd taken the leave for granted and gone below, so I drank my cocoa and finished my watch by myself.

I may as well tell you about the two young beauties. Bob Temple was, unfortunately for me, my cousin—a scraggy, freckled, untidy midshipman, who hadn't the brains to get into mischief, or to get out of it again, but for his pal the Angel. What had made them chum together I don't know, for the Angel (Tommy Sparks) was the exact opposite of Bob—as spruce and ladylike a chap as you ever saw, always beautifully neat and clean, with a face like a girl's, light hair, and blue eyes. He looked as though butter couldn't possibly melt in his mouth, and devoted every moment when he wasn't asleep or eating to getting himself and my *dear* young cousin into a scrape. It was one of his latest efforts which had cost them watch and watch for three days, and that was why they were keeping the 'middle' with me that night; so you can guess why they were so keen on the coaling signal, and had streaked down below. It didn't matter to me a tinker's curse how many watches the Angel kept, but with Cousin Bob it mattered a good deal. His people looked on me as his bear-leader, and every time he got into a row sooner or later I heard about it from them, or from his sister Daisy. I'm hanged if you are going to hear any more about her, except that she used to think me a brute whenever his leave was stopped, or he had 'watch and watch,' and put it all down to me. I hadn't had to cane him yet, but I knew that would have to happen sooner or later, and I guessed that when it did happen, she'd write me a pretty good 'snorter.'

Don't think that Bob would peach—not he, intentionally—but I knew exactly what he'd write home —something like this :

'The Angel sends his love—he and I cheeked the Padré at school yesterday—we had awful fun—old Billums (that was I) caned the two of us after evening quarters. This morning we both pretended we couldn't sit down, and groaned when we tried to, till the Padré went for old Billums for laying it on so hard. We've got our leave stopped for trying to catch rats on the booms with a new trap which the Angel has invented. The Commander caught his foot in it. You should have heard him curse.'

That was the kind of thing that used to go home, and his father and mother, and my mother too, to say nothing of Daisy, put it all down to me.

I had to turn the hands 'out' at seven bells, to rig

coaling screens, the whips, and all the other gear for coaling, turned over my watch to the fat marine subaltern who relieved me, and got a couple of hours' sleep before the coal lighters bumped alongside.

It was a case of being as nippy as fleas after that, because we *had* to beat the *Hercules*. You should have seen the Angel and Cousin Bob in blue overalls, with white cap covers pulled down over their heads, digging out for daylight down in my coal lighter among the foretopmen, all of them as black as niggers, shovelling coal into baskets, passing them up the side, dodging the lumps of coal which fell out of them and the empty baskets thrown back from the ship. There wasn't much of the Angel left about either of them then.

At the end of the first hour we'd got in 215 tons, and as the little numeral pendants 2–0–7 ran up to the *Hercules* foreyard-arm to show how many tons she had taken in, our chaps cheered. We'd beaten her by eight tons.

'I bet she cheated even then,' I heard Bob tell his chum.

We were still a ton or two to the good after the second hour, and then the 'still' was sounded in both ships, and every one went to breakfast.

You should have been there to have seen us in our coaling rigs—simply a mass of coal dust and looking like a lot of Christy Minstrels—squatting on the deck outside the gun-room, and stuffing down sardines with our dirty hands, every one talking and shouting and as merry as pigs in a sty. Even young Marchant, the new clerk, had got into a coaling rig of sorts and worked like a horse—he was so keen to beat the hated *Hercules*.

I gave them all a quarter of an hour to stuff themselves, and then down we clambered into the lighters again and began filling baskets—nobody, not even the Angel, shirking a job like this, when there was the chance of getting even with the *Hercules*.

The men came struggling down after us, long before the breakfast half-hour was finished, and we could see the *Hercules*' people swarming down into her lighters as well.

In all the lighters we must have had sixty tons or more in baskets before the bugler sounded the commence, the ship's band upon the booms banged out 'I'm afraid to go home in the dark,' the drum doing most of it; the men began cheering and singing the chorus, and the baskets began streaming on board again.

By the end of the fourth hour we were as hard at it as ever, but then Commander Robinson—we didn't care for him much, as he was such a bully —began bellowing at us, because the *Hercules* was fifteen tons ahead. We could hear her chaps cheering.

The band banged out again 'Yip-i-addy,' and the Skipper, with his eyeglass tucked in his eye and his long hair straggling over his neck, walked round the upper deck singing down to the lighters, 'Go it, lads, we must beat 'em.'

Down in my lighter the men were working like demons. They looked like demons too, got up in all sorts of queer rigs, and only stopping to take a drink from the mess tins of oatmeal water which the 'Scorp'[1] lighterman ladled out for them.

'Look out how you're trimming your lighter, Wilson,' the Commander had bellowed.

'Aye, aye, sir,' I shouted back, but never thought what he really meant—thought he meant we weren't working hard enough.

'We can't do no more 'ardly,' Pat O'Leary, the captain of the foretop, panted. 'The foretop men be pulling their pound — anyway, sir,' and he seized basket after basket and hove them on the platform rigged half-way up the ship's side, doing the work of three men.

'Keep it up, foretop,' I shouted, shovelling for all I was worth, Bob and the Angel keeping me busy with empty baskets. Then there was a warning shout from up above, a lot of chaps cried, 'Look out, sir!' and, before I knew what had happened, I was in the water, all my chaps were in the water, the lighter had turned turtle, and twenty or more tons of good coal was sinking to the bottom of the harbour.

The first thing I thought was, 'We can't beat them now,' knew it was my fault, and felt a fool. The

---

[1] Natives of Gibraltar are often called 'Scorps' (Rock Scorpions).

Commander was bellowing for me to come aboard, and Bob and the Angel, with their faces rather cleaner and bursting with laughter, were bobbing alongside me. Then O'Leary spluttered out that the 'Scorp' lighterman was missing, and we both up with our feet and dived down to find him.

The water was so thick with coal dust that we couldn't see a foot away from us, but O'Leary touched him as he was coming up for breath and brought him to the surface, pretty well full of water and frightened out of his wits, though otherwise none the worse.

I did feel a fool if you like. What had happened was that we had dug away all the coal on one side, and I had never noticed—I was so excited—that the lighter was gradually heeling over, till over she went—upside down. The band had stopped, the whole of the coaling had stopped, the men looking over the side to see if any of us had been drowned, till the Commander, hoarse with shouting, shrieked for them to carry on again, whilst we clambered up the ship's side like drowned rats, O'Leary helping the lighterman. Well, there wasn't the faintest chance of our beating the *Hercules* now. Every one knew it, every one slacked off, and there was no more cheering and shouting of choruses.

It was my stupidity that had spoilt everything.

The only thing that I could give as an excuse was that I'd never been in charge of a coal lighter before, but I jolly well knew that the Commander would say,

'And I'll take care you never have charge again,' so I kept quiet whilst he stormed at me, shouting that he'd make me pay for the twenty tons. When he was out of breath, he took me, dripping with coal water, to the Captain, who was very angry and very disappointed about the *Hercules* part of it, but he hated the Commander bellowing at people, so wasn't as severe as he might have been. He sent me away to right the lighter, and it took us—me and the foretop men—a couple of hours to do it, fixing ropes round her under water. We shouldn't have done it even then hadn't Stevens—one of the Engineer Lieutenants and a chum of mine—switched on the current to the electric fore capstan, and we hauled her round with this.

Another loaded lighter had been brought off from the shore to make up for the coal I'd tipped into the harbour, and then we were sent to empty her, whilst the rest of the ship's company sat with their feet dangling over the side, jeering at us.

By the time we had finished we were all in a pretty bad temper, all except O'Leary, who kept up his 'pecker' till the last basket had been filled and hauled up the side. 'I ought to have told you—anyway, sir; I've coaled from lighters time enough to have known better,' he said, trying to buck me up.

I reported myself to the Commander, had another burst of angry bellowing from him, and then every one had to clean ship.

Bob and the Angel were shivering close to me, so

I sent them down below to get out of their wet things, but they were up again in a couple of seconds, and could hardly speak for excitement.

'We're off to Santa Cruz. They've collared a steamer as well as those Englishmen, and we're off to give 'em beans. Isn't that ripping?'

It jolly well was, but the youngsters had had just about enough of working in their wet clothes, and were shaking with cold, so I sent them down again and went on with my job—it didn't make any difference whether hoses were turned on me or not, I was so wet. Presently, old Bill Perkins, our First Lieutenant, came limping along, his jolly old red face beaming all over. 'Never mind, Wilson, we'll beat 'em another time; lucky none of you were hurt or drowned.' He saw that I too was about blue with cold, and took my job whilst I changed into dry things.

Old Ginger came over after dinner from the *Hercules*. 'They're having a sing-song in the gun-room, but I thought I'd give you a look up,' he told me—'awfully sorry about the lighter business.' Of course he'd come across to cheer me, and he did too, both of us talking twenty to the dozen about Santa Cruz and the chances of our having a 'scrap.'

My chaps presently started a bit of a jamberee, old Ginger singing a couple of songs and joining in the choruses. We were just beginning to forget all about the coaling, when a signalman came down and handed Barton, the senior mid., a signal. 'Senior Midshipman, *Hercules*, to Ditto, *Hector*.—Hope none of you are any the worse for your nice little swim.'

The mids. were too angry to speak for a minute, and then the storm burst, and they called the *Hercules* gun-room all the names they could lay hold of, old Ginger looking very uncomfortable, and very angry too.

'Never mind, Billums,' he said. 'We've done our best to make 'em friends, and they won't be,' and then sang out, 'Gentlemen, I apologise for that signal—don't answer it—its beastly rude, and I'll cane the senior midshipman to-morrow morning.'

There was no more sing-song after that, old Ginger went back to his ship as angry as we were, and I turned in, knowing jolly well that my chaps would hate Ginger's all the more, and that Ginger beating the senior mid. would only make things worse.

'Let's hope we get mixed up in a 'scrap' or two out in Santa Cruz,' Ginger had said as he went away, and I knew that that was about the only thing that would do the trick and make them friends.

That was a bad day's work for me. I'd shown myself a fool, the Commander wouldn't forget my carelessness for months, and the Skipper would feel he couldn't trust me.. That made me want to kick myself.

CHAPTER II

A Revolution Imminent

Written by Sub-Lieutenant William Wilson, R.N.

EARLY next morning, just as the sun was lighting up
the signal station at the top of the Rock, we and the
Hercules slipped from our buoys and shoved off into
the Atlantic, the *Hercules* two cables astern of us.

We rounded Tarifa Lighthouse; the jolly old
Rock, sticking up like an old tooth, was hidden by
the Spanish mountains; we saw the white walls of
Tangier under the snow-capped Atlas mountains, on
the African side, and then we began to tumble about
merrily in the open Atlantic. The *Hector* wasn't
still for a minute at a time, and my mids. had something else to think about than the latest *Hercules*
gun-room insult. Most of them felt pretty 'chippy,'
though of course it had nothing to do with us rolling
and pitching. Rather not! None of them were seasick, perfectly absurd! They were only a little out
of sorts; didn't want any breakfast, or got rid of
what they did eat pretty rapidly; much preferred
lying down in a corner inside the battery screen, out
of the wind, and took a deal of 'rousting' out of it

before they'd do their job.   For all that, they'd have
been awfully angry if any one had suggested that
they were seasick.   The gun-room messman had
given us the strongest of kippers for breakfast that
morning—this was his idea of a joke—and as we
couldn't keep a single scuttle open, and there was
practically no ventilation in the gun-room, you can
imagine that you could almost cut the atmosphere
with a knife.

Pearson, the A.P., the engineer sub, Raynor, and
I were alone in our glory when we began tackling
the messman's kippers; but soon the mids. came
along, and it was worth a fortune to watch them put
their heads inside the gun-room, take a 'sniff,' and
go away again.   Presently Bob and the Angel came
dashing down, and we three chuckled as they rushed
in, got a breath of it, stopped dead in their tracks,
pretended they didn't mind, and sat down as near the
door as they could get.   We watched them 'peck' a
bit, Bob's freckles showed up more than ever, the

Angel looked perfectly green, and they were both as silent as mummies.

The ship gave a big roll to starboard, a green sea slapped over the glass scuttles and darkened the whole gun-room; there was a crash of crockery smashing in the pantry; Bob and the Angel grabbed their plates, back the old *Hector* tumbled to port; Bob's coffee-cup slid gracefully into his lap—he could stick to it no longer—and rushed away.

The Angel lasted another lurch, but that finished him.

'Afraid I—caught—cold—in the water—yesterday—afraid Bob did too—I'm not—very hungry—I'll see what's the matter with Bob,' he gulped, swallowing every word; and, clapping his hand over his mouth, he disappeared after his chum.

More than half the mids. never ventured further than the gun-room flat, where they caught the first whiff of kipper, and those who did, didn't stay long.

'We'd get a fine mess surplus if they'd only keep like it,' the A.P. grinned; 'but, confound them, they won't.

'They'd enjoy an hour down in the engine-room now. Wouldn't they?' Raynor chuckled.

Of course they were as right as a trivet in a couple of days, and you may bet that they made up for those lost meals.

Every one on board expected that there might be a bit of a scrap when we got across to Santa Cruz, and you can guess how we got hold of Brassey's *Naval Annual* and Jane's *Fighting Ships* to see if Santa Cruz had any ships good enough to give us a show.

They hadn't; that was the worst of it. Three or four miserable out-of-date cruisers, half-a-dozen gunboats, and a couple of torpedo boats built in the year one. There certainly was a cruiser building for them at Newcastle, a ship named *La Buena Presidente*, a big monster like our latest cruisers, and even bigger and more powerful than the *Hector* herself; but Raynor had seen her in the Tyne since she was launched, knew all about her, and was certain that she couldn't be ready inside six months.

'What a pity they didn't wait till they'd got her!' Bob said, with his mouth open. And that was about what we all thought.

Still, though there wasn't likely to be any sport with their wretched Navy, we might have to bombard a fort or two, which would be good enough business; and, more exciting even than that, we might have to send a landing-party ashore.

We didn't waste much time all these eight days we were at sea, the Commander, Bill Perkins, and Montague, the Gunnery Lieutenant, slapping round, from morning to night for all they were worth. The marines, three companies of seamen, two field-guns' and two maxim-guns' crews, and a stretcher party of stokers were told off to land. Their leather gear, haversacks, water-bottles, and rolled-up blankets

were all got ready, hung over their rifles in the
racks, and, morning and evening, we made an
evolution of 'falling in' on the quarterdeck and
fo'c'stle, and getting on our gear in double quick
time.

Ten of my sixteen mids. were told off to land, and
were as happy as fleas in a blanket, fitting their
leather gear and sharpening their dirks all day long,
and thinking about what they'd do when they got
ashore half the night.

Marchant, the young clerk—he'd only just joined
the Navy, and this was his first ship—was told off to
land as 'Old Tin Eye's' secretary.

He was being pretty well bullied and knocked
into shape by the mids., and made to feel what a
hopeless worm he was; but now there were six of
them who'd have given their heads to change places
with him, and he absolutely swelled with pride and
importance.

Three days after leaving Gib. the weather became
gloriously warm, the sea simply like a sheet of
glittering glass, the sun glaring on it all day long.
It was grand to be alive, and we all—officers and
men alike—went into training, and were doubled
round and round, morning and evening, till the
sweat rolled off us. Every evening, too, the parallel
bars and the horizontal bar were rigged on the
quarterdeck, and the ward-room fellows and we
gun-room people did gymnastics for an hour or so,

finishing up with a follow-my-leader round the battery till we nearly dropped. On board the *Hercules* they were doing gymnastics and the new Swedish drill, on the fo'c'stle, the whole day long. But the sight of all was the fat blue marine subaltern—the Forlorn Hope, we called him—doubling up and down the quarter-deck, on his own, to work off his fat, so that he could march properly when he landed—his cheeks flopping from side to side, and running with perspiration. I'm sure you would have died of laughing, especially when his opposite number—the Shadow—the awfully thin red marine subaltern, doubled round after him, trying to work up an appetite, and put on *more* weight. It was the terribly earnest faces they shipped that made one laugh. When you come to think of it, the whole thing was really jolly odd. Here were these two great grey ships, with their long grim 9.2's and 7.5's, and their twelve hundred odd men, pounding steadily along for eight days and nights, to a country hardly any one of us had heard of before, and every one on board both of them was digging out to make himself and them as fit as 'paint,' in case there was a job for us when we did get there.

The Commander even stopped bellowing at people, and brimmed over with good temper.

We had two great heroes on board—at any rate the mids. thought they were—one of the lieutenants —Bigge—who had been with Sir Edward Seymour in the Relief of Pekin force, and Mr. Bostock, the

Gunner, who had been through the siege of Ladysmith during the Boer War.

Some one told the story how five Chinamen had
attacked Bigge whilst he was trying to blow in a gate
or something like that, and how he settled the whole
lot of them with his revolver.   Whether it was true or
not—and I believe it was—the mids. simply hung
round him now, and tried to get him to tell them
some of his experiences.   They looked at the little bit
of yellow and red ribbon on his monkey-jacket, and
simply longed for a chance to earn something like it,
and have a bit of ribbon to stick on their chests.
Although they never could get *him* to talk about
his show, Mr. Bostock would talk about the siege of
Ladysmith, and how the naval brigade helped the
sappers, that awful morning on the crest of Wagon
Hill—would talk as long as they'd like to listen.

He'd sit smoking ship's tobacco in his cabin—it
hadn't any scuttle or ventilation whatever of any
account, so you can have an idea what the smell was
like—and the mids. would crowd in, those who
couldn't do so squeezing into the doorway, and
listen by the hour.   Nothing else but war was talked
about from morning to night.

Well, on the ninth day out from Gibraltar, we
sighted Prince Rupert's Island, ran in through the
northern channel, and anchored two miles off Princes
Town in a great wide bay, with the dark mountains
of Santa Cruz just showing up on the horizon away

to the west. Somewhere up among them old Gerald was teaching his natives to play cricket.

The Skipper went ashore immediately in the picket-boat, to call on the Governor and get news and fresh orders ; so you can guess how excited we all were when she was seen coming tearing off again, and the Skipper ran up the accommodation ladder. I believe every officer in the ship was up on the quarterdeck to hear the news, and you can just imagine what we felt like when we saw that the Skipper had shipped a long face, and when he shook his head at us and went down below.

In three minutes we knew the worst—it was all over the ship. The Englishmen and the English steamer had been released ; old Canilla, the President, had apologised handsomely, and all was peace. Wasn't it sickening?

'Ain't it a bally shame,' Montague, the Gunnery Lieutenant, said, 'stoppin' our gun-layers' test at Gib., just as we were in the thick of it ; bringin' us lol-loppin' along here, and nothin' for us to do when we get here—no landin' party, no nothin'.' And he sent word down to Mr. Bostock to re-stow and pack up all the leather gear and water-bottles.

'It do take the 'eart out of one,' Mr. Bostock told the sympathising mids., 'not a blooming chawnce to let off so much as a single ball cartridge,' and he went below to see that none of his landing party gear was missing.

The Governor himself came off to return the Skipper's call, and brought off some of the shore chaps with a challenge to play us at football, hockey, tennis, cricket, polo, or anything and everything we jolly well liked.

That bucked us all up a bit, and Clegg, our Surgeon—a great, tall chap and a grand cricketer —who ran the sports on board, sent for me to fix up things.   Between us we fixed enough matches to last the first ten days.

'Can't play you at polo,' we told them, 'we've only got one chap who's ever played in his life.'

'Well, I'll tell you what we'll do,' one of them said, 'we'll lend you ponies to practise for the match, and if you'll lend us one of your boats, we'll practise in her, and pull a race against you in ten days' time. What d'you say to that?   That'll even up matters a bit.'

'Let's get this little lot finished first,' we said, laughing.

They *were* a sporting crowd.   This was a Tuesday. On Wednesday we were to play Princes' Town at rugby—it made me sweat only to think of it, although this was what they called their winter—whilst the *Hercules* was to play the Country Club.   On Thursday we were to change rounds, and on Friday the two ships were to play the whole of Prince Rupert's Island.

On Saturday they thought we might have a cricket

match—if it wasn't too *cold*! 'Right you are,' we said, 'if there's anything left of us—though we shall probably be melted by that time.'

There were dances every night, and picnics and tennis parties for those who weren't playing anything else.

'We're going to have a fizzing time, Wilson, after all,' Dr. Clegg said, as we watched them go ashore, after having had no end of a job to get their boat alongside, because there was such a crowd of native boats swarming round the foot of the ladder, loaded down to the gunwales with bananas, oranges, melons, and things like that, the buck niggers on board them quarrelling, and squealing, and laughing, dodging the lumps of coal the side boys threw to make them keep their boats away from the gangway.

Most of the boats had their stern-sheets weighted down with black ladies, dressed in white calico skirts and coloured blouses, trying to look dignified and squealing all the time, holding up bits of paper whenever they caught sight of an officer, and singing out, 'Mister Officah, I vash your clo's—I hab de letter from naval officah—I good vasher-lady, you tell quatamasta, let me aboard—all de rest only black trash.'

They were allowed on board presently, and down into the gun-room flat they swarmed—old ones, young ones, fat ones, and thin ones, all trying to get our washing to take ashore. 'Me Betsy Jones, me vash for Prince George, sah! I know Prince George when he so high, sah! Betsy good vasher-lady, you give me your vashing.' They were all round the 'Angel.' 'Ah! bless your pretty heart, my deah, you give your vashing to Matilda Ann; I vash for Prince George and for Admiral Keppel—verrah nice man Admiral Keppel.' He was pulled from one to the other, and when he escaped into the gun-room they followed him. He was jolly glad to hear the picket-boat called away and escape.

It was all very well to arrange matches; but a wretched collier came creeping into the bay that very afternoon with three thousand tons of Welsh coal for the *Hercules* and ourselves, and, instead of playing football, we jolly well had to empty her between us. There was no going ashore for any one except the paymasters, and for two whole days we were busy. The heat of it and the dirt of it were positively beastly. It took us twenty-two solid hours to get in 1400 tons, because the men couldn't work well in that heat. It was bad enough on deck, but down in the collier and down below in our own bunkers the heat was simply terrific.

We felt like bits of chewed string when we did go ashore on the third day to play the combined match, and chewed string wasn't in it after we'd been playing ten minutes. I don't think that we could have possibly held our own, but that game never ended. We were waiting for the 'Angel' to get back his breath after being 'winded,' and were wiping the sweat out of our eyes, when a marine orderly came running on to the ground with orders from the Skipper for us to return on board at once.

We stuck the 'Angel' on his feet, told the other chaps what had happened, bolted for our coats, and were off through the town to the Governor's steps as fast as we could go, the marine orderly puffing behind us and the nigger boys, thinking we were running away from the Prince Rupert's team, shouting rude things after us.

Boats were waiting there, the ward-room and gun-room messmen came along, followed by strings of niggers carrying fruit and live fowls and turkeys—everything was bundled down into the stern-sheets—there was no time for ceremony—and we were only waiting for Perkins, the First Lieutenant, who was lame and couldn't run. He'd being doing touch judge.

Cousin Bob was the midshipman of the boat—the second barge. 'What's up?' I asked him. 'Somebody's died—over in Santa Cruz—and we're ordered off to Los Angelos at once. We're to attend the funeral or something like that.'

'Funeral!' we groaned; 'fancy spoiling a football match for a funeral,' and the 'Angel,' who'd recovered by now, squeaked out that he'd already engaged most of his partners for the dances—'ripping fine girls, too, you chaps.'

Perkins came hobbling along, his red face redder

than ever, hustled his way through the laughing, jostling crowd of niggers at the top of the steps, and jumped down among us, mopping his face. 'All in the day's work, lads ; shove off, I'm in the boat.'

'Hi, Bill!' some of the ward-room people sang out, 'some one wants you,' and they pointed to where an enormously stout black lady was elbowing her way to the front.

'Hi, Massa Perkins! Hi, Massa Perkins! How d'ye do, Massa Perkins—me Arabella de Montmorency —you sabby Arabella—Arabella see your deah red face—vash for you in de flagship—de *Cleopatra*—you owe Arabella three shillin' and tuppence—you pay Arabella—vat for you no pay Arabella—Arabella vash for you when you midshipman in de *Cleopatra*.'

'All right, old girl,' Perkins sang out, waving his stick cheerily at her, 'I sabby you, you come aboard, by an' by, when we come back—give you some ship's baccy—come aboard the *Hector*.'

'Shove off,' he told Bob, and off we pulled, the crew grinning from ear to ear, and the niggers all cackling with laughter, dancing about and singing out, 'Three cheers for the red, white, and blue,' 'Old England for ebber,' and Mrs. Arabella's voice following us, 'I mak' de prayer to de good Lo'd for Massa Perkins—Him keepa Massa Perkins from harm— Arabella want de three shillin' and tuppence.'

'You've got some nice friends, Bill,' the ward-room officers chaffed him.

The cable was already clanking in through the hawse-pipe as we got aboard, and in half an hour the *Hercules* was following us out through the eastern passage, and we headed across for the mainland and Santa Cruz.

It was my morning watch next morning (from four to eight), and it was a grand sight to see the sun rise behind us, flooding the calm sea with red and orange colours, whilst the little wisps of clouds which hung about the sides of the fierce - looking mountains of Santa Cruz, in front of us, kept on changing from gold to pink and from pink to orange.

O'Leary was the quarter-master of the watch, and I saw the old chap looking at them. He shook his head at me, ' Better than an " oleo "—that—sir. That's God's own picture.'

Even the stokers who'd just come off watch and were cooling themselves, down on the fo'c'stle below us, stood watching the grand sight, and then, down at the foot of the mountains, a long white line showed up.

' That's the breakwater at Los Angelos,' fat little Carlton, our navigator, told me.

As we forged along through the oily, glistening sea, and got closer, we could see the masts and funnels and fighting-tops of the little Navy of Santa Cruz shelter-ing behind it, all tinged with the sunrise ; and the hundreds of windows in the lighthouse and the houses clustered at the foot of the mountains were all glowing as if they were on fire. If old Gerald had heard we were coming, it was quite likely that he'd come down from the estate and might be snoring on his back behind one of them, snoring like a good 'un and dreaming about the last football match he'd played in.

Then high up the side of the dark mountains a ball of white smoke shot out, hung there in the still air for a second or two, and melted away, changing colour as it disappeared.

'That's the sunrise gun, sir, from one of their forts, sir. Them Dagos be half an hour adrift, I'm blowed if they ain't,' O'Leary said.

The bridge was crowding up now, for the Skipper and the Commander and a host of mids. had come along to bring the ships to anchor.

'Pretty sight that,' the Skipper grunted, squinting through his eyeglass.

'Like pink icing on a wedding cake, sir,' the Commander added, thinking he'd said something funny.

'Yes, sir; beautiful, sir,' chipped in the navigator, really wondering what the Skipper was referring to, but very eager to agree with him—he would have licked his boots if he thought the Skipper would like it.

'Bring ship to an anchor,' snapped out the Skipper, and the boat's'n's mates piped, 'Watch, bring ship to an anchor—duty-men to their stations—away second barges.'

The anchoring pendants were run up to our mast-head—the answering pendant on board the *Hercules* got to her masthead almost as soon—and we moved slower and slower in towards the breakwater.

The navigator reported, 'On our bearings, sir;' the Skipper nodded to the Commander, who bellowed down to the fo'c'stle, 'Let go;' the signalman hauled down the pendants; the starboard anchor splashed into the sea, and the cable began rattling out through the hawse-pipes.

Down went the pendant aboard the *Hercules*, and her anchor splashed behind us.

'Full speed astern both,' snapped the Skipper to the man at the engine-room telegraph and the water churned up under our stern.

'Going astern, sir,' sang out the leadsman, with an eye on the water.

'Stop engines,' the Skipper snapped again, and the old *Hector* was once more at anchor.

At eight o'clock we saluted the Santa Cruz flag; the fort, up in the clouds, which had fired the sunrise gun, returned it after a while, and the swarthy little port doctor came out from behind the breakwater, in a fussy little steam-launch, to see if we had any infectious diseases on board, and as we hadn't, to give us 'pratigue '—take us out of quarantine.

After a lot of silly rot, he bowed and scraped himself on board, said '*bueno, bueno,*' about a hundred times, bowed and scraped himself down the ladder into his boat, and went fussing back behind the breakwater again.

He'd brought some letters from our Minister at Santa Cruz, and it turned out that it was the President's wife who had died. She was to be buried next day, so we were a trifle early.

'We might have finished that "footer" match after all,' I heard the Angel grumble to Cousin Bob.

I rather hoped that Gerald would have written, but he hadn't—he was a terrible hand at writing letters.

The Skipper—Old Tin Eye—went ashore to call on the Military Governor, who returned his call almost before he could get back.

He was a long, lean, hollow-cheeked Spanish kind of a chap, in a white uniform and marvellous hat with green and yellow plumes, his chest covered with medals and orders—a grand-looking old fighting-cock. He brought with him his two A.D.C.'s—one of them as black as your hat, and the other fat and short, with an enormous curved sabre ten sizes too big for him and gilt spurs so long that he could hardly get down the ladders, even by walking sideways. He looked just like a pantomime soldier.

He brought his black pal down to the gun-room to leave the Governor's cards, and, as he could speak a little English, we got on all right.

I noticed him looking at me rather curiously, and at last he said, 'You know Señor Geraldio Wilson?'

'Old Gerald! he's my brother. Why?' I asked.

'You have the same,' and he pointed to his face

and hair. Old Gerald has the same yellowish hair and grey eyes that I have.

Funny that he'd spotted me, wasn't it, for we never thought each other much alike?

'You know Gerald?' I asked him.

'All peoples know Señor Geraldio,' he replied, very courteously, but with an expression on his face as if he wasn't going to say any more.

We took them on deck, and whilst their boat was being brought alongside, and they were waiting for the Governor to come up from the Captain's cabin, they were awfully keen on the after 9.2 gun.

'Make shoot many kilometres?' the fat chap asked.

'About thirty,' I told him, doing a rough calculation in my head, and he told his black pal, and they jerked their thumbs towards the mountains. It didn't take much brains to guess that they were wondering whether we could shell the city of Santa Cruz itself. They looked at that gun jolly respectfully after that.

Later on that day, we learnt a lot about local politics from two English merchants, who came off to call and feel English 'ground'—as they expressed it—under their feet again. They looked jolly cool in their white clothes and pith sun-helmets.

'It's a mighty change from a week ago,' they said. 'All the Europeans and Americans here at Los Angelos and up in Santa Cruz were practically prisoners, some had actually been thrown into San Sebastian—the old fort of Santa Cruz—and we were all expecting notice to quit the country, when they heard that you were coming along, apologised to the chaps in San Sebastian, and let the rest of us along.   We're glad to see you, you bet we are, for there's trouble coming.'

'What? Where?' we asked, frightfully keen to know, all the mids. crowding round and keeping as silent as mice.

'Revolution! that's what's coming.   It's as certain as we're sitting here.   Old Canilla, the President, is hated everywhere, except in his own province of Santa Cruz and the city itself.   The country will revolt directly the Vice-President—de Costa—gives the word. It's been coming for years, but Mrs. President, the old lady who's to be buried to-morrow, was the Vice-President's sister, and, though they hate each other like poison, she kept the peace between her husband and her brother.   'Every one called her *La Buena Presidente*, and now she's gone '—they shrugged their shoulders—'we don't know what will happen.   The very day *La Buena Presidente*, poor old lady, died, General Angostina was shot in the back—he was the most popular general in the country and backed the de Costas—and no attempt has been made to arrest his assassins, who boast about it at the Military Club.   In fact, the paper this morning says that one has been promoted for "services to his country."'

'*La Buena Presidente?*' the A.P. sang out; 'that's the name of the new cruiser building for them at Newcastle.'

'Named after her,' one of them said. 'She's big enough to sink the whole of the rest of their fleet, and that's where the trouble comes in. The fleet is loyal to the President just now, but he's in a terrible funk lest the crew he is sending to England to bring her here alter their minds. If they do, they can make cat's-meat of the rest, and then old Canilla's up a tree, for he can't scotch a revolution in the provinces to north and south of him, unless he holds command of the sea and prevents them joining forces.

'When's this revolution to start?' we asked rather chaffingly.

'To-morrow at 1.25 sharp. That's the official time for the funeral service to end, and till then Canilla and de Costa will be friends. To-morrow night there won't be a single friend of the Vice-President in Santa Cruz, unless he's shot or in San Sebastian. De Costa himself won't be in Santa Cruz either, unless he's shot or arrested as he leaves the cathedral. He'll be off to his own province of Leon. Now you can guess why we're glad to see you.'

'I'm jolly glad we didn't stay to finish that footer match,' the Angel sang out, as they took their leave. 'We're going to have some jolly fun, ain't we, Bob?'

'D'you know a chap called Gerald Wilson, a brother of mine?' I asked one of them, a very fat chap, whose name was Macdonald. 'A chap with yellow hair something like mine and a jaw like an ox.'

'Know him!' he answered quickly; ''pon my word, I've been looking at you and wondering whom you were like. Why, you're as like as two peas, though he's a bit broader and taller.'

'Do we know Gerald Wilson? Don Geraldio? Why, my dear chap, every one knows your brother,' the other Englishman joined in. 'He's the maddest chap in the country, and if our Minister doesn't get him out of it pretty quickly, he'll get his throat cut.'

'Or be a general in the revolutionary army,' Macdonald added. 'He's right "in" with the de Costas.'

Well, that was exciting if you like—to me, but the mater would be awfully upset if she knew—poor old mater.

'Where's he now?' I asked excitedly. 'I've not seen him for five years.'

'Up in Santa Cruz, he lives at the European Club,' Macdonald answered. Then an idea struck him, and he continued, 'Some of your people are going up to the funeral. If you like to go, I'll take you; get ashore to-morrow morning by 6.30. I'm driving up. The funeral will be worth seeing, even if you hadn't your brother up there. I'll find him for you.'

'Thank you very much, I'll try and get leave,' I told him, as he went down into his boat.

'You can bring a couple of your midshipmen if you like,' he shouted up.

I was so excited I hardly knew what to think or

do, it was so worrying about Gerald, from the mater's point of view, and so splendid from mine.

To-morrow was my day ' off,' the Commander gave me leave, the two mids. were, of course, the Angel and Cousin Bob, and they were too excited to do anything else but walk up and down the quarterdeck with their eyes glued on the mountains, where Santa Cruz lay, in the clouds, five thousand feet above them.

CHAPTER III

The Revolution breaks out

Written by Sub-Lieutenant William Wilson, R.N.

A WHOLE crowd of us from the *Hector* and the *Hercules*, all bound for Santa Cruz, went ashore at six o'clock next morning.   On our way inshore, after we'd pulled round the head of the breakwater, we had a good view of the Santa Cruz ships.   Rotters they all looked, slovenly kept, nothing seamanlike or shipshape about them, with their 'wash clothes' hung about the rigging and even over the quarter-deck railings—anyhow.

And a funny-looking crowd of soldiers they had too, falling in on the wharf where we landed, ready to receive the two Skippers when they came ashore— in uniform—to attend the funeral on duty.   They were all South American natives or full-blooded niggers, half of them bare-footed, none of them dressed alike.   Some had hats like the French army *kepi*, others, broad-brimmed felt or straw hats ; their shirts were of every colour under the sun, and a pair of loose dirty cotton trousers seemed to be about the only uniform they had.   They all had

48

rifles—of sorts—a bayonet, and a leathern belt hanging loose over their hips to support a cartridge pouch, but many had lost their bayonet frogs and scabbards, and simply stuck the naked bayonet inside the belt.

My chum with the gilt spurs and enormous sabre seemed to be bossing the show, and was too busy trying to get the men into something like order to notice me.

We all pushed our way along through a not at all friendly mob of people, Bob and the Angel sticking to me like leeches. Then we lost the rest of our people, and felt pretty lost ourselves till a grinning native caught hold of my sleeve.

'*Buenos! Señor!* You *Señor* Wilson? *Señor* Macdonald send me. I his boy.'

We were jolly glad to find any one who would take us to him.

'How did you find me in the crowd?' I asked him.

'*Señor* Macdonald say you like *Señor Geraldio*. All peoples know Señor Geraldio.'

'Blowed for a yarn,' I thought. 'Old Gerald wouldn't be very flattered.'

We stepped out briskly enough then, and you ought to have seen the Angel strutting along in the middle of the road, in a blue suit and straw hat, the trousers beautifully creased, the latest thing in ties round his neck, the most startling thing in socks showing under his turned-up trousers, looking as if he was off to a tea-party in Southsea. Even the niggers smiled at him and got out of his way. We came upon Macdonald in a minute or two, waiting for us at a corner, with a carriage and six grand-looking mules—the carriage was like a big two-wheeled governess cart with an awning over it, and he was so enormous that he almost filled it.

In we jumped, the two mids. managed to squeeze themselves alongside the native driver, our guide kicked the mules in the stomach, one after the other, just to wake them up; the driver cracked his whip, and away we went bump-terappity along the bumpy road, the bells on the harness jingling like fun.

We clattered along past rows and rows of red mud cottages, dogs flying out at us from every door, and giving the two mids. a grand time with the whip, pack mules tied up to the door-posts frisking about and kicking up their heels as we went past, and long-legged fowls scattering like smoke in front of us.

'You're extraordinarily like your brother, now you're in plain clothes,' Mr. Macdonald muttered, with his mouth full—for he'd started on the hampers already.

'Jolly proud of it,' I answered, but he only made a face and shrugged his shoulders.

We started climbing soon after, and the mules had a pretty hard time of it for the next three hours, zig-zagging up the most appalling road, panting and grunting.   The mids. and I walked the steepest parts, but neither the driver nor Mr. Macdonald budged from their seats.   The higher we got the more cheerful we were.   It was grand looking down at Puerta and the sea, with the *Hector* and *Hercules* like toy ships lying inside the breakwater, but **Mr.** Macdonald did not let us stop anywhere for more than a minute at a time, because there was a whole line of jangling mule carriages coming up after us, and he didn't want to be overtaken.   The mids. didn't either, for there were four *Hercules* mids. in the one next behind us, and they were not going to be beaten by them if they could help it.

Every now and again, at the corners where the road zig-zagged, we came across thirty or forty native soldiers, evidently guarding the way.

'That looks as if they were expecting trouble,' Mr. Macdonald told me.   'It's most unusual.   D'you see the colours they have in their hats?'

Nearly all of them had a patch of yellow and green stripes sewn on.

'I've never seen the regular troops wearing them,' he said.   'Did you notice that the stripes were *vertical*?   That means that they are President's men.   The de Costa's colours are black and green, but the stripes are worn *horizontally*, and of course they aren't allowed to wear them.'

He shook his head very ominously.

'Things are going to hum to-day.   You'd have

been wiser to stay on board. You're too like your brother.'

You can guess that this only made it more jolly exciting.

Every now and then we met long trains of mules or donkeys, with huge bundles on their backs, pacing wearily down the road.

'They're carrying rubber or cocoa down to Los Angelos,' Mr. Macdonald said. 'The President makes them bring all their rubber through Los Angelos; that's one of the grievances they have against him.'

Jolly interesting everything was, and once the men with one long mule train took off their big hats, bowing and saying, '*buenos*.'

'They're doing it to you, not to me,' Mr. Macdonald said. 'They're from Paquintos, close to your brother's estate, and think you are he.'

It was a jolly funny feeling to land at this out-of-the-way spot and find so many people appear to know me; don't you think it was?

By this time we had left the shade of the tropical trees below us, and the road and the side of the mountain were simply bare rock—the heat terrific. At half-past ten we were at the top, and got our first glimpse of Santa Cruz spread out in a hollow beneath us, with mountain ridges all round it. Our mules roused themselves into a trot, and we slung along at a good rate, kicking up a cloud of dust. The *Hercules* mids. had been gradually drawing closer, and now they came along at a gallop, and would have passed us, singing out rude remarks, but the Angel seized the whip and beat our poor brutes into a gallop too, and the teams simply tore along, side by side, the drivers having all they could do to keep on the road. The two carriages bounced along close together, I thought the wheels would lock every other second, and the mids. were hitting at each other with their sticks and shouting.

Luckily we didn't meet anything, but I saw that, just ahead, the road narrowed, and that we couldn't possibly get through there side by side.

'Let them go ahead,' I shouted, and leant over to help the driver pull in the team, but then one of the *Hercules* mids. sang out, 'Who upset the coal lighter?' the others shouted, 'The rotten *Hectors*!' —and that made me as mad as a hatter. I didn't care whether we all went to glory or not so long as we beat them—after that.

'Pull up, you fools!' Mr. Macdonald shouted, but the mules were quite out of hand.

We came to the narrow part, the leading mules bumped into each other, then the others, till the wheelers were touching; our axles bumped once or twice, there was a lurch and a crash, the other carriage toppled over on to the bank, the wheeler mules were on their backs, and the mids. shot out head over heels as we flew past, the Angel and Bob cheering wildly.

Before we were out of sight we saw the four mids.
and the driver on their feet again, trying to right the
carriage, so I knew they weren't hurt.

Mr. Macdonald simply wagged his head from
side to side. ' It was my weight brought us through
—you'd have upset but for me.'

I do actually believe he enjoyed it.

We were in the city itself by now, and the mules
had steadied down on the rough stone streets crowded
with people on foot or riding horses or mules. There
were soldiers at every corner—quite smart chaps
these—and they all had the vertical green and yellow
stripes in their helmets or hats. The same colours,
hoisted with the stripes vertical, hung at half-mast
from nearly every house, and the few women, we saw,
had the same colours too.

' There are some of de Costa's people,' Mr. Macdonald sung out, as we passed a group of sunburnt
men outside a café. I looked, and saw that they had
patches of green and black stripes worn horizontally.

' They call the two parties the Verticals and
Horizontals,' Mr. Macdonald told me. ' Those are
countrymen ; you can see that by their rig.'

' Hi ! ' he sung out; ' look up there, up to the left,
that's San Sebastian, where our chaps were put in
" chokey " a fortnight ago.'

It was a crumbling old fort perched on a rocky hill
just above the big building, and we three looked at
it jolly keenly.

Then we got into the better part of the town, dazzling big white houses with gratings in front of every window, and women peering out from behind the curtains in most of them. Everywhere were soldiers, and the yellow and green flags drooping at half-mast.

Next we drove through a great open place, white with dust and dazzling in the sun, with a grand old weather-beaten cathedral on one side, and on the other some public garden with palms and huge tropical ferns. We had to draw up to let a regiment march into the square, and then we wedged our way out of it, into a side street, turned a corner, and stopped in front of a big door with strong iron gates, sentries with fixed bayonets on each side of it, and a whole jumble of French, English, German, American, and Dutch ensigns hanging down from a flagstaff above it. There was a wizened little black chap leaning up against the wall; he started when he saw me, and let his cigarette drop out of his mouth. He *was* an ugly-looking little beast.

'The European Club,' Mr. Macdonald said. 'Out you jump. I bet your brother's in here.'

We followed him into a cool courtyard with a splashing fountain in the middle of it, and through the open French windows I heard the click of billiard balls—a jolly homely sound—and, looking in, there was Gerald, with his coat off, watching the other chap making his stroke, his jolly old lion head with the long yellow hair brushed back and his grand square jaw—not a bit like me.

He didn't see me as I went in and touched him on the back. 'Hello, Gerald!'

'Hello, Billums! What the dickens are you doing here? How's the mater? Well played, Arnstein (this to his opponent). Wait till I've "knocked" him. Won't be a second.'

He won quite easily, and then he stood us all lunch at the Club. I did my best to pump him about the revolution, but he kicked me hard under the table, so I didn't say any more about it. The mids. had a grand time, hardly uttered a word, but simply ate steadily through course after course, not even the excitement of hearing regiments of infantry tramping past every now and again, with their bands playing, putting them off their feed.

'Come along,' Gerald said presently, 'I've got a window from which we can see everything ; there'll be room for all of you.'

But Mr. Macdonald wasn't coming, so we left him.

'Be here by three o'clock,' he said, 'not a minute later, and I'll drive you back.'

As we left the gate I noticed that the sentries looked rather puzzled at Gerald and myself.

'I couldn't say anything in there,' Gerald began, when we'd got out into the crowded street ; 'you never know who may be listening. We're going to have a revolution, and I'm rather mixed up in it. You saw that little plain-clothes chap at the gate, he's one of the President's secret police, and has been shadowing me for the last four days.'

I had seen him, the one who'd been so startled when I went in.

'Don't you carry a revolver or anything?' I asked nervously.

'My dear old Billums, I've never thought of it.'

I bothered him to get one in case anything happened.

'All right, old chap, I'll think about it.'

There was too great a crush in the narrow streets to do much talking, and we had a lot of trouble to push our way along. There were quite a lot of people wearing the *horizontal* black and green stripes in these streets, and you could tell they were strangers by their weird-looking clothes and by the way they flocked along with their eyes and mouths open.

We presently passed a lot of officers standing outside a doorway.

'That's the Officers' Club,' Gerald told me, as he took his hat off, and they all clicked their heels and saluted, looking from Gerald to myself with that same puzzled look—they seemed very unfriendly. We waited a minute or two to let a battery of field artillery rumble past—the guns were 'horsed' with mules—turned down another side street, and entered a cool courtyard with more fountains splashing. There were any number of people in it; they nearly all had black and green rosettes with horizontal stripes, and all bowed very cordially to Gerald.   He spoke to several, looked as if he had heard bad news, and took us into the back of the Hotel de L'Europe, up some narrow wooden stairs, opened a door on a narrow landing, and there we were in a corner room with a large French window opening on to an iron balcony and overlooking the great square.   The cathedral tower, with its arched entrance and broad steps, wasn't fifty yards away.

'You'll get a grand view here—it's cool too—you'd get sunstroke outside—stay where you are—I'll be back presently—I've just had some important news,' Gerald jerked out, and left us to watch the people and the soldiers pouring into the square—'Plaza' every one called it.   These soldiers were jolly smart-looking chaps, well dressed and well set up, very different to those we had seen at Los Angelos.   They all had the vertical green and yellow stripes in their white helmets, and even we could see that they were pretty rough in dealing with the people.   We saw several of the ward-room fellows hunting about for a good place to see the procession, and the two Skippers drove up to the cathedral, in uniform, the soldiers making a way for their carriage, and driving the people back by prodding them in the stomach with the butt-ends of their rifles.

Gerald came in again looking worried.

'Everything all right?' I asked.

He nodded, and sat down in a corner,

'The soldiers don't treat the people very gently,' I said, and he told me that they were all Presidential troops in the city that day, and that there was no love lost between them and the country people, who had poured into the city to pay respect to the President's wife. 'If you look closely, you'll see that a great many of these are wearing the badge of the de Costas—the horizontal green and black stripes.'

'I heard to-day,' he went on, 'that the President's wife, just before she died, made her brother, de Costa, and her husband, José Canilla, shake hands and promise to keep the peace after she was gone.'

'Will they?' Bob asked, with his mouth open.

He only smiled and shrugged his shoulders—quite like a Spaniard. 'They called her *La Buena Presidente*, and she was a good old lady and kept the peace, but she's kept back progress and reform for years. There's no such thing as freedom in the country. There will soon be a change now.'

'They named that ship which Armstrong's building after her, I suppose?' I asked him, and he nodded.

I tried to pump him about her, but he'd tell me nothing, except that she would be ready very soon, and was strong enough to blow the rest of the Santa Cruz Navy out of the water. I knew that well enough.

I wanted to ask him if there was any chance of her new crew favouring the Vice-President's party—as Mr. Macdonald had suggested—and a whole lot of other things, but a frightful din started in the 'Plaza.'

Bob, pointing down below, yelled for us to look, and we saw a drunken-looking countryman waving his broad-brimmed felt hat, with an enormous black and green rosette fastened to it, in the face of one of the officers with the troops.   He tried to take no notice of it, but in a second or two lost his temper, seized the rosette, tore it off, threw it on the ground, and stamped it into the white dust with his patent-leather boots.

There was a roar of anger at this, booing and hissing from people crowding in the windows of a house close by, and the mob beneath us began pushing and shouting; knives were drawn, the few women there began screaming, and the soldiers, standing in line, turned round to drive the people back.   Some cavalry came galloping up, and began hitting at the people with the flat of their swords.   One of them was pulled off his horse and disappeared in the struggle, people were pressing in from all sides of the Plaza, and things began to look jolly ugly, when we heard a pistol fired, and a very smart-looking young cavalry officer, who was trying to get his men together, reeled in his saddle and fell on the ground, his fiery little horse plunging away down the swaying lines of soldiers.

Women screamed, every one stopped struggling and drew back, leaving him lying there, by himself, all doubled up in a heap, in the dust, blood trickling from his mouth.   Almost before we'd realised what had happened, a young priest, in black cassock, dashed across from the cathedral steps, knelt down, and lifted the officer's head on his knee.   We saw him press a little black crucifix to his lips, but it was too late, the poor chap was as dead as a door-nail.

Then there was another wild burst of shouting and hooting from the mob and from the people at the windows.

'They've got the man who fired the shot,' Bob squeaked—he was so excited—and we could see a lot of soldiers struggling with a very tall man.   He wrested himself free, knocked down one or two, burst through the line of troops, and went running away from the cathedral, the crowd trying to prevent the soldiers following.   I'd never seen anything so exciting.   He dodged, and doubled, and got clear again for a second, running towards one corner, but there were soldiers everywhere, one of them tripped him with the butt-end of his rifle, and he fell sprawling on the pavement right under our window.   Before you could say a word, a couple of soldiers had driven their bayonets through him—we could actually hear the points knocking against the pavement.   In a moment the mob were on them, and a fierce fight commenced. What would have happened I don't know, but then the loud crashing music of the Dead March in 'Saul' sounded from the opposite side of the square.

'Thank God,' I heard Gerald mutter, 'here comes the procession.'

Officers dashed up again, shouting and cursing, the soldiers fell back into line, the mob hid their

knives and took up their places, the space in front
of the cathedral was cleared in a twinkling, Bob,
leaning out of the window, told us that they'd brought
the body of the officer into the hotel, and that the
other body had disappeared, the purple velvet hang-
ings which hid the cathedral entrance from us were
drawn apart, and, right in the middle, on the top step,
a tall old priest, gorgeously dressed, was standing
with his arms lifted up. He must have been a bishop
at the very least, because directly the people saw him,
they fell on their knees in the dust, leaving only the
soldiers standing erect.

This really was a most extraordinary effect after the
noise, and yelling, and struggling of a few moments
before. Now nothing could be heard, except, some
way off, the funeral march, the clatter of cavalry
horses, and the grating of the wheels of the funeral
car, a dark mass we could see just entering the square.

Behind the cavalry marched a couple of companies
of sailors from the ships at Los Angelos, their white
uniforms stained with sweat ; then came eight horses,
with velvet cloths flowing almost to the ground,
dragging the great state funeral car covered with more
purple velvet, the troops reversing arms and the
kneeling people crossing themselves as it passed in
front of them.

Walking two or three yards behind the car were
two men, and then a gap in the procession.

'There they are,' Gerald said excitedly. 'The little

wizened chap in uniform, with the grey moustaches, is the President, and the fat man in plain clothes the Vice-President.'

The two walked slowly past under our window, and we got a jolly good view of them. The little chap was covered with orders and medals, and looked a grand little soldier and jolly fierce, whilst the big chap, clumsily built, slouched along, one step behind the President, and didn't seem at all at ease. He was perspiring very much too—his collar was all limp—and he kept on looking from side to side as if he didn't much care for his job.

'You wouldn't if you were he,' Gerald half shouted. He had to shout, because the massed bands were now passing beneath us kicking up the most appalling din.

After the bands had gone by, long rows of people, some in uniform, others in plain clothes—notable people of sorts, I suppose—went shuffling past, looking hot and uncomfortable.

We saw the cavalry and seamen halt, forming a guard on each side of the cathedral steps, and then, as the big hearse drew up at the foot of them, a great discordant bell clanged out from the tower above, and a second later there was the loud boom of a gun.

'That's the first minute-gun from San Sebastian,' Gerald said.

The bands suddenly ceased, from the open cathedral doors we heard the grand rolling sound of an organ, and, as the coffin was borne up the steps, choristers broke out into a shrill anthem—an awfully melancholy sound, which made me catch my breath for a second.

The little President and the lumbering great Vice-President, mopping his forehead, walked after the coffin side by side, and disappeared into the gloom of the cathedral, followed by all the untidy string of notables, who scrambled in after them in a very undignified manner, as though they wanted to get out of the heat.

As the last one crowded in, the velvet curtains were drawn across the door again and shut out the noise of the singing.

' That's the last time any one will see those two together again in peace,' Gerald muttered, and turning round I saw that he was looking fearfully worried and anxious.

' What's the matter?' I asked.

' There's hardly a Vice-President's man among that lot,' he whispered.

' What's that mean?'

' They've cleared out, Billums—fled to the country —it's the beginning. Something's gone wrong. It's beginning too soon.' He was very excited, and could hardly sit still. In a minute or two he jumped up, sang out that he must find out how the land ' lay,' and told us to stay where we were.

' If there's any shooting, lie down on the floor —there may be some.'

' Let me come with you?' I asked, awfully keen to go, but he shook his head, and went out.

I wished he'd have let me go with him.

The mids. hadn't noticed him go, for they were tremendously excited again. Some more cavalry were clattering along between the lines of soldiers, and in front of them, his black horse flecked with white foam, they had recognised the Governor of Los Angelos and his two A.D.C.'s, the fat little chap looking a jolly sight smarter on a horse than he did climbing down ladders on board the *Hector*. They stopped opposite the cathedral, dismounted, the Governor strode up the steps, the black A.D.C. handed him a big blue paper, and he stood there looking nervously first at the velvet curtains drawn across the entrance, and then at the troops and the kneeling masses of people behind them. A battery of field artillery began unlimbering on each side of the steps, the guns pointing straight across the Plaza, more infantry marched up and formed a semicircle, four deep, round the base of the steps, and the line of soldiers, turning round, forced the people to rise from their knees, and pressed them back away from the cathedral. There wasn't the least doubt that something was going to happen, and I remembered that Mr. Macdonald had told us that the Vice-President might be arrested or shot directly after the service— perhaps that blue paper the Governor of Los Angelos had in his hand was the warrant.

All this time the huge bell in the cathedral tower above us clanged and jarred, and the minute-guns from San Sebastian shook the air, and made it feel even hotter than it was. We were so excited that, for a moment, I forgot about Gerald.

Suddenly we heard the organ inside the cathedral throbbing, the velvet curtains were drawn aside, the Governor of Los Angelos, unfolding his blue paper, sprang forward, and the little white figure of the President appeared. The massed bands blared out some weird tune—probably the Santa Cruz National Anthem—the troops presented arms, the Governor saluted, and then seemed uncertain what to do. He was looking for some one—the Vice-President, I felt certain—but his clumsy figure didn't appear, only the long string of notables. I saw the Governor shake his head and disappear into the cathedral, one of his A.D.C.'s dashed down the steps, and the President, without looking back or moving a muscle of his face, mounted a white horse, which was waiting for him, and cantered away at the head of a cavalry escort, all the troops presenting arms and shouting, ' *Viva el Presidente.*'

Once or twice since we'd been in that window, hawkers had tried to make us buy things by shoving up little baskets, of sweets and fruit, fastened to long poles. They went from window to window and did a roaring trade. Now as we watched the President cantering away, another basket was thrust up. I pushed it away, but it came again. I shook my head at the man down below who had done it, and saw something strange in his expression. He nodded, and motioned with his free hand as if he wanted me to pick something out, shoving the basket right under my nose.

I looked in, and there, under some small oranges, was a piece of folded paper. I seized it, the basket was drawn down again, and I unfolded it. Hurriedly scrawled there was, 'Can't come back. Get back to the Club quickly, and stay there.—Gerald.'

'Phew!' I went cold all over with excitement. I didn't know what to think.

I looked at my watch, it was 1.30, and remembered that Mr. Macdonald had told us chaffingly that the revolution would begin at 1.25 sharp. I wasn't going to move yet, especially if there was going to be any fighting; we hadn't to meet Mr. Macdonald till three o'clock, and we might as well see all the fun there was going on.

The soldiers began clearing the square now, crowds of people passing along under our windows, Bob and his chum spotted some of our mids., and yelled to them and to the four *Hercules* mids. who came by too, but the noise was so great, and they were so busy shoving and pushing in the hot crowd, that they didn't hear them.

Presently Captain Grattan—Old Tin Eye—squinting through his eyeglass and smiling at the crowd, Captain Roger Hill, sitting bolt upright and looking bored, Perkins, and the Fleet Surgeon drove past in a

carriage.   They were all in uniform, and the soldiers
made a way for them through the people.

'There's not going to be any firing after all,' the
Angel said sadly.   'Look how peaceably all the
people are clearing out.'

'Well, come along,' I sang out, 'we'll go along to
the Club,' so we picked up our hats and sticks,
opened the door, and ran 'slick' into the arms of that
ugly little chap I'd seen outside the Club—the one
Gerald said had been shadowing him.

He had half-a-dozen sturdy nigger soldiers behind
him, and he held up a blue paper in front of me,
grinning cunningly—hateful little beast.

I couldn't read the lingo, but there was Señor
Gerald Wilson written among the print, and a
scrawling 'Jose Canilla' at the bottom, so I guessed
at once that this was a warrant for Gerald's arrest, and
that he must have given the little beast the slip.   The
nigger chaps began closing round me, and had the
cheek to try and seize hold of my wrists.

Well, I'm pretty strong, and I'm pretty bad-
tempered too, and this was too much for me.   I'd
torn the warrant to bits, punched Gerald's friend good
and hard in the face, and laid out the first two chaps
who'd touched me—banged their heads against the
woodwork of the narrow passage, before I'd thought
of it—but then the others drew their revolvers,
and that wasn't playing the game.   I yelled to
the mids., shoved them back into the room, banged

the door, and slipped two bolts in as the chaps charged it.

'Lean out and try to get some of our fellows to help us,' I sang out; 'I'll hang on to the door.' It was the first idea that came, but then it flashed through my head that the longer I kept them fooling round after me, the more chance Gerald would have of escaping—I knew now that that was what he must be doing.

'Slide down into the street—over the balcony—get to the Club—and tell the Skipper I've been arrested,' I yelled out.

'Ain't going to leave you,' the Angel and Bob cried, and came in again and got their shoulders against the door. 'There's not a single one of our chaps about,' they panted, pushing against the creaking door.

My Christopher! it *was* a shoving match. Luckily the passage outside was so narrow that only two people abreast could shove properly, but the screws in the clasps of the bolts at the top of the door began to 'draw,' and I knew we couldn't hold them for long. Then they fired a pistol through the door—high up—the bullet smashing against the opposite wall.

I knew it was no use staying any longer, I didn't want a bullet in me. 'Clear out, and I'll come too,' I sang out, and we bolted to the window, climbed over the balcony, and shinned down the iron uprights.

As my feet touched the pavement, a dozen soldiers threw themselves on top of me ; I hadn't a chance to strike out, my head was covered with a cloak, and the next I knew I was inside the hotel bar, being trussed like a turkey.

As soon as he could do it safely, the little brute who'd had the warrant came and kicked me in the stomach and spat at me—I must have had my pipe in my hand when I hit him, for he had a gash across his forehead—and the two whose heads I'd banged came along and kicked me too.

Thank goodness, Bob and his chum weren't there —I guessed that they'd been cute enough to cut away to the Club.

Even then I rather enjoyed it (not the kicking part —I'd be even with those swine some day), thinking how disappointed they would all be when they found that I wasn't Gerald.

Some more soldiers poured into the room, the little brute pulled a dirty greasy cloth off a table, I was covered with it, carried outside like a sack of potatoes, and dumped into a cart. Something else soft was dumped in beside me, half-a-dozen chaps sat on me to keep me quiet, and off we drove. I could hear horses' hoofs on either side of the cart and the clatter of scabbards and jingle of accoutrements, so knew I had a cavalry escort, and felt jolly proud that Gerald was such a big 'pot' in the revolution business as to require one.

We went slowly after a little while—going uphill.
I wondered whether they were taking me to San
Sebastian, but didn't wonder long, because a minute-
gun was fired—about the last of them—and it sounded
quite close.

In a minute or two we bumped and rattled across
a wooden bridge, and then stopped.

As I was hauled out, they pulled the cloth away
from the soft thing beside me, and it was the body
of the officer who'd been shot in the square. Ugh!
that was rather beastly. An old chap came along
—the boss of the fort, I suppose—and jawed to me in
French and Spanish, and got savage when I couldn't
understand him. He thought I *wouldn't*.

He soon got tired of this, and I was led across the
courtyard by a band of ruffians with fixed bayonets
and loaded rifles (I saw them load their magazines).
We passed behind the crumbling old walls, where a
party of soldiers were cleaning out the saluting guns,
and I was shoved into a kind of store-room, dug out
of the rock or in the thickness of the walls, and shut
in there by a big iron gateway of a door, on the outside of which a miserable little beast of a half-nigger
sentry leant and smoked cigarettes.

There were seven others in there, all quiet indi-
viduals in plain clothes, who rose and bowed to me
when I was brought in, thinking at first, I suppose,
that I was Gerald. They looked very relieved when
they saw that I wasn't. Two of them had rosettes of

black and green with the stripes horizontal, so I knew why they were there. One very courteous old gentleman put a cigarette between my lips, lighted it with his own, and then slacked off the ropes round my wrists and arms, the sentry, turning round to watch us, simply shrugged his shoulders when my arms were free again, and I commenced whirling them round and round to try and do away with the numbness and the ' pins and needles.' He just half opened the breech-bolt of his Mauser rifle, pointed very suggestively at the cartridges inside, turned round again, and went on smoking. Somebody offered me an empty cartridge-box and I sat on it, watching the other chaps busy writing things in notebooks or even on their shirt cuffs.

It struck me that possibly they were writing their ' wills.'

Well! that was a funny ending to my first day ashore, if you like, though so long as Gerald got clear away I didn't mind, and so long as Bob and his chum had fetched up at the Club I knew that things would turn out all right.

It was jolly hot in that hole of a place, and as the afternoon went on the sun shone straight in through the gratings of the door and it was like an oven.

I sweated like a pig.

Every now and then I heard a cart rattle across the drawbridge. That generally meant a fresh arrival, some other Horizontal caught, and he'd be

C 197

"HIS EYES SPAT FIRE

shoved in with us.   At first I was terribly afraid lest
I should see Gerald brought along; but four o'clock
came, Gerald evidently hadn't been caught, and I
began to feel quite easy in my mind about him.

I did wonder why nobody from the ship had come
along, but wasn't particularly worried.   Things
would 'pan out' all right, and this was a rummy
enough experience for any one.

Just after four o'clock there was great excitement
in the courtyard outside.   Soldiers ran about hunting
for their rifles and formed up behind the saluting
guns, trumpets sounded some kind of a 'general
salute,' I heard a lot of horses' hoofs clattering over
the drawbridge, and a few minutes later round the
corner stalked the little President and a crowd of
officers, the Governor of Los Angelos and his two
A.D.C.'s among them.

He'd evidently come along to count his day's 'bag,'
for he walked along the grating looking in at us.
My aunt! he had the cruellest eyes I'd ever seen.

He first caught sight of the old chap who'd un-
fastened my ropes.   Phew! he did give him a piece
of his mind through the grating! and then the old
fellow was dragged out and marched off to a bit of
blank wall between two of the saluting guns.   The
fat little A.D.C. went up to him, and then I knew
what was going to happen, for I saw him offer to tie
a handkerchief across his eyes—he was going to be
shot.   But he wouldn't have his eyes covered, and

for a moment I saw him standing bolt upright with his arms folded in front of him. Then some soldiers ran up, stood in a line between him and me, an officer gave an order, their rifles went up to the present; I turned my head away and saw the other prisoners clutching the gratings, their throat muscles all swollen, and their eyes starting out; there was a scraggy volley, and the President came back again.

Two more men were hauled out and shot, and I shall never forget the face of one of them as he was marched away. It was just like picking a fat hen out of a coop, and we were the hens. Then back the President came a fourth time, and I was dragged out.

He knew that I wasn't Gerald right enough, but his eyes simply spat fire, and he stamped with rage and was more furious than ever because I couldn't understand him.

The fat little A.D.C. was called up to ask questions. He gave me a friendly wink, and I notched up a point in his favour.

He jabbered away to the President and I heard 'Wilson no Don Geraldio' and '*Hector buque de guerra—Inglesa—Los Angelos.*'

He asked me if I knew where Gerald was. Of course I didn't and shook my head, 'No! old chap, I don't.'

The President didn't believe it when this was told him.

'El Presidente say shoot you if do not say where is Don Geraldio.'

Of course that was only bluff, and I smiled.

Then the firing party were called across, but that was still only bluff, I thought, and it didn't frighten me in the least till I saw the fat little A.D.C.'s face turn yellow under his brown skin.

Well, then I was in a mortal funk, if you like, and something inside me went flop down into my boots.

'Our cannon—cannon of *Hector*—shoot thirty kilometres,' I jerked out, remembering how impressed the A.D.C.'s had been with our after 9.2, my tongue feeling a bit sticky and my knees not altogether steady.

The old Governor, the two A.D.C.'s, and several other officers were evidently doing their best for me. I heard 'kilometres' mentioned once or twice, and then the President waved his hand majestically and I was taken back and the grating locked behind me.

My head was buzzing, and I don't mind telling you that I felt a jolly sight more comfortable inside than outside—just then. The little President and all his staff went away, and I heard their horses clattering over the drawbridge. Before he went away, my fat little pal came along and held out his cigarette case through the gratings. I bowed and smiled and took one cigarette; but he shook his head, he wanted me to empty it. I did this and then had a brilliant inspiration. My cigarette case was a pretty decent one, so I offered him mine.

'We change cigarette cases—for remembrance—
I shall always remember,' I said.

The kind-hearted little chap seemed quite pleased,
took mine as I took his, bowed, said '*Adios*! I also
shall remember,' and went after the others as fast as
his spurs and his sabre and his fat little legs would
let him.

I sat down on my cartridge-box and wondered
what the dickens 'Old Tin Eye' was doing and what
had become of Bob and the Angel, smoked one of my
pal's cigarettes, examined the cigarette case—it was
an oxydised silver one with black enamel work,
probably made in Paris—and watched some black
convicts with chains round their ankles filling in
three graves under the wall opposite.

Phew! there might have been four if I hadn't
remembered about the 9.2's and the thirty kilometres.
I shivered and felt jolly sick, and wished to goodness
I was back again in the *Hector's* gun-room.

CHAPTER IV

The Rescue of the Sub

Written by Midshipman Bob Temple

'Cut along to the Club and find the Skipper,' Billums had sung out as we slid down from that window at the Hotel de L'Europe, and when we jumped to the pavement we saw all the soldier chaps —dozens of them—pouncing on him. They didn't pay any attention to us, and it was no good stopping there, so my chum, the Angel, and I scooted away as fast as we could go.

We wormed our way round the corner, out of the square all right, and then we lost ourselves, and were wedged in among an awful crowd of people, carts and mules, cavalry and artillery all jumbled up together, jostling and shoving and cursing. We could hardly move at all, or see where we were going.

We did get along presently, and kept looking down the side streets to try and see all those flags over the Club gate, but we'd forgotten exactly which turning it was. We'd work our way to the outside of the crowd and dart down a side street, looking for the flags and those two sentries, and dart back again into

77

the main street, holding on to each other so as not to
get separated, and push and push till we got to the
next side street.   It was awfully hot work; we couldn't
find it and I simply felt terrified about Billums, when
we ran into those four *Hercules* mids. whom we'd
upset in the morning.   I'd never been so glad to see
any one before.

'Hello! Coal lighters!   What's the hurry?' they
sang out.   'Looking for coal?'

We didn't mind that in the least.

'Where's the Club?' we gasped.   'Quick! tell
us! Our Sub's been arrested, and we want to find
our Skipper.'

'We've just come from there,' they shouted.   'My
aunt! what a lark!   Come along!' and they
turned back and all six of us pushed our way along.
It was hot work, if you like.

'What's he been up to?' one of them asked me.

'They think he's an insurgent; he is just like his
brother who is one.'

We saw the flags almost directly, dashed through
the gateway into the Club, the *Hercules* mids. after us,
and saw Mr. Perkins sitting under a punkah trying
to get cool.

'Where's the Captain, sir?' we asked.

'Don't know!   Was here ten minutes ago.'

We hunted everywhere—he wasn't in the Club—
and ran back to Mr. Perkins.

'The Sub's been arrested, sir; they're half-killing

him. They think he's his brother and have carried him off. What can we do?' Mr. Perkins whistled and scratched his head.

That big German man who had been playing billiards with cousin Gerald in the morning was sitting close by and jumped up, 'What you say? Gerald Wilson caught?'

'No,' we both piped out, 'not Gerald, his brother Bill, our Sub; they've collared him at the hotel near the cathedral.'

'Phew! that's awkward! Something must be done at once. They'd shoot Gerald Wilson if they caught him, and they may shoot his brother.' He spoke very rapidly.

'What can be done?' Mr. Perkins asked, his red face getting quite white.

'I'll drive you to the British Minister—it's a long way out of the town—he's gone there, I know—that's the only thing we can do—you'll have to wait till my carriage comes.'

We did wait, waited for half an hour—it seemed hours, and though Mr. Perkins stood us lemon squashes and cakes we were much too worried to eat anything. The *Hercules* mids. waited about—the greedy pigs—till Mr. Perkins had to order some for them too, and they finished the whole lot of cakes, ours as well as theirs. Then the big German called us, and he and Mr. Perkins and we two drove away. It was a quarter to three and Mr. Macdonald would be expecting us in a quarter of an hour—whatever should we do ! The Angel and I couldn't keep our feet still—we felt so awful—because we could have walked faster than the carriage went in the crowded streets.   When we turned down a side street, the nigger driver lashed the horses into a gallop, we got out into the country, and presently pulled up at a big white house with the Union Jack flying above it.

Oh ! It was so comforting to see it.

Out we jumped, the German hurried us through a courtyard, a black footman in livery led us through a lot of beautiful cool rooms into a garden with palms and fountains, and we saw a whole crowd of people —English ladies too—sitting in the shade.   We forgot to be shy, we were so frightened, caught sight of Captain Grattan and Captain Roger Hill, and, without waiting, simply ran up to them through all the ladies, and told them all about it.

'Tut, tut, tut, tut,' our Captain said, jumping out of his chair and screwing in his eyeglass. 'Tut, tut, that's serious.   Come this way,' and he took us in to the British Minister—a big tall chap with a nose like a hawk and great bushy eyebrows, dressed in white duck clothes.   We had to tell our story again, clutching each other; he made us so frightened, looking at us so fiercely.   You couldn't tell from his face what he thought of it, but he told the Captain that he'd change into uniform and take us to the President right away.

' It's serious,' he said. 'Gerald Wilson is too openly mixed up in politics to claim our protection, and things may go badly with his brother.'

We felt so jolly relieved that something was at last going to be done that we did have some tea then, the ladies crowding round the Angel and helping him, though they weren't so keen on me—they never are, which is a jolly good thing. ' If I'd a face like a girl's they'd fuss round me too,' I told the Angel, and he was beastly rude and called me ' Old Pimple Face,' and made them all laugh at me. I could have kicked him.

The Minister was back again before we'd finished stuffing, and then hurried us away—he and the Captain in one carriage, and Mr. Perkins and we two in another.

We drove as fast as ever we could back to the town, and the soldiers we passed looked as if they'd like to shoot us. They scowled so much that I was jolly glad that the Minister was in his gorgeous gold braid uniform and the Captain and Mr. Perkins were in theirs. We had to pass close to San Sebastian, and we told Mr. Perkins that that was probably where Billums had been taken. ' Mr. Macdonald told us they take all the revolutionary people there.'

Just as we'd told him this, we heard a scrappy kind of a volley from inside the walls.

' Good God ! ' Mr. Perkins nearly jumped off his seat, his red face turning quite yellow ; ' they're

shooting people already. Why can't we go faster?'
I almost blubbed.

We were back again in the city now, the streets
simply filled with soldiers, leaning up against the
walls, trying to find a little shade and some of them
shouting rudely at us as we passed.

At last we stopped opposite some big iron gates
through which soldiers were coming and going in
hundreds. The sentries there wouldn't let the
Minister pass through at first, till an officer came
along. Then we all got out and walked in, following
the Minister, who stalked along, head and shoulders
taller than any of the officers standing about, and
pushed his way into a big room crowded with very
excited people, most of them officers, half of them
niggers and the other half not much lighter. They
left off chattering as we appeared, and bowed and
clicked their heels when they saw the Minister, but
didn't look at all pleased.

'They hate us English,' I heard the Minister tell
the Captain. 'Most of us favour the Vice-President's
party, though only Gerald Wilson has been fool
enough to do so openly.'

We stuck very closely to him whilst officers and
orderlies kept on streaming in and out of a small door
leading into another room. Most of their uniforms
were jolly smart—either white with yellow facings or
khaki with white facings. Cavalry officers had a
light-blue striped cotton tunic fitting very tightly and

very bulging khaki riding-breeches. They looked awful dandies, and all wore stiff white shirts with cuffs although it was so hot—the blacker they were and the more like niggers, the more stiff white cuffs they showed.

What the Angel and I noticed chiefly about the infantry officers was that they didn't seem to worry so much whether their clothes fitted them, and they nearly all wore patent-leather ' Jemima ' boots, with the elastic generally worn out and quite loose round the ankles.

' The President is not here—won't be here for some time—he's gone to San Sebastian,' the Minister said in a low voice.

You could never tell whether he was worried about it or not—his voice and his face never changed. 'We shall have to wait. He's a fiery little chap—thinks he is the Napoleon of the west, and loves to show off before us Europeans. He'll be in a pretty bad temper to-day. He meant to arrest the Vice-President, de Costa, as he left the cathedral, but he and his friends got wind of it and left by a side door ; smuggled away as priests or nuns, some say, and have slipped through his fingers. He meant to "scotch" the revolution which is coming, and he's failed badly, so he'll be a pretty handful to tackle.'

' Well, *he* might be able to tackle him,' the Angel whispered, and we both thought that he looked perfectly grand in his uniform. Then there was a great clatter outside ; we could hear officers calling their men to attention ; trumpets were blown, all the officers in the room took their cigarettes out of their mouths, stood bolt-upright, and in came the President just as we'd seen him in the procession.   Every one made a lane for him to pass into the room beyond, and he spotted us, but hardly took any notice of the Minister's salute or of our Captain's either, which made the Angel and me very angry, though we were really too frightened at his very cruel-looking eyes to be angry.

Several people followed him—all very gorgeously dressed—covered with medals and with green and yellow sashes over their shoulders, and the last to come in was the little A.D.C. from Los Angelos with the big spurs and the curved sword.

The Minister spoke to one of them, who seemed to be doing 'orderly' officer, but he only shrugged his shoulders, went into the little room.   We heard a few fierce words and back he came, shrugging his shoulders all the more.

'He says the President is too busy to see me,' the Minister told the Captain, who was gradually getting angry at being treated like this.   Then there was another commotion, and in came the grand-looking old Governor of Los Angelos and the black A.D.C.   He seemed to be a friend of the Minister, for he stopped and shook his hand, bowed and yarned quite pleasantly. He too went into the other room.

'I've told him that I must see the President,' the Minister said, and we waited again, though even he wasn't successful, and came back shrugging his shoulders and spreading out his hands, his great sword clanking along the floor.

The Minister's face never altered the slightest bit. 'He refuses to see me—will only receive the senior foreign Minister—that is the Comte de Launy, the Frenchman. It's no use waiting here any longer—we must go and find him—it will take an hour.'

His voice never altered in the slightest degree, but the Captain was 'tut tutting' and polishing his eyeglass, whilst Mr. Perkins was bubbling over with wrath.

As we went out we saw the officers all sneering at us, but the Governor sang out something very angrily, and they stood to attention and he himself bowed us out. We were jolly glad to get out, I can tell you, because it was such a horrid feeling to have all these strange fierce-looking officers all round us without being able to understand a word they said, and to feel certain that they'd like to murder us.

'Well, the old Governor's a gent, isn't he?' the Angel whispered.

We drove back to the Residence—I was feeling awfully sick with funk about Billums—and there we were left whilst the Captain and the Minister drove away again to find the Frenchman.

It was long after four o'clock; Mr. Macdonald would be on his way down to Los Angelos, and we hadn't the least idea how we should get back; but we didn't want to go back so long as old Billums was shut up in San Sebastian, and might be shot any minute.

There were only three ladies there now, the Minister's wife and her two daughters, and they did their very best to cheer us up. The Angel was in great form—he always was when ladies were about—and sang his rotten songs ; but as I couldn't sit still, I wandered out into the courtyard, and fed some gold-fish in one of the fountains. It was fairly cool there, and every time I heard wheels I ran to the gateway, but they didn't come back till nearly six o'clock, and when I rushed out, hoping to see Billums with them, there was only a dried-up little man in another gorgeous uniform—the French Minister.

'No good, Temple,' the Captain said, looking awfully serious.

'He won't let him go till his brother surrenders—does it to humiliate us.'

'What are you going to do now, sir?' I asked him, but he didn't answer.

They all three drove away again, and Mr. Perkins told me that they were going to collect all the foreign Ministers, and intended to see him in a body.

Then he and we two mids. had to do more waiting —it was terrible. The sun went down, it got dark quite suddenly, and we couldn't help thinking of the awful road down the mountains to Los Angelos and how we were going to get down there at night.

The Minister's wife gave us some dinner and tried

to be jolly, but I couldn't be, and couldn't eat anything. She and the girls were pretty nervous too, because, all the time we were pretending to have dinner, there were noises as if a riot was going on in the town. We were all fidgeting, and the black men-servants in their scarlet liveries were very jumpy. You could see by the way they moved about that they were frightened too.

The Minister's wife made them close the big windows and that drowned a good deal of the noise, and I couldn't see the dark creepy shadows of the palms outside and felt less uncomfortable. She kept on saying, ' I wish your father would come back,' and, just as we were going to have some coffee, we heard the banging of rifles. The black footman dropped his tray, and all of them simply trembled. It was no use to sit any longer at the table, the two girls began to cry, and then it was our turn to do something to help.

The firing sometimes seemed to be coming our way, so we three went round the garden and made sure that all the gates were locked—a jolly creepy job it was out there in the dark, and I jumped every time I heard a rifle go off. The servants were all standing about, whispering and looking frightened, which made it all the more horrid ; so, to give them something to do, we sent them to close all the shutters, though we couldn't get them to go into the street to close some there, and had to do that ourselves. Then we made the three ladies come into the drawing-room, lighted all the lamps, and tried to cheer them up.   The Angel played the piano, and Mr. Perkins, who hates singing, bellowed out some sea-songs and made them join in the choruses.   That wasn't much of a success, so he scratched his funny old head and did a few tricks. One was to stand straight upright and then sit down on the floor without bending his knees, and he did it so jolly well that it nearly shook the ornaments off the mantelpiece, and the bump frightened them all. Then he showed them how he could fall flat on his chest without bending his knees, and did it, but banged his chin hard on the polished floor, so that wasn't quite a success either.

We couldn't think of any other tricks.

Nine o'clock came, and ten o'clock—there was no firing now—and half-past ten came before we heard several carriages coming towards the house, and went out into the courtyard to the street gate.

The Minister, the Captain, the tall German, who turned out to be the German Minister, and was in a grand-looking uniform, the little Frenchman, four or five others, and the United States Minister in ordinary evening dress, got down, and then several ladies, closely wrapped up, came in too.

All the Ministers disappeared into another room by themselves, only the Captain and the ladies coming into the drawing-room.   He was saying 'tut, tut' all the time, and all we could get out of him was, ' We've been treated like children—tut, tut—by a miserable half-bred savage—he won't listen to us.'

' A lot of firing going on in the city, isn't there, sir?' Mr. Perkins asked.

'Only a few drunken soldiers letting off their rifles,' he grunted, and then he was sent for, and a few minutes afterwards a man-servant came in to ask the Minister's wife to speak to her husband. She went out, and we could hear her speaking to him, and back she came looking very pale. 'Captain Grattan' (that was our Captain) 'has asked us to stay on board the *Hector*, my dears ; we are going down with him to-night.'

She tried to look cheerful, but they and we knew what that meant—that it wasn't safe for them in Santa Cruz any longer—and the girls began to cry again. All three of them went away to get ready.

' Phew ! Great smokes,' Mr. Perkins whistled, 'it's come to a pretty pass—that ass of a Sub has stirred up a hornets' nest, if you like.'

' It wasn't his fault, sir,' I said ; 'he couldn't help it.'

Just then the Captain and the Ministers trooped in. They looked as though they'd come to some decision which pleased them, and it made the Angel and me feel more happy about poor old Billums up there in San Sebastian. We both wondered whether he'd had any dinner, and what he thought had become of us—all this time. Some more ladies came in, all wrapped up

in furs because the night was very cold, and in the
middle of all the hubbub we heard a lot of cavalry
coming along. They stopped outside the house, and
a moment later the Governor of Los Angelos, with his
two A.D.C.'s, came in. Weren't we pleased to see
him, that's all! There was more bowing and scrap-
ing, coffee was handed round, and we two edged
alongside the little A.D.C. who had talked English
in the gun-room yesterday. He recognised us then
and said, smiling, 'We take you to Los Angelos
to-night—the *señoras* and the *señoritas* also—we
have many horse soldiers—the road it has much
danger.'

'How about Billums—William Wilson—our Sub?'
we asked, 'up in San Sebastian.'

He smiled, and pulled out—what d'you think?—old
Billums's cigarette case—I knew it jolly well—and said,
'I give him my—he give me him,' but shut up like
an oyster, shrugged his shoulders, and shook his head
when we asked him if Billums was coming with us.
That made us miserable again, and we went out to see
what the cavalry escort were like. They had dismounted, and were swaggering into the courtyard,
looking absolute villains, most of them niggers,
their carbines and bandoliers over their shoulders,
revolvers in their belts, and swords, which clanked
and rattled whenever they moved. The servants
were giving them cigarettes and some food, but,
for all that, they didn't seem at all friendly, and the

whites of their eyes showed up under the swinging lanterns, and made them look more like brigands than ever. The Angel palled up to them and made them show him their rifles, but I felt too frightened and only hoped that the Governor was coming with us. The carriages drove up, all the ladies came out and were put into them, the dear old Governor of Los Angelos handing them in and bending down to kiss our Minister's wife's hands in such a jolly manner that the Angel and I could have hugged him.

We felt that he could be absolutely trusted, and weren't we jolly glad again when his horse was led up and he and part of the escort rode away with the ladies.

In the last carriage the Captain, Mr. Perkins, and we two mids. were stowed, and away we went after them with the two A.D.C.'s bobbing behind on their horses and the rest of the escort, leaving the Ministers all standing together under the lamp which lit up their faces and all their beautiful gold lace.

'They don't look very "sniffy," do they?' I whispered to the Angel, 'I should if I was letting my wife go away like this.'

'Not if you'd got those uniforms on and had a Frenchman or a German or a Dutchman watching you,' he whispered.

I expect he was right.

The Governor came clattering back on his great horse to see that we'd started, and then went on ahead again, the black A.D.C. bumping along after him.

You can imagine what a row we made, and how, as we got into the streets, all the shutters of the windows were thrown back and people peered at us from behind the bars ; dogs, too, flew out and barked from every doorway.   It was a wonderful night—a big moon and millions of stars, the tops of the mountains showing up all round us.   Jolly cold it was, too, and the Angel and I were glad to snuggle together under a rug.

We seemed to go a long way round, skirting the city, and though sometimes at street corners pickets and patrols challenged us, they were quite satisfied. Presently we passed close to a great shadowy building high up on our right.   It had a funny little tower at one corner, and we recognised the shadow at once—it was San Sebastian.

The Angel and I squeezed each other to buck our-selves up, and kept our eyes on it all the time.   It looked most awfully gloomy, and it seemed horrid to think that only twelve hours ago Billums had driven past it with us, and now he was inside and we were going back without him.

'What will he think of us?' I gulped.   'Poor old Billums !'

Well, we got on to the main road, left the city be-hind us, and presently began to go downhill.   Mr. Perkins went to sleep soon, his jolly red face rolling from side to side as the carriage bumped, and the Captain snuggled down in the other corner, and we

knew when he went to sleep, because his eyeglass fell
out, and he didn't 'tut, tut,' and put it back.

We didn't go to sleep for a long time—we were too
miserable and cold—and watched the troopers riding
on each side of us with their blankets over their
shoulders, and every half-mile or'so, flaming fires at
the side of the road, with soldiers sitting round them.
We could hear them challenging the carriages in
front, but when we got up to them, they only stared
at us, or called out to the escort, and wrapped their
blankets round them more closely.   There was a
huge nigger chap riding on my side of the carriage,
and both he and his wretched thin horse seemed
nearly asleep.   I watched him bobbing and lurching
from side to side in his saddle, waking up with a
start whenever his poor brute stumbled, and then
must have gone to sleep, because the next I remember was finding that we were going past rows
of houses—pitch dark, with not a sound coming from
them—and knew that we'd got down to Los Angelos.

I was colder than ever, because the Angel had all
the rug, but the smell of the sea was grand.

We drove down to the wharf where we'd landed in
the morning.   The carriages all stopped—I could
hardly stand when I got out because my legs were so
cramped—and two of our barges were waiting for us,
their mids. holding up lanterns and singing out to let
us know where they were.

The cavalry escort clattered away, the old Governor

kissed the hands of all the ladies as he helped them into the boats, the two A.D.C.'s, looking frightfully sleepy, clicked their heels and bowed, the Captain said, 'Tut, tut,' a good many times and shook the Governor by the hand, the Angel and I managed to get hold of the fat A.D.C. and shake his hand, and off we all went.

It was simply splendid to be in a boat again and to hear the oars go 'click, click' in the rowlocks, and when we'd got round the end of the breakwater to see the lights of the *Hector* and *Hercules*.   The other chaps who had gone back before us had taken orders for the two barges to wait in, all night, if necessary ; that was why we'd found them there.

The Angel and I were both of us dead tired, and went down below to turn in, but there was a lot of scurrying up above; we heard the Gunnery Lieutenant sent for, and the Captain's Clerk was turned out. Evidently something exciting was going to happen, so we ran up on deck again and, peeping down the ward-room skylight, saw our Captain and the Captain of the *Hercules*, the Commander, and most of our senior officers all sitting round the table, which was littered with papers and confidential books.

We stole away, because the officer of the watch whacked us over the back with his telescope, and were undressing in the gun-room flat when the bugler sounded the 'officers' call' and 'both watches fall in.' We heard 'Clear lower deck' being shouted along the mess decks and bugles sounding aboard the *Hercules*, so instead of undressing we shifted into uniform, whilst every one else tumbled out of their hammocks and shifted into theirs.   We all clattered up on deck.

' Everybody aft ' was piped, and the men came streaming through the dark battery door into the glare of the group light on the quarterdeck, buttoning up the tops of their trousers and stuffing their flannels down them.

The master-at-arms reported ' Lower deck cleared, sir,' to the Commander, he reported to the Captain, and the Captain, standing on the top of the after 9.2 inch turret, coughed, said 'tut, tut,' a good many times, and then told the men that Billums had been collared because he was so much like his brother, who'd mixed himself up in politics, that the President was going to keep him till Gerald surrendered, and that all the foreign Ministers were agreed that steps had to be taken jolly quickly to get him out of San Sebastian.

The men were as quiet as lambs, waiting for the exciting part and to know what he intended doing. You couldn't hear a sound.   ' I want you to clear for action—now—do it quickly—I'm going to take the *Hector* inside the breakwater at daylight, whilst Captain Roger Hill '—he called him ' Old Spats,' but corrected himself—' gets under way in the *Hercules* and prepares to tackle the forts.   They've got some —you've seen them—up on the hill above the town—

but won't give us much trouble. If Mr. Wilson is not at the landing-stage at noon, the foreign Ministers will be, and they and all the Europeans who wish will come aboard this ship. That being the case, I shall then—acting under the Ministers' orders—take possession of the five Santa Cruz cruisers and gunboats inside and shall tow them out.'

You could feel the men getting excited, and then he gave several more 'tut, tuts,' and told us that a revolution had started, and that, as the revolutionary people came from both the provinces to the north and south, and the mountains separated them and made it impossible for them to combine successfully by land, the only way they could do so was by the sea, and as long as the President had his cruisers and gunboats he could prevent them doing so, and keep the upper hand.

'If we capture his ships, the insurgents can do what they like,' and he finished up with, 'There are ladies aboard—we couldn't leave them in Santa Cruz —so work quietly. Carry on, Commander!' We dug out like smoke, turning the boats in and filling them with water, getting down davits and rails, lashing the rigging, and working hard till daylight came.

Then all us mids. scrambled down below to get some hot cocoa and bread and butter, and were up on deck again in a jiffy, for the buglers sounded 'cable officers,' which meant that we were just going to weigh anchor, and we didn't want to miss any of the fun.

The *Hercules*, cleared for action, just astern of us, was looking awfully grim, her long guns simply bristling over the sides, and white ensigns lashed in her rigging.

Petty Officer O'Leary came up to ask about Billums —he was very worried about him—and, just as we began to steam ahead, a cloud of smoke shot out from one of the forts above the town.

'They're going to fight,' I sang out, not quite certain that I wasn't frightened.

But O'Leary growled, and said, ' No such luck, sir, anyway, that's only the sunrise gun—late as usu'l, sir.'

'General quarters' was sounded—we could hear it too aboard the *Hercules*—and we all had to rush to our stations.   Mine was in the starboard for'ard 9.2 turret, and you may bet your life that directly we'd cleared it away, and had things ready inside, I got my head jammed outside the sighting hood to see what was going on.

We headed straight inshore, and then made a wide sweep round the lighthouse and the end of the breakwater.

As we turned, the white forts about the town came into view, and we tried to get our gun to bear on them, but though we gave it extreme elevation, cocking it up in the air, we couldn't elevate it nearly enough.

Mr. Bigge, the lieutenant in charge of my turret,
was very angry about it, but of course nothing could
be done.   That was why the *Hercules* was steaming backwards and forwards, far enough outside the
breakwater for her guns to bear.

As we crept up to the town, I kept my telescope
glued on the forts, but couldn't see any sign of life
in them.

'They aren't going to fight, sir, are they?' I asked
Mr. Bigge, and he didn't think they were, which was
very disappointing—one doesn't mind being fired at
when one is inside a turret.

On the port side—the breakwater side—we were
now right alongside the Santa Cruz Navy—miserable
dirty little ships when you saw them close to us.
Their people were awake and on deck, but hardly
bothered to look at us, and were fishing over the
side, smoking cigarettes, and spitting in the water,
some of them washing clothes and hanging them up
in the rigging.   They did hoist their colours—the
vertical green and yellow stripes—after a time, but
that was the only thing they did.   Not very exciting,
after all we had been hoping for, was it?

Just before we got up to the end of the breakwater
we'd dropped a kedge anchor made fast to our
biggest wire hawser, and as we went along we paid
the hawser out astern.   Then when we'd got just
beyond the landing-stage we dropped an anchor, and
there we were in a pretty close billet, not enough

room to turn, but our kedge ready to haul us out stern first, and everything as snug as a tin of sardines. We were not a hundred yards from the wharves where that guard of honour had been yesterday, but only a few people and some mules were moving sleepily about, and a lonely-looking sentry leant against a great pile of cocoa bales and yawned.

Well, we'd taken them by surprise right enough, and there was nothing to do but to wait till noon and see what happened. It was a jolly long wait, and I don't really know whether I wanted most to see Billums come off, or to capture the cruisers if he didn't. I know that all the other chaps didn't want him to come off. Outside the breakwater the *Hercules* still steamed backwards and forwards, with her guns trained on the forts in case anything happened, and during the forenoon got down her topmasts and wireless gear. This made her look all the more ferocious, and our Commander began bellowing and cursing 'that he'd have to do the same and spoil all his paint-work.' It took us a couple of hours, but it was much better than doing nothing, and later on in the morning crowds of people came down on the wharves to look at us, and watch us working. My eye! but it was appallingly hot in there.

At about ten o'clock the forts began to show signs of life, hoisting yellow and green flags and training their guns round and round. They had two dynamite

guns in one of them—so the books said—and we
felt as though they couldn't possibly miss us if
they had fired.   That sounded far too exciting—
dynamite seemed rather unpleasant—but the Gunnery
Lieutenant's ' Doggy ' brought the news that none of
the guns in the fort could be depressed enough to hit
us, which was rather a relief—really—though the
others didn't think so.   The cruisers, too, began to
get up steam, let down their gun ports, and ran their
guns out.   We could see them being loaded, and
then they were trained on us, which was very exciting when you remember that they were only fifty
yards away.

Directly they had the cheek to do this our port
guns were trained on them—the foremost 9.2 on one,
the port for'ard 9.2 on another, two of the 7.5's on a
third, and so on, with orders to fire directly the Santa
Cruz ships fired.

Of course these poor little things wouldn't have
stood a chance, but they kept their crews at their
guns, and if they'd only been able to let off one broadside it would have swept our decks.   This made it
jolly interesting for all of us who were getting down
the topmasts and had to work in the open.

I had never thought about how Billums or the
Ministers were coming off, and when at seven bells
the first and second barges were called away, you can
imagine how excited I was, because the second barge
was mine.   They lowered us into the water, planked

a Maxim gun in the bows, revolvers and cutlasses were served out to the crew, and I had my dirk and revolver.

The Commander bellowed down that we were to go inshore, lie off the steps at the landing-place, and wait for Billums or the Ministers.

I was in white uniform with a white helmet, and it was so boilingly hot that, though the men only had on straw hats, flannels, and duck trousers, they sweated under their cutlass belts before they'd pulled half-way inshore.

As we got close to the wharf it was more exciting still, because the people crowding there and the soldiers began shouting and jeering at us, shaking sticks and throwing stones—not to hit us, but to splash us. They weren't brave enough to do any more, because they could see all the starboard twelve-pounders on board the *Hector* trained on them. I felt jolly important, and when Blotchy Smith—the midshipman of the first barge and a pal of mine—sang out for me to 'lay on my oars,' we bobbed up and down only about ten yards away and pretended we didn't see them.

We waited and waited; eight bells struck aboard the *Hector*, there wasn't a sign of any one coming, and the black ruffians on the wharf became more irritating than ever. Several lumps of mud and dirt had been thrown into the boats, and one had struck my clean helmet, but I still pretended not to notice anything.

It got so bad soon that Blotchy Smith sang out to me to train my Maxim on the crowd, and you would have laughed if you'd seen the brutes clearing away.

Then the *Hector* signalled across that carriages could be seen coming down the road from Santa Cruz, and after another long wait we heard the mob ashore groaning and hooting, and a lot of cavalry and several carriages came clattering and rattling along the wooden wharves.

You can guess how we wondered whether it was Billums coming or only the Ministers. It wasn't Billums, for we saw all the foreign Ministers, and knew that they would not have come with him.

Some soldiers made a way for them, and then we had to pull backwards and forwards, taking them and a lot of Europeans—Mr. Macdonald among them —off to the ship, and afterwards go back for their luggage.

'Well, we'll have a bit of a "dust up" after this, sir,' my coxswain said, and that was about the only comfort.

The Angel told me afterwards that when the Ministers got on board their wives came up and made asses of them, they were so jolly pleased to see them, but they'd all been sent below by the time my boat had been hoisted in. Then we had to collar the cruisers.

Well, even that was disappointing, because they never made any resistance, the officers simply shrugged their shoulders when we hauled their colours down and hoisted our own white ensigns, and ordered their men to pull ashore. You couldn't really blame them, because our 9.2 shells would have blown them to smithereens; but, for all that, it was very tame.

By half-past one we'd got hawsers aboard their flagship, the *Presidente Canilla*, and by three o'clock hawsers had been passed from her to the others, and we simply went astern, hauling on our kedge anchor till we were clear of the breakwater, and then steamed astern with the whole of the Santa Cruz Navy coming along after us like a lot of toy ships on the end of a string. It looked perfectly silly, and the last one— a gunboat as big as a decent Gosport ferry-boat —fouled the end of the breakwater till our chaps aboard of her shoved her off, and along she came after the rest of them. By five o'clock we and the *Hercules* had anchored, and all the prizes as well.

It was a jolly tame ending to all the excitement, and we all wondered what we should do next to make them give up Billums. The A.P. said that we should probably land and take possession of the Custom House.

He bucked us up a good deal, but not even that came off, because before we finished making everything shipshape for the night, out puffed the port launch, flying a huge white flag in her bows and the yellow and green ensign in the stern, bringing out our friend the Governor and his two A.D.C.'s. They

came along to make complete apologies, and say that
Billums should be given up next morning. He
brought a letter from the President simply grovelling
to the various Ministers and imploring them and the
merchants to come ashore again. Wasn't that grand,
although, you know, we couldn't help feeling that
we'd been rather playing the bully?

When it got dark, the Angel, and I, and Mr.
Bostock, the Gunner, with half-a-dozen hands, were
sent aboard one of the ships, the *Salvador*, an old
torpedo-gunboat kind of affair, to keep watch through
the night. We had revolvers served out to us in
case any chaps from shore tried to play the idiot;
but they didn't, and we simply sat down under an
awning with our coat-collars turned up, and took it
in turns to keep watch, or, if we were all awake, got
Mr. Bostock to tell us tales of Ladysmith.

In the morning we all went back to the *Hector*, and
at five minutes past ten o'clock old Billums came
along in the port launch, the Governor bringing him
off and making more apologies. Billums *was* glad to
get back again—he wanted a shave and a clean collar
most awfully—and you can guess how jolly glad
we were to have him. The Commander bellowed
at him that he'd make him pay for all the paint-work
which had been spoilt by clearing for action, but it
was only his way—he couldn't help it—and the
Hercules gun-room sent a signal, 'Sub to ditto.
We are all jolly glad to get you back,' which was

nice of him, though his beasts of mids. didn't join in
with the signal—just like them.

Well, the Ministers and the merchants went ashore
jolly pleased with themselves, but they left all the
ladies on board, as they thought it wiser for them to
go to Prince Rupert's Island with us till things had
quieted down in Santa Cruz.

We gave Billums a rousing good sing-song, till
the Commander ordered us to chuck it, and was
appallingly rude to him; and next morning we left
the Santa Cruz Navy for its own people to take back
behind the breakwater, and shoved off for Prince
Rupert's Island.

You should have seen the Angel looking after the
Minister's two daughters! It was too asinine for
words, and I told him so. He said I was jealous, and
we jolly nearly came to punching each other's heads
about them.

CHAPTER V

Gerald Wilson captures San Fernando

Written by Sub-Lieutenant William Wilson

THOSE thirty-six hours in San Sebastian are over and done with, and I shouldn't care to go through them again. They were the longest hours I have ever spent, and they, at any rate, taught me what it does feel like to be a prisoner, and to look through an iron gateway and envy everything outside it, and everybody. The other chaps—*insurrectos* they all were— had been jolly decent to me, although I could not understand their lingo, and the way they settled down and took things as a matter of course was simply extraordinary. Even when two more were dragged out the morning I was released, and shot against that parapet, the others only shrugged their shoulders and simply smoked cigarettes all the harder. You could only imagine that they were but half-civilized, had known no other way of carrying on the politics of the Republic, and were so used to violence and murder that, when their turn came to go ' under,' they simply bowed to the inevitable, their only consolation being that probably in another few weeks or months,

if luck favoured their party, that same stuffy room
would be crowded with President's men, and quite possibly the same villainous-looking firing-party would
just as cheerfully prop them up against that wall and
shoot them down.   These same miserable - looking
convicts, whom I'd seen with chains round their ankles,
would almost certainly be there to dig fresh graves.

Of course, all those hours I wondered what our
chaps were doing to bail me out, but didn't worry
much—I knew things would come right in the end—
and of course they did.

But I did worry about Gerald and what his hare-
brained adventures would lead him to.   He had
always been getting into trouble at home, and that was
why the pater and mater had shipped him out to
Santa Cruz, though they little thought that he'd take
a leading part in a revolution, and the poor old mater
would be fearfully worried when she heard about it.
It was jolly to know that an Englishman, and my own
brother, was such a boss among these fierce, bloodthirsty, half-Spanish people, but that wouldn't be
much comfort to the mater if he was stuck up against
the parapet of San Sebastian, which would certainly
be his fate if he ever fell into the clutches of the
President.

It was my chum of the cigarette case who actually
fetched me down and took me aboard the *Hector*.
Even whilst I was trying to thank him, the Commander began bellowing that ' He'd make me pay for

the paint he'd spoilt clearing for action and housing the topmasts.' He was as rude as it was possible to be, but every one else—'Old Tin Eye' included—was all right, and Ginger signalled congratulations from the *Hercules*.

Of course my adventure was known all over Princes' Town before we'd anchored more than an hour or two, and reporters from the local papers and Reuter's Agent came bustling on board for more details, but were told nothing, except that I'd been arrested by mistake, and that, as a hint to the President to let me out again, 'chop, chop,' one or two of the Santa Cruz gunboats had been seized. We had all been ordered to give no political information to anybody, but you may imagine that their ears were rigged out for something more exciting than that, and you can jolly well guess who gave it to them—the Angel backed up by Cousin Bob. They saw their way to getting a cheap 'blow out' at the Savannah Hotel, and actually had the cheek to tell the two local reporters that if they'd stand them a dinner there, they would tell them all they knew about it.

They had put their names down in the leave book for the late boat and went ashore, but of course I had no idea what their game was. I had turned in early, and they woke me, by knocking at my cabin and asking if they could come in.

I switched on my light, and there they were, in their best blue suits, grinning from ear to ear.

They both began talking twenty to the dozen. 'We've given you such a "leg up"—we've had a topping feed at the Savannah, and you'll see all about it in the papers to-morrow!'

'All what?' I asked.

'All about you fighting dozens of soldiers, knocking them over, and of our trying to rescue you.'

'We put in a lot of extras to make it look better,' Bob squeaked.

'We told them all about knocking over the rotten *Hercules* mids., and about you being so like Cousin Gerald.'

'What!' I sang out, sitting up in my bunk. 'You blessed idiots, what rot have you been up to? You know you had orders not to speak of it.'

'We didn't say a word about politics, not a word,' Bob said rather nervously. 'It's quite all right; we never mentioned politics.' The Angel added, 'We didn't tell them the real way you escaped.'

'Out with it! What did you tell them, you fools?'

They were backing out of the cabin—rather sulky —but I yelled for them to come back. 'Now, none of your tomfoolery. What did you tell them?'

'Well, we gave ourselves a bit of a leg up too,' the Angel began, looking down his nose as good as gold.

'It really was all a joke,' Bob interrupted, 'it was their fault if they believed it. We told them that we waited till night under the walls of San Sebastian, wriggled over the parapet, and found your dungeon.'

'We told them that we'd whistled "Rule, Britannia!" —very softly—till—we—heard—you—whistle back,' the Angel stuttered out, choking with laughter, 'and that the sentry was asleep, and we only had to knock him down—and gag him—steal the key—open the door—all of us crawling away again over the walls and tramping it on our flat feet down to Los Angelos.'

'You don't mean to tell me that they believed all that rot?'

'We think they did—wasn't it a joke?' Bob said —he was beginning to see that I didn't think it a joke. 'We gave them the key of the dungeon—an old brass key we'd found on the armourer's bench before we went ashore.'

'It was the key of the bread-room that was broken yesterday,' the Angel gurgled, when he could stop laughing. 'And we said we'd all swum off to the ship in the dark.'

I wasn't in the humour to see how it was funny, and sent them out of it. 'If anything does come out in the papers, I'll beat you both,' I told them.

'Well, the feed was worth a hiding, and the joke too,' Bob mumbled, as they went away—thank goodness the Angel was no relation of mine and had no mother or sister who could write snorters to me, so he didn't dare to be rude.

You can guess how angry I was next morning,

when the wretched local papers did come aboard, and saw in big letters : 'Romantic Escape of British Naval Officer—Plucky Middies effect Rescue,' and underneath it was the silliest nonsense you could possibly read. Honestly, even now I don't know whether it was put in as a joke, and whether, instead of Bob and the Angel pulling the reporters' legs, they were pulling ours. Angry! I was too angry to speak!

They described me as Sub-Lieutenant William Wilson, the celebrated United Service half-back, and the brilliant naval officer, specially appointed to command the *Hector's* gun-room by the Lords of the Admiralty as a mark of their appreciation of my services! Angry! My blessed potatoes! I sent for my dear cousin and the Angel and gave them six of the best over the gun-room table—as hard as I could lay it on—the first three for making their Sub look a fool, and the last three for disobeying the Captain's orders. I know which were the hardest whacks, and I didn't care a biscuit what Bob's sister, Daisy, thought or wrote. They went away muttering that the dinner was worth it—every time—which was meant to be rude, because they both had got it into their noddles that they'd actually given me a 'leg up,' and couldn't see that they'd only made a laughing-stock of me.

First of all the Commander sent for me on the quarterdeck. He had Perkins there as a witness, and before I ever had a chance of saying anything, bellowed out, 'You're the "brilliant naval officer," are you? You're a fool, and an idiot, and a useless idiot. You can't keep order in the gun-room, and the sooner you get out of the ship the better.' He bellowed till the maintopmen, painting masts and yards up aloft, left off painting to listen to him. He didn't ask me to speak, so I didn't—said not a word—which made him almost apoplectic with rage, his ugly red face getting perfectly crimson. Every time he stopped for breath, Perkins kept on trying to tell him that perhaps it wasn't my fault, which sprung him off again, and at last he turned round and cursed him for interfering.

Perkins twisted round on his heel and hobbled off, but the Commander called for him to come back, and he did, his jolly face all tightened out.

'Did you hear the Commander curse me on the quarterdeck?' he asked very quietly.

'I did, sir,' I said; and he turned to the Commander, 'Very well, I shall see the Captain about it. I'm not going to stand any more of it.'

You should have seen the Commander's face. His mouth opened, and he looked as if he would willingly have murdered the two of us, then he bounced off the quarterdeck, and into his cabin just inside the battery, and banged the door, like the childish bully he was. As he didn't come out again, I went below.

Then the Skipper sent for me. He was grinning all over his face : 'Those two boys have made a fool of you, Wilson; tut! tut! stop their leave—whack 'em both.'

'I've beaten them, sir, already,' I told him, 'and given them six apiece—as hard as I could,' and explained to him that I had no idea why they went ashore.

'Tut! tut! no harm done; they got their dinner all right; tell 'em to lunch with me, tut! tut!—if they can sit down—I'd have done it myself for a good dinner—thirty years ago.'

Old Ginger and I had arranged to go for a walk together that afternoon, to shake up our livers, and I was not particularly keen, after what had happened, to ask leave from the Commander, but I screwed up my courage and did so, and was flattened aback when he said, 'Very good, Wilson. Come and have "chow" with me in the ward-room to-night—celebrate your release.'

That was the rotten, or rather the irritating, part about him. After he'd been as rude as a fishwife, and long before you'd got over bubbling with anger at the sight of him, he'd come up as if nothing had happened and take the wind out of your sails.

Of course I had to say 'Yes,' although at the time I'd have much preferred to take him on with bare knuckles and punch his head to relieve my feelings.

Old Ginger met me at the Governor's steps, where we landed, and we had a fifteen-mile walk as hard as we could go—tearing along till we hadn't a dry rag between us.

Fifteen miles in that climate takes more out of you than twice the distance in England, so you can guess we were pretty well 'done' by the time we got back to the landing-steps.

Whilst we waited for our boats we sat under the shade of the fruit market and watched the niggers —all as cheerful as sand-boys—unloading a cargo of cocoa-pods from a small schooner. The washer-ladies were coming ashore, too, from the *Hector* and *Hercules*, cackling like hens because of the huge bundles of clothes they'd got. Perkins's friend, Arabella de Montmorency, was the first to waddle up the steps, grinning from ear to ear, and carrying a huge bundle. 'The good Lo'd be praised,' she sang out to a buck-nigger waiting for her, 'Massa Perkins pay Arabella the three shilling and tuppence —Massa Perkins know Arabella good vash-lady— no black trash for Massa Perkins. I pray de good Lo'd keep Massa Perkins in His strong hand.' She went back into the boat for more washing, but the other washer-ladies had bagged it, and there was a fine row. All their men friends joined in shouting, and yelling, and shaking their fists at each other, and we hoped to see a good free-fight, but the Sikh policeman on duty stepped majestically forward, said a few sharp words, and they all burst out laughing, Arabella waddling away with her man carrying the disputed bundle, and trying to look dignified, telling everybody : ' Arabella no black trash —Arabella vash for de British naval officah.'

It was too funny for words, Ginger and I were simply doubled up with laughter, when I felt some one touch my shoulder, and, looking round, saw a thick-set native chap, as brown as leather—like those soldier chaps we'd seen on the wharf at Los Angelos—in a blue striped cotton vest, which showed his lumpy chest muscles through it, and a pair of loose cotton drawers, his brown legs and feet naked.   He was bowing and holding a broad Spanish grass hat in front of him with one hand.   ' William Wilson,' he kept on saying.

' What is it, old cock? me William Wilson—all light—belong ploper.   What's your game?'

His face beamed, and he pulled a dirty crumpled letter from under his vest and handed it to me.

It was addressed to me in Gerald's handwriting, and I tore it open, his face beaming again as he pointed a thin brown finger first to the address, and then circled it round my face, saying, ' William Wilson.' It was the only English he seemed to know.   I read :

' DEAR OLD BILLUMS—Sorry to have cleared out so hurriedly the other day—just managed to give them the slip in time—heard news of your adventure and the Navy business—wish you chaps would collar the lot of them for good.   Keep a look-out for that little chap who was shadowing me ; he'll try and get even with one of us. Tell the mater I'm having a ripping time — better than planting — will pay better than planting if our side wins. Tell her those socks she made me are A1. Look out for yourself—you're too much like me for this corner of the world. Don't send an answer.—GERALD.'

The nigger was still beaming and bowing, and he pointed to my hair. I'm jiggered if he hadn't spotted me by it.

That was a funny go, if you like, and I was jolly glad to know that Gerald was all right. It didn't worry me a ha'penny candle about that detective chap —I'd be only too jolly glad to see his ugly face and smash it. Ginger and I thought that the little messenger must have come in one of the many trading-schooners which slipped across from the mainland at night when the land breeze sprung up. We gave him all the small change we had in our pockets, and he smiled, and bowed, and disappeared among the merry crowd round us. He couldn't speak a word of English except my name, and my Chinese pidgin-English wasn't a success.

This was the only excitement and the only news I got from Gerald for several weeks. In the mean-time the *Hector* and the *Hercules* carried out the gunnery practices which had been interrupted at Gibraltar, returning to anchor off Princes' Town every Thursday night till Monday morning, so we managed

to get in a good many football matches.   Ginger and
I borrowed grounds and had some more gun-room
matches as well, but they didn't smooth things over,
rather the reverse, for when we beat the *Hercules*
at rugby by a try, which, they swore, wasn't one,
matters went from bad to worse.   There actually was
some doubt about it, for Perkins had been referee
(we couldn't get any one else) and couldn't keep up
with the ball on account of his game leg.   We had to
separate the two teams in the pavilion, and after that
my mids. seldom came back to the ship from a tennis
party, picnic, or dance, or anything in fact, without
having some furious tale to spin.

Old Ginger and I pretty nearly washed our hands
of them and let them go their own way.

There was no regular news from Santa Cruz all
this time, because the President had closed the
Telegraph Company's office, but the Pickford and
Black steamers still called at Los Angelos twice a
month before coming to Princes' Town, and they
brought news of what was going on.

As it chiefly came from Santa Cruz, it was from the
President's point of view, and if it was at all correct,
most of de Costa's people were already in San
Sebastian or flying in front of the President's
invincible troops.

Our fat friend, Mr. Macdonald, appeared at the
Princes' Town Club one day when I happened to
be there, and he, too, gave me anything but cheering

news.   Nearly every week, he told me, the guns of
San Sebastian fired a salute in honour of another
victory over the *insurrectos*.   'They're not showing
fight anywhere; the President's troops are scouring
the provinces and driving them from place to place,
whilst his cruisers and gunboats scour the coast and
prevent any arms or ammunition being smuggled
ashore.'   This made me jolly nervous about Gerald,
and very miserable too, for he also had told me that
Gerald's rubber plantation had been entirely destroyed
in revenge for his taking up arms.   It may have
served him right, but it was beastly hard luck on the
pater, who had bought the place for him.

Of course we seemed to be in the thick of everything, because Prince Rupert's Island was only fifty-
two miles from the nearest point on the coast of Santa
Cruz, and, as it was the centre of all the foreign trade
of the Republic, the revolution, which was going on
there, was practically the only thing talked about.
By listening to the English merchants and officials
talking at the Club we got to know quite a lot about
the military position and the chances of the two
parties.

You see the Republic of Santa Cruz stretches for
almost a hundred and fifty miles along the eastern
shore of South America, and is made up of three big
provinces.

Starting from the south, there was the province
of Leon, with its vast swamps, forests of mahogany,

and other valuable trees, and its rubber and cocoa plantations. It was on the northern border of this province that Gerald had his plantation.

The capital and centre of its trade was San Fernando, situated at the top of a narrow inlet of the sea called La Laguna. Most of this trade was in the hands of Europeans, and the town itself was held for the President by a General Moros with about a thousand troops. From what we heard, he didn't worry much about anything, except to loot the Custom House occasionally or take bribes from the merchants and captains of trading-ships. The President always had a 'down' on this province, and hindered its trade as much as he could without stopping it altogether ; and, after his old General had had a 'picking' at San Fernando, every ship had to stop at the narrow mouth of La Laguna and pay more dollars. The President had a pretty modern fort there — El Castellar — to make them heave to if they forgot to stop, and directly the revolution started he had given orders that no ships whatever were to be allowed to pass, so you can pretty well imagine how the English merchants cursed. Then northward of the province of Leon came the towering mountain ranges and plateaus of Santa Cruz, arid, and scorched, and dusty, rising almost precipitously from the forests of Leon, and falling again in terrific ridges and chasms into the northern province of San Juan, the eastern slopes falling into the sea as we had seen at Los Angelos.

The mineral wealth—copper, gold, and silver—of the
Republic was in these mountains, and they absolutely
cut off the southern province of Leon from any com-
munication with the northern province of San Juan.
There were mountain paths and dangerous mule-
tracks, but what I mean is that no armies could
possibly assist each other across them, and old Canilla
could sit up in Santa Cruz, at the top of his
mountain, and jolly well choose his own time to
crush any rising in the provinces spread out at his
feet, and, so long as his Navy was loyal, could prevent
any insurgents from one province getting to the other
by sea.

However, there was one thing 'up against' the
President. The province of San Juan bred all the
cattle and live-stock of the Republic, and he was
obliged to keep a big army down in the northern
plains to guard them. Once the insurgents got the
upper hand in San Juan he would have to depend
entirely on importing cattle from the neighbouring
Republics or from Prince Rupert's Island—not so
much to feed his troops, but Santa Cruz itself.

Now you will have a rough idea how the land
lay, and can understand that, so long as his Navy
was loyal to him and prevented the two insurgent
provinces on either side of him from combining, the
President would be cock of the walk.

That was the opinion of nearly every one in
Princes' Town, and, though they all favoured the

insurgents and wanted them to win, they'd shake their heads and say that old Gerald's chances were pretty bad.

Then came news, from Santa Cruz, that there'd been a great battle fifty miles or so to the north'ard of San Fernando, and that de Costa's insurgent troops had been defeated with great slaughter. There was a rumour going through the Club that Gerald had been killed, but I couldn't find how it had started.

'Don't you worry. All my eye!' my chum 'in the know' said; 'de Costa isn't such a fool as to try a pitched battle yet. Wait for another six months. The President is only trying to bluff the people who are finding the money to keep his end up.' Then he told me something more about that big armoured cruiser *La Buena Presidente.*

He had an idea that de Costa's people were trying to get hold of her. 'If they do,' he said, 'she can simply wipe the floor with all Canilla's rotten old tubs, and his game will be finished in a couple of months.'

I couldn't help worrying about Gerald and the mater—when she heard the news—for she thought he was still tapping his rubber trees. It may have been because of that, but I played abominably against the Prince Rupert's Island team that afternoon. It was fearfully hot, the sweat seemed to make my eyes all hazy; my fingers were all thumbs, I fumbled my passes, and if I did gather them properly, could think of nothing except to get rid of the ball quickly, without passing forward. I was playing centre three-quarters, so messed up the whole of our attack and we lost badly. The Angel at 'half' kept looking at me with a puzzled face, wondering what was wrong, and all our chaps were shouting themselves hoarse, 'Buck up, Wilson,' but nothing would go right, and directly after the match I trudged down to the Governor's steps by myself, to smoke a pipe and wait for our boat.

You know what it feels like to have lost the game for your side; so I wanted to be alone, slung my heavy sweater over my back, with the arms tied round my neck, put on my coat over it, and sat down where old Ginger and I had sat that time before.

I smoked and watched a crowd of niggers hustling round me unloading a lighter which had come ashore from one of Pickford and Black's steamers lying off in the harbour—she had come in from Los Angelos that morning—and had just taken off my straw hat to light another match inside it, when I heard a naked footstep behind me, a fierce kind of a grunting hiss, and something struck my shoulder.

I was on my feet and had turned in a second, and there was that little brute who had been shadowing Gerald, and had nabbed me up at Santa Cruz. He had a long knife in his hand, and I knew him at once, although he was dressed as a coolie, by the scar on his forehead—the one my pipe had made.

I had hold of his wrist in a jiffy, but it was all oily. He wriggled himself free, I made another grab at him, but he was like an eel, and bolted through the crowd of niggers. It was all done so quickly that no one seemed to have noticed him, and, though I dashed after him, I lost sight of the little beast. Something warm began trickling down inside my jersey, and I gave up following him to see what damage had been done. The knife had made a gash in the skin over my left collar-bone, and I was bleeding like a pig. Like an ass, I must have fainted, for when I woke up my head was resting in the huge lap of Arabella de Montmorency, who was pinching up the skin near the gash; there were crowds of jabbering niggers all squashing round me; the tall grave Sikh policeman had his notebook out, and I heard her chattering away: 'The good Lo'd be praised. He send Arabella to sab de life of de British naval officah—some black trash hab done dis—no buckra niggah from Princes' Town—oh, de pretty yellow hair.'

Luckily for me Dr. Clegg and the rest of the football team came up and rescued me, or the old 'washa-lady' would probably have kissed me.

Of course I was all right directly, and Dr. Clegg stitched me up when we got aboard, but I was on the sick list for a week. The knife had cut clean through the knot in the sleeves of my sweater, and this had probably saved my life. Strangely enough, when I got on board, there was a letter waiting for me from my friend the fat A.D.C., telling me, in very bad English, that Pedro Mendez—that was the name of the ugly brute—had been dismissed the police force for bungling Gerald's arrest, and had left Santa Cruz burning to be revenged on us both. The letter and the ex-policeman had probably come across together in the Pickford and Black steamer which I'd been watching.

It was awfully decent of my A.D.C. chum to have taken all this trouble to warn me, because it must have been jolly hard work for him to write a letter in English.

He signed himself Alfonso Navarro, and I shouldn't forget his 'tally' in a hurry. It wasn't his fault that the letter had been a bit late, and it didn't make me the less grateful.

The Angel and Bob, pale with excitement, came rushing into my cabin directly Dr. Clegg had finished with me, and of course they wanted to see the letter. Bob wanted the stamps and begged the envelope. He gave a whoop. 'Look at that, Billums—on the back—it's in French!'

Scrawled in pencil very hurriedly was *Votre frère est blessé seulement dans le bras droit.*

Phew! then there had been a battle after all, and I felt sick all over, because it struck me that my brother might have been captured, otherwise how would the A.D.C. know? And if he was captured, I knew it meant San Sebastian and a firing-party.

It was mail day too; I had to write home, and it was jolly difficult not to tell the mater what I'd heard about Gerald. I couldn't tell her about the little brute either—only about my having done so badly at football.

It was lucky I didn't say anything about Gerald, because three days later—Dr. Clegg still kept me in my bunk—one of our boats brought off another note to me.

'One of those nigger kind of chaps gave it me, sir,' the coxswain of the boat said. 'Didn't seem to talk English—nothing but your name, sir. He cleared out directly he'd got rid of it.'

I thought of Gerald's messenger and thought it must be from Gerald, though it wasn't in his handwriting. It *was* from Gerald, for all that, and I soon knew why the handwriting was so funny, for he wrote:

'We've had a bit of a scrap—got a bit of a shell in my right arm. Learning to write with my left—don't tell the mater. We got a bit of a hiding—my fault—I'm all serene barring the arm. You'll hear news, important news soon.—GERALD.'

Well, he wasn't a prisoner, which was the great thing, and I felt jolly cheerful again.

'Wouldn't it be ripping if we could get some leave and go over there and chip in?' Bob and the Angel said, their mouths and eyes wide open.

Of course that was what we all wanted to do, and wondered all this time why the English Government allowed the President to go on stopping our trade. It was jolly galling to all of us to see the fleet of local British steamers lying in Princes' Town harbour doing nothing, simply because the President up at Santa Cruz wanted to punish the insurgents. The English merchants were grumbling furiously, and wanting to know what use the *Hector* and *Hercules* were if they weren't to be used to protect their trade. Everybody was saying that it was a thousand pities that more people hadn't followed Gerald's example and gone in for the revolution 'bald headed.' In fact, Gerald had become a popular hero, and you can imagine how proud it made me. But then I got rather a nasty jar. The Captain sent for me, and I found him in his cabin with a lot of papers in front of him. He tut, tutted and hummed and hawed a good deal, and then burst out with : 'Look here, Wilson, you'd better give that brother of yours the tip to keep clear of Princes' Town or an English man-of-war. I've got orders to arrest him if I can get my hands on him. Look at this!' and he showed me a big document beginning,

'Whereas it has been represented to us by our Minister resident in Santa Cruz in the Republic of Santa Cruz that a person, Gerald Wilson—known as Don Geraldio—being a British Subject, has taken up arms against the Government of Santa Cruz Republic, that Government being at present on terms of friendship with his Britannic Majesty's Government, all

law-abiding subjects of his Britannic Majesty are
hereby warned, on pain of being indicted for felony,
to abstain from affording any assistance to the aforesaid Gerald Wilson.'

I got very red in the face, and then came to the
part,

'The utmost endeavour is to be made to arrest the
aforesaid Gerald Wilson should he enter British
Territory.'

That was roughly what I read, though I can't
remember now the actual words, but it was so full of
legal phrases that it made me feel cold all over.   It
seemed so beastly cold-blooded too, as if he hadn't
already done more actually for old England than all
the rest of us English out here put together.

'Well, boy, give him the tip to keep clear—that's
all,' the Skipper said, screwing his eyeglass in and
running his fingers through his long hair.

'I can't, sir,' I told him.   'I don't know where he
is.   He's wounded too, sir.'

Then I told him about the letters I'd received and
how I'd got them.

'Well, well, boy, I can tell you.   Tut, tut !   Read
that—I got it from our Minister this morning—brought
across in a trading-schooner.   You're not to speak of
it till the news comes out.'

He was simply bubbling with pleasure, and handed
me another paper.

'Received reliable news that General Moros abandoned San Fernando yesterday — insurgents, under Don Geraldio, occupied it immediately—Vice-President de Costa has formed a Provisional Government there. General Zorilla, Governor of Los Angelos, left Santa Cruz hurriedly this morning to take command of President's army in the south.'

That, then, was the important news Gerald had written to me to expect. I simply felt hot and cold all over with excitement and the pride of imagining him, with his yellow hair and his arm in a sling, head and shoulders above every one else, marching into San Fernando at the head of his troops; and to have the fierce old Governor of Los Angelos on his track—their best fighter—even that was simply glorious.

'Surely, sir, he won't be arrested if the insurgents win?'

The Skipper shrugged his shoulders. 'Those are my orders, whether he's a hundred Generals rolled into one, or even the President himself, so you'd better give him the tip.'

I went away feeling very proud of Gerald, but very upset about the other thing. It did seem such jolly hard lines after he'd risked everything to help the side that was friendly to Englishmen, and had made a great name for himself in the country, and made all these half-civilized people respect all Englishmen because of him. I was worrying about this in my cabin, and how I could manage to warn him, when Ginger came banging at the door.

'Look here, Billums, old chap, I've just come across from the *Hercules*. This has got to stop. D'you know what has happened now? One of your chaps in your picket-boat has smashed up our steam pinnace, rammed her whilst she was trying to get alongside the Governor's steps—cut her down to the water—did it on purpose.'

I had heard about it in the morning; Bob, who was running the picket-boat, had told me. Her pinnace had tried to get alongside before our boat, neither would give way, because the two mids. disliked each other so much, and there'd been a collision.

'It was your boat's fault, Ginger; she cut across our bows. I've reported it to the Commander.'

'Be blowed for a yarn. Our Padré was in the boat and said it was done on purpose—the whole boat's crew said it was. The mid. tried his best to get out of the way, and had his engines full speed astern. It was done on purpose, I tell you.'

'It wasn't,' I said, getting angry with Ginger. 'It was your confounded mid. who tried to cut across our bows, our Engineer Commander was in the boat and told me so. The picket-boat has had to be hoisted in with her stem smashed in. D'you mean to say you don't believe me?'

'Well, if it comes to that, d'you mean to say you don't believe me?' Ginger jerked out.

'No, I'm hanged if I do! you've got hold of the wrong end of the stick,' I said hotly.

'But, my dear chap, the Padré said——'

'I don't care a hang for your Padré—our Engineer Commander——'

'Then you won't take any notice of it?' Ginger was getting excited now.

'None,' I said, 'except to report your mid.'

'You won't cane your chap?'

'No, I'm hanged if I will. It was young Bob Temple, he's too stupid to try and do a thing like that. Your boat was simply poaching—I'm hanged if I'll cane him.'

Ginger's face looked as angry as mine felt, and he burst out with: 'Thank goodness, I haven't got a cousin aboard my ship, and ain't in love with his sister!'

Well, that finished me, and I swung off that if he thought that was why I didn't cane him he was welcome to think so for the rest of his blooming existence.

'All right,' he muttered angrily, 'I'll not trouble to try and patch things up again.'

'I hope you jolly well won't. If your chaps want to cut across our bows, tell 'em to look out—that's all.'

'You absolutely refuse?' he said very coldly.

'Absolutely,' I answered, just as icily, holding the door curtain back.

'All right; sorry to have troubled you,' and Ginger had gone up on deck before I could think of anything more, and I knew that we'd jolly well parted 'brass rags' at last—after all the times we'd sworn that we'd never let the gun-room quarrels make any difference to us.

I wanted to rush off to the *Hercules* and make it 'up' on the spot, but that beastly remark about Bob being my cousin—and the other thing—simply set me tingling all over, and I'd see him in Jericho first. If he thought that every time our midshipmen had a row, mine were to go to the wall, he was jolly well mistaken.

There was bound to be a row about the damaged boats, and there was—a regular Court of Inquiry—and a lot of hard swearing on both sides, the only result of which was that Ginger and I—we'd been glaring at each other all the time—got badly snubbed for not keeping better control over our gun-rooms.

Well, all this, coming directly after the worry about Gerald, made me feel pretty bad-tempered. I wanted Ginger to yarn with more than any one, but that was 'finish,' and, as my shoulder wasn't quite all right yet, I had nothing to do but wander about the ship like a caged monkey.

Every one knew about San Fernando in two or three days, and by the time my shoulder was all right and I could go ashore—you bet I kept my eyes skinned to see that chap who'd knifed me—news began coming pretty regularly from that town, brought by small sailing-boats which managed to get through at night—and most of it was pretty bad news.

Gerald and the insurgents had certainly got possession of San Fernando, but El Castellar, the strong fort at the narrow inlet to the bay, was still in the hands of the President, and still stopped all trade. Not only that, but, worse still, the Santa Cruz gunboats slipped up there and amused themselves by bombarding the defenceless town. The whole insurgent army didn't possess anything even as big as a field-gun, so the gunboats could fire away in comfort as long as their ammunition lasted. We heard that the warehouses and offices along the seafront had already been practically destroyed by shellfire. As these nearly all belonged to English firms, whose headquarters were at Princes' Town, the whole colony was in an uproar; and, much to our joy, our Skipper was ordered—from home—to take the *Hector* up to San Fernando and report on the state of affairs.

You can imagine how excited we all were, and how I looked forward to seeing old Gerald bossing round in his General's uniform.

That chum of mine ashore—the man who seemed to be 'in the know'—came up to me in the Club, the day before we were to sail, and made me introduce him to the Skipper. ' I want him to take a few things to San Fernando for me,' he told me. ' I've got some machinery for one of our estates—it's been lying on the wharves for the last six weeks, and they can't get on without it.'

I didn't hear what passed between them, but knew that the Skipper was in such high spirits that he'd have done anything for anybody just then. And so it turned out, for that evening a lighter came alongside, and I had the job of hoisting in four large crates of hydraulic machinery, some boxes of shafting, and dozens of smaller crates. The Commander was furious, but the Skipper had said ' yes,' and although his jolly face fell when he saw how ' chock-a-block ' the battery deck was, with all these packing-cases, he wouldn't go back on his word.

After we'd finished I was getting a bit of supper in the gun-room when O'Leary came knocking at the door and wanting to speak to me. He wouldn't come in. ' Beg pardon, sir, but I wants to 'ave a word with you, private like.'

' What is it ? ' I asked, taking him into my cabin.

He carefully pulled the curtain across, and then said in a half-whisper, ' We let down one of they small crates rayther 'eavy like, sir, and started one of the boards, sir.'

' That doesn't matter,' I said.

' Eh, but it do, sir ! I banged 'im in again, but not

afore I'd seen inside it—a hammunition box—sir—the same as what we've got for our twelve-pounder.'

My aunt! that made me all jumpy.

'Are you quite certain?' I gasped.

'As certain as I'm astanding 'ere, sir. That ain't no bloomin' 'ydraulic machinery—they boxes marked " shafting " be guns, sir, that's what they be.'

Hundreds of things rushed through my head.

'Did any one else see it?' I asked, and was jolly glad when he shook his head.

'N'ary a one, sir; I covered 'em up too quick; and I ain't going to tell no one neither, sir, for I 'ears your brother is takin' a leadin' part in this 'ere revolution, and maybe he'll be wantin' a goodish deal o' 'ydraulic machinery before he's through with it. That's why I tells you, sir. I couldn't keep it all to myself—in my chest—without tellin' some one.'

My brain was so hot that I couldn't think properly.

'Don't mention it to a soul; I'll think over it,' I told him.

'No, that I won't, sir; good-night, sir;' and O'Leary left me.

Well, if he was correct, and it was ever found out, the Skipper would get in an awful row; if any one found out that I knew about it, it would mean the 'chuck' for me, and if I told what I knew, and it turned out to be true, old Gerald wouldn't get his guns.

You can pretty easily guess what I did—kept as

mum as a mummy—and how I gloated over all that
jumble of boxes and packing-cases and the long boxes
marked 'shafting for hydraulic machinery' when I
walked through the battery next morning on my way
to the bridge.

As we passed under the stern of the *Hercules* I
saw Ginger on watch, and I was just going to wave
to him when I remembered that we'd parted 'brass
rags' and didn't.   I wished to goodness that we
hadn't quarrelled.

All that watch, as we drew nearer and nearer to the
mainland, I kept on thinking of these crates and boxes,
frightened lest any one else should have any suspicion
about them, and couldn't help remembering the words
in that document which the Skipper had shown me,
'All law-abiding subjects of his Britannic Majesty are
hereby warned to abstain from affording assistance
to the aforesaid Gerald Wilson, on pain of being
indicted for felony.'

'Felony' has a jolly nasty sound about it.   And
there was another thing.   Suppose Gerald came off
to the ship when we anchored at San Fernando.
Well, they couldn't arrest him unless he actually
came aboard, and I determined to stay on deck all
the time, and warn him off before he could get alongside.   I'd tell all the watch-keeping lieutenants, and
the 'Forlorn Hope' and the 'Shadow' too, for they
kept watch in harbour.

CHAPTER VI

The *Hector* goes to San Fernando

Written by Captain Grattan, R.N., H.M.S. 'Hector'

As the English merchants in Prince Rupert's Island were kicking up no end of a fuss about the stoppage of their trade with Santa Cruz, I received orders from home to take my ship to San Fernando and report on the state of affairs there; so one morning I left old 'Spats' comfortably anchored off Princes' Town and toddled across. Young Wilson—my Sub-Lieutenant—has told you about that fort at the entrance to La Laguna, the fort which had been firing on our merchant steamers and stopping all trade to San Fernando, at the head of the bay, fifteen miles farther on, and as we steamed towards the gap in the high cliffs which marked the entrance, all of us on the bridge were anxious to know whether the insurgents had managed to capture it yet. We could see the little white lighthouse on the port side, the rambling white walls of the fort itself, perched high in the air, on the starboard side, and presently the yeoman of signals reported that a small cruiser, lying close inshore, was flying the Government colours—you could tell

"IS THAT GERALD WILSON ABOARD?"

them because the stripes were vertical—so we guessed
that it still remained in the President's hands.

The heat, however, was so great that the glare
from the water and the mirage from the baking rocks
made it difficult to see anything distinctly, and it was
not till we drew nearer that we made out a large
yellow and green flag, hanging limply down over
the fort itself.   That settled the question.

In another quarter of an hour we were passing
through the entrance, when—well, I couldn't believe
it myself, and I saw it, so can hardly expect you to
believe it—the miserable sons of Ham in that fort had
the colossal cheek to fire a shot across my bows.

'Accident, my dear boy !' I told Wilson, who was
officer of the watch ; 'of course it was an accident;
but I'm blowed if, before we'd got a cable length past
the entrance, a second shot didn't come along and
make as neat a furrow across my fo'c'stle deck-planks
as you'd see anywhere.   It scattered the stokers and
bandsmen basking under the awning, and I quite
enjoyed their little obstacle-race into the shelter of
the battery.

'My dear boy, they don't mean it; but just put
your helm hard a-port and go full speed astern starboard—if you please.   Give 'em back a 9.2 common,[1]
please, Commander ; they've only fired by accident,
but accidents are bound to happen sometimes in the

---

[1] 'Common' = common shell.   A thin-walled shell with a heavy bursting
charge.

best-regulated ships.' Round we swung on our heels—we just had room—and I dropped my eyeglass to laugh more easily, because that little cruiser—one of those piffling little things I'd towed out of Los Angelos six weeks ago—had hauled down her flag, and was scurrying off as fast as she could go. The poor idiots who'd had their little accident in the fort thought, I suppose, that we were running away, so didn't ease off again, and by the time Montague, my Gunnery Lieutenant, had reported the for'ard 9.2 cleared away, and the fo'c'stle awning had been furled, we'd turned and were coming back past the fort.

'Have your accident, Montague—as soon as you like ; but I'll only give you one, so don't miss.'

His accident was quite a success, and when the smoke of the bursting shell had cleared away, there was a hole in the walls through which even my coxswain could have steered the galley without breaking an oar, and that yellow and green monstrosity was being hauled down with a run.

Angry ! Rather not ! I can't afford to get angry ; it's bad for my gout ; I'd had my accident, and proceeded on my way quite ready to apologise for my gross carelessness directly they apologised for theirs. I suppose I should have had to be angry if that shell, or whatever it was, had killed any of my people— except my coxswain, and then I should have blessed them, for he was the most exasperating idiot I'd ever known.

An hour later we came up to San Fernando—a miserable deserted-looking collection of dingy white walls and warehouses, fizzling in the awful heat, and, 'pon my word, there was another dirty little cruiser there at anchor, with the yellow and green ensign flying, calmly potting at the town—firing a gun every other minute. We could not see what damage she was actually doing, but the white walls along the sea-front were riddled with holes, and that was good enough for me.

'Front row of the stalls, old chap,' I told my navigator, and though he'd have walked about on his head, or shaved it, if he thought it would please me, he hadn't a sense of humour, and looked puzzled. 'As close to her as you can,' I explained, 'between her and the town;' and there we dropped anchor, and awaited the next item on the programme. It was jolly lucky for her that she didn't have any *accidents*. We hadn't been comfortably anchored for more than five minutes before dozens of black and green flags were hoisted over the town, people began to venture out into the front street, and I had hardly gone below, when one of the signalmen came running down. 'A boat's pulling this way, sir, from shore, sir, with a black and green flag flying.'

My coxswain—I called him the 'Comfort' because he was such a nuisance to me—pulled my cap out of my hands and gave it me, seized my telescope from under my arm, rubbed the bright part up and down his sleeve, and handed it back, gave me two right-hand kid-gloves from the table, and I was ready to receive anybody, the Insurgent Provisional Government, or the Queen of Sheba, on my quarterdeck. A clumsy white boat, with a huge ensign, came wobbling off, very careful to keep us between her and the little cruiser. The crew were rowing atrociously, each man pulling the time that suited him best, and it occurred to me that perhaps the Provisional Government might possibly accept the services of the Comfort for their official barge. Then they were near enough for me to see that there was a white man there, among several dark-skinned people, under the stern awning—a white man with yellow hair and his right arm in a sling, my Sub's brother, as sure as life. I looked round and saw Wilson himself, the colour of a sheet, trying to attract the boat's attention, and looking piteously at me, 'Here! Hi! give me a megaphone—some one!' I sung out. A dozen people fell over one another to get one, and I shouted through it, 'Lay on your oars,' and when my Sub's brother had made them stop, I sang out, 'Is that Gerald Wilson aboard?'

'Yes,' he shouted, putting his head out from under the awning. 'Then, for goodness' sake, don't come aboard my ship, or I'll have to arrest you. I've got your warrant on board. You can come alongside, but don't leave your boat.'

'Thank you,' he shouted; and it amused me to

see my Sub's face. I believe that he was even grateful enough to stop the mids. doing physical drill early
in the morning over my head on the quarterdeck.
The Provisional Government—for that it actually
was—did manage to get alongside, and the first man
to tramp up the ladder was the Vice-President—de
Costa himself. I recognised him at once from having
seen him in the cathedral at Santa Cruz. Poor
chap, he had on a black frock-coat and beautifully
brushed tall black hat—in that awful heat too. No
wonder, if it was necessary, as head of the Provisional
Government, to wear it, that he looked ten years older
than when I saw him last.

His face looked more yellow and flabby, and his
black eyes more shifty than ever. He bowed, and I
bowed, and then he waved his secretary at me—a
little chap in another frock-coat and silk hat who
followed him. The little chap's patent-leather boots
were giving him trouble, and he came along the
quarterdeck on his toes, like a cat walking along
a wall covered with broken glass. Fortunately he
could speak a little English, and whilst his boss was
mopping his forehead, he said, 'Presidente de Costa
thank you for coming,' almost breaking himself in
half, he bowed so low. Four or five more chaps
came along, every one of them with an enormous
black and green rosette in his coat. These were
soldiers—two of them niggers—and very mild-looking
soldiers they were, just the sort you'd imagine would

hang about at headquarters, and get soft jobs where there weren't many bullets flying round. However, I was wrong in thinking so.

They spent half an hour on board, explaining that the Dictator's flag (Canilla's) flew nowhere throughout the province of Leon, except over El Castellar—the fort which had had the accident two hours before —and of course swore that they were now strong enough to march on Santa Cruz itself, and intended to do so very shortly. The upshot was that they demanded official recognition from the Foreign Powers. That was the whole matter; they wanted recognition so that they could buy warlike supplies from abroad openly, for of course at the present time no Foreign Power would allow its subjects to assist them. 'We have this policy foreign, we encourage the merchants, and we permit all trade very much of the foreign peoples, and very much the *Inglesas* also. Always they shall be first now that the noble *Inglese* ship of war visit San Fernando —the first ship to come,' the little secretary told me.

He looked so diminutive and so important, and was evidently in such discomfort with his boots and his tight frock-coat, that I had to screw my eyeglass into my eye till it pained — I wanted to laugh so much.

Not a word did they say about the little cruiser which was lying close by, waiting for a chance to pot them on their way ashore, or about the shell-

marks on every wall.   Not much, for that would have
drawn attention to the perfectly obvious fact that
they could do nothing till they had command of
the sea, and also to the fact that they were absolutely
without any artillery.   A couple of well-fought six-
pounder guns, if they'd had them, would have been
quite sufficient to drive off the wretched little cruiser-
gunboat kind of affair.   Poor chaps! you couldn't
help seeing that they were terribly in earnest, but I
couldn't possibly give them any hopes of their Provisional Government being recognised, the most I
could do was to forward their demand by 'wireless' to
the *Hercules* at Princes' Town for her to cable home.
I saw them over the side, and interrupted the brothers
Wilson yarning at the bottom of the gangway.

'Ask your brother if he'll show me round the
place if I come ashore for a toddle,' I sang out.

'Certainly, sir; he'll be only too pleased,' my Sub
answered.

'If he dyed his hair I might ask your brother to
dine with me to-night,' I told him, as we watched
them slowly splashing ashore; 'I shouldn't recognise
him with his hair dyed—not officially.'

Botheration take it! I'd never said anything
about that wretched hydraulic machinery I'd been
bullied into bringing across.   Still, you can't talk to
Provisional Governments about packing-cases, can
you?   However, my Sub relieved my mind on this
point,

'I told Gerald that we had a lot of things for a firm here, sir,' he informed me. 'He's going to tell them.'

'Good lad! Good boy!' I said, and went below.

The commander of the cruiser wasn't showing any signs of calling on me, in fact he was beginning to raise steam, so I got ready for my toddle ashore.

'Yes, please; usual leave to officers,' I told the Commander, who hammered at my door (he always was noisy, thought it made him breezy—it didn't), and sent the Comfort with my compliments to Dr. Watson, my Fleet Surgeon, and would he come ashore with me for a walk. He was so lazy that he wouldn't be able to walk far, and would therefore act as a check on my Sub's brother if he wanted to rush me over the country. I had thought of taking my Sub himself, but he couldn't come, had to get out that hydraulic machinery.

The Comfort and five loafing sons of sea-cooks, whom the Commander had given me as my galley's crew, pulled us ashore, and a miserable-looking place it was, a long sloping beach covered with rubbish and stinking seaweed, dead dogs here and there, and live ones, not much more healthy-looking, prowling about in search of food.

We ran alongside a crumbling wooden jetty, and Wilson was waiting for us, dressed in white duck riding gear, smart brown gaiters, and with a smart white polo helmet on his head. His arm in the sling

gave just the wounded-hero appearance to complete the
picture.   He had a carriage waiting for us, but before
we got in he pointed out a very weather-beaten pillar
of granite, about five feet high, standing on the shore.
'Pizarro landed there with thirteen men in 1522 or
thereabouts to conquer this country—thirteen men,
their armour, and ten horses.   Just think of it!'

This pillar was one of the most sacred things in
the Republic, and there was a white flag flying close
to it, so that the gunboats could give it a wide berth
when they shelled the rest of the town.   There were
traces of shell-fire everywhere, but it was astonishing
to see how little actual damage had been done.
'Five men and a little girl killed, and they've fired
over six hundred shell into the town during the last
fortnight,' Wilson told me.   There was one two-
storey house close by with at least twenty holes in
the side facing the harbour, and yet it seemed little
the worse—rather improved, from my point of view,
because the holes increased the ventilation.

The place was swarming with people, practically
all were men, and nine out of ten of them had rifles
slung round their necks—a ragged unkempt-looking
lot of scaramouches they were, you couldn't call them
soldiers.   Most of them had no equipment at all—a
cotton bag to hold cartridges slung with string over
their shoulders, a loose white shirt, and a ragged pair
of cotton drawers, legs and feet bare, and very often
nothing on their heads at all, or, if they had, a rough-

plaited, wide-brimmed grass hat.   Their attempts to
salute, as Wilson and we drove along, were praise-
worthy but ludicrous.   There were shrill cries of
' *Viva los Inglesas!* ' and they would have followed
us if Wilson had not stopped them, but they were
eminently respectful, and the slightest word he spoke
seemed law to them.

' You're a bit of a nob here,' I said.   I wanted to
say ' my boy,' but I'm hanged if I could.   He was
two or three sizes too big for me, was Gerald Wilson.
I'm a pretty big boss on board my ship, but I'm
hanged if I was in it compared with him on shore.
I've cultivated the ' for goodness' sake, get out of my
way ; don't you see it's me ' air pretty successfully,
but he'd got it to perfection, apparently without knowing it, and when he stopped the carriage, and we got
out, he strode along with the chin-strap of his polo
helmet over his grand square jaw—simply a blooming
emperor.

He was taking us to the cathedral, on one side of
the usual Plaza you find in all Spanish types of
towns, and as we passed the ' Cuartel de Infanteria,'
two or three hundred so-called troops were hurriedly
forming in front of it.   The trumpeter was the only
chap in anything approaching a uniform.

' Kicked out of the regulars for blowing so badly,'
Wilson said ; and I didn't doubt his word when I
heard him try to sound some kind of a salute.

' My dear chap !'   Thank goodness, I stopped

myself in time and didn't say that, but wanted to ask him if he thought it possible to knock the troops I had seen in Santa Cruz with these he had here.

There was something in his face, 'a keep off the grass' look, that made me, me a Post-Captain commanding one of the finest armoured cruisers in the Royal Navy, take soundings jolly carefully before I spoke to him.

He saw what I was thinking, and smiled, 'I'm licking them into shape gradually. We've only just begun.'

He took us into the cathedral, a crumbling old place with a huge crack across one side—the result of an earthquake some years ago—and the cool, musty, religious gloom inside was very comforting after the dazzle and glare of the sun outside. Two little stars of light, far away at the end of the chancel, made the gloom all the more mysterious, and then, as our eyes became more accustomed, we could make out the gaudy image of the Holy Virgin, looking down, with calm patient eyes, on the high altar and its tarnished gaudy tapestry.

At the foot of the steps, below the altar-rails, many women, shrouded in black hoods, were praying before it.

'They come here when the gunboats start firing; the cathedral is spared,' Wilson whispered, as we tip-toed out into the glare again.

'Where do the men go?' I asked.

'They carry on with their work,' he answered ; and that came with rather a 'thump' after seeing the men. Perhaps they were better chaps than they looked.

'Not one shell in twenty bursts,' he said, as an afterthought.

Then he took us across the square to the English Club, the only clean, cool-looking building there, with a shady creeper-covered verandah all round it, and long easy wicker-chairs simply inviting rest.

'I shan't get you away from here, doctor, I fancy,' I said to the Fleet Surgeon, who was already streaming with perspiration, and I didn't. He went to sleep the whole of the afternoon in one of those chairs. We always chaffed him about the book he said he was writing : 'Clubs I have slept in.'

In the reading-room all the dear old English papers and periodicals, ten weeks old, were neatly laid on a table, and about a dozen thin, lantern-jawed Englishmen had come to welcome us. De Costa, looking nervous and uncomfortable, was there too, with his secretary (he'd changed his boots). We all had a green bitters, and I was given the longest cigar, and the best I'd smoked for many a day.

I wanted to do as Watson had already done— stretch myself on one of those long chairs on the cool verandah, with my feet up, and stay there till it was time to go aboard—but I was much too afraid of Wilson, and drove away again. 'I'll take it out of my Sub if his brother bullies me too much,' I

chuckled to myself as we bounced along into the
country to see what preparations were being made to
defend San Fernando against the army which fierce
old General Zorilla was leading to attack it.   Luckily
the carriage had an awning, but it was horribly hot
all the same.

We got out of the town, passing along shady
lanes, with little palm-hidden villas standing back
in the shadows of olive groves and vineyards, and
gradually clattered up to some high ground, a regular
tree-covered ridge, at the back of San Fernando, from
which we had a grand view of the town at our feet,
the square cathedral tower, the grand sweeping bend
of the head of La Laguna, and, far away to the
left, the faint outline of the rocks which marked its
inlet—El Castellar could not be seen because of the
dazzling haze and mist which hung on the water.
The wretched little cruiser had just weighed, and was
steaming slowly past my ship, covering her with
black oily smoke.   I only hoped that the Comfort,
or the officer of the watch, had had the 'savvy' to
shut my stern windows.

Wilson turned me round to look inland.

Sloping gently downwards at our feet was some
open ground, dancing in the heat, and pigs and goats
and some wretched cattle were lazily browsing there.
The road in which we were standing ran down it, a
broad red streak, to a sluggish stream at the bottom,
crossed it by a ford, and gently rose over some more

bare, parched, open ground, and was swallowed in the dark shade of a forest. Everywhere beyond, look which way I would, there was nothing but forest, stretching away in the distance in every direction till the outlines of the trees were lost in a dim confusion of mist on the horizon. The town of San Fernando, but for that bare ground on each side of the stream which swept round it, was simply built in a great clearing, and it gave me the impression that that dark motionless forest was silently awaiting the opportunity to claim its own again and swallow it up.

'That is our first line of defence, and our last,' he said, sweeping his arm round the horizon.

'Sometimes, when it is not so hot, you can see the dim outlines of the mountains of Santa Cruz away over there,' Wilson said, pointing to the north. 'You see that road—Queen Isabella's road they call it—it runs straight as a die for fifty miles through the trees. Three hundred years ago the Spaniards cut it through the forest, and from here to Santa Cruz you could travel by coach in five days, but now the part through the mountains has been destroyed by earthquakes.'

'But where are your defences—your trenches?' I asked.

'We have none,' he said, 'we don't want any. General Zorilla is marching down that road to attack us. He is a grand old man' ('I know him : he is,' I said, beginning to understand), 'and a grand soldier, but his only way through fifty miles of virgin forest is along that road.   It is a big job, and he knows it. Six days ago he and his army plunged into it, and they will never leave it, for my little brown forest-men, with rifles and *machetes*, hover all round him. We are drawing him on, the farther he gets away from Santa Cruz, the greater difficulty he has to feed his troops—he has four thousand of them and artillery—and is already short of food, sending out strong parties to forage, but they find nothing, and we capture fifty or sixty of his men every day.

'You see that dark mass over there?' he pointed.

I pretended I did see it.

'There's a big clearing close there—just twenty-four miles from here—and his army camped in it last night.   My little chaps gave them a rotten time.'

I could not help thinking of those little brown-skinned, half-naked natives, with their bags of cart-ridges and their rusty rifles, gliding from tree to tree, through the thick undergrowth, and never giving the regulars a moment's rest, day or night.   At night-time too!   I shuddered to think of it, and began to have a most wholesome respect for those tattered ragamuffins of his.

'How many have you?' I asked him.

'I don't know,' he said.   'We have something like five thousand rifles, but whenever there is a spare rifle there are hundreds to claim it,   Here come some who

would be soldiers—that is, riflemen ; they are taking
food to the front.'

A long train of heavily laden mules came past us,
ambling wearily down towards the stream, each mule
led by a little native.   As each passed he doffed his
hat to Wilson, who stopped one of them and made
him show me the *machete* he carried in his waist-
band—a long curved knife something like a bill-hook,
only heavier, and not so curved and the blade broad
at the end.   I felt the edge ; it was very keen.

'They can cut an arm clean through at a stroke,'
he said ; ' these *machetes* are better than rifles—at
night,' and I shuddered again as the little man, with
a grin of pride on his face, ran after his mule.   It
wasn't the kind of warfare I'd been brought up to.
We watched them all splashing across the ford,
forcing their mules through it as they tried to stop and
drink.   Before the last mule had entered the forest,
the head of another train began to emerge from it.

'Those aren't mules,' I sang out, as they came
towards us.

'They're horses,' he said, and walked down
towards them.

There were thirty or more thin, hungry-looking
beasts, with military saddles and equipment, each led
by a little native, whose eyes sparkled with pleasure
as he saluted Wilson.

'That's good news,' he said, after speaking to one
of them ; 'we cut off a whole squadron of Zorilla's

cavalry early this morning. These are some of the horses. Look at the boots the men are wearing ! '

I hadn't noticed them before, but now I couldn't help smiling, for the little half-naked men were shambling along with big cavalry boots on their feet, the soft leather ' uppers ' half-way up to their knees.

' Quaint little chaps, aren't they? Their whole ambition is to be proper soldiers. The first thing they want is a rifle, and the next boots. They'll wear these now till their feet are so blistered that they can't walk with or without them.'

' Surely Zorilla will have to fall back,' I said, as we drove back to the town.

He shrugged his shoulders. ' My only fear is that he will break away towards El Castellar. About sixteen miles along that road there is a forest track leading there, and he may have to fall back on it; but he'll have to leave his wagons and his guns if he does, and his reputation will be lost. He's been ordered to attack San Fernando, and the fierce old man will do so, even if he and his two " A.D.C.'s " are the only ones left.'

We rattled past the string of captured horses, and drove down to the shore where I had landed, calling at the Club, on the way, to wake the Fleet Surgeon and bring him along.

Two big lighters were aground at the bottom of the beach, and hundreds of natives were swarming round them, wading into the water, bringing ashore the packing-cases of hydraulic machinery, and making a noise like a lot of bumble-bees as they dragged them up the sloping foreshore.

Thank goodness we'd got rid of them at last, for the Commander had been like a bear with a sore head ever since those cases had lumbered up his battery.

'Why the dickens don't they get rid of their rifles when they're working?' I asked, because most of them had rifles slung over their backs.

Wilson smiled, 'That's a regulation I've made. If a man drops his rifle for any purpose whatsoever, any man without one may pick it up and becomes a soldier and a *caballero*—a gentleman—and has a *machete* man to carry his food for him on the march. That's why they won't part with them!'

That was a quaint idea if you like.

My galley was waiting alongside the little tumble-down jetty, and the Comfort pushed his way through a crowd of awestruck natives to give me a signal-paper. 'The Commander thought you'd like to see it, sir—a "wireless" from the *Hercules*.'

I read, '*La Buena Presidente*, under command of Captain Pelayo, left the Tyne yesterday.'

I thought it would interest Wilson, so I read it to him.

His eyes gleamed. 'What! Captain Pelayo! That's Captain don Martin de Pelayo—our man—a de Costa man—he's managed to get hold of her after all,' and he sang out some gibberish to the natives standing round.   In a moment they had leapt in the air, shouting and waving their hats, and hugging each other, bolting away towards the town screaming shrilly, '*La Buena Presidente! La Buena Presidente! Viva Capitaine Pelayo!*'

I had some inkling of what had happened.

'Don Martin was the best captain in the Navy,' Wilson told me; 'chucked out because he demanded ammunition for his ships.   We sent him to England, and if that telegram is correct, he has managed to get hold of the big cruiser.   In three months de Costa should be President of Santa Cruz.'

I could not help telling him—not officially, of course—how glad I was; and as my lazy crew pulled us aboard, the town seemed to be buzzing like a bee-hive, the bells in the cathedral ringing joyously, and green and black flags hanging over every building.

'Your brother wants you to ride out to the front with him to-night,' I told my Sub.   'You can go when you like.'

As usual, the most beautifully cool crisp night followed the terrible heat of the day, and the town of San Fernando looked extremely picturesque, a mass of white roofs and clear-cut shadows, bathed in the light of a full moon.   The road leading up the ridge behind the town stood out a silvery streak, and the mere thought of it, plunging into the appalling shadows of that grim forest beyond, made me shiver as I held my breath and listened for sounds of the struggle I knew must still be going on twenty miles away. Huddled together in some clearing of the forest, or strung wearily along the road, brave old Zorilla and his half-fed men were still surrounded by those fierce, silent, little forest-men with their terrible *machetes*, their bags of cartridges, and their rusty rifles.   I turned in feeling rather creepy, and hoped that my Sub wouldn't do anything foolhardy.

What he did he will tell you himself.

CHAPTER VII

General Zorilla falls back

Written by Sub-Lieutenant William Wilson, R.N.

You may bet that I was glad to see Gerald, and to know that, although he still kept it in a sling, his arm was practically well again. I had a long yarn with him in that boat alongside, and told him my suspicions about the so-called hydraulic machinery we had brought across from Princes' Town. He knew that two 4.7's on field-carriages, four field-guns, and two pompoms, with plenty of ammunition, had been waiting there for weeks, so I pretty well guessed that they weren't very far away now, and implored him to send lighters off for them as quickly as he could, before any one else gave the show away. He had to wait for the Provisional Government, but could not have wasted a moment after he did land, for hardly had the Skipper and the Fleet Surgeon gone ashore than lighters came hurrying off, and I had the job of hoisting all those packing-cases into them, my heart in my mouth all the time lest anything should happen. Careful! Why, I lowered them down as if they were new-laid eggs or valuable china.

'What the Moses d'you mean by taking such a confounded time?' the Commander bellowed, and stood by my side yelling down orders to hurry. Thank goodness, O'Leary was in charge of the working party, and wouldn't be hurried for any one, although the Commander kept on shouting that he was a disgrace to his uniform, and that he'd disrate him to ordinary seaman.

Didn't I feel relieved when the last little lot had shoved off from the ship and was on its way ashore, the Santa Cruz cruiser taking no notice whatever. She didn't seem to suspect anything, got up her anchor, and steamed down towards El Castellar.

When we received that wireless message from the *Hercules*, nobody had the slightest idea that *La Buena Presidente* had actually been collared by the insurgents, so you can imagine how happy I felt when the Skipper came off and told me. He was as pleased as I was. 'Fine chap, your brother! The Provisional Government isn't in the running with him. He's the boss.'

He told me, too, that Gerald wanted me to ride out to the front with him that very night, gave me forty-eight hours' leave, and, fearfully excited, I dashed below. Bigge, Montague, Perkins, the Forlorn Hope and the Shadow, Dr. Clegg—nearly every one, in fact—came along to have a word with me, whilst I tumbled into riding breeches, flannel shirt, and jacket —they would all have given anything to be going

too. The Angel and Bob filled my 'baccy' pouch,
and I stuffed some sandwiches into a haversack ; the
Angel lent me his panama hat, and then I jumped
into the skiff, and was just shoving off when O'Leary
came running down the ladder.

'The petty officers, sir, are going to ask leave
to-morrow, sir. I'm thinking that that 'ere 'ydraulic
machinery kind of wants a little putting together, sir.'

'What the dickens d'you mean by delaying my
skiff?   Shove off in that boat or you can swim
ashore,' the Commander bellowed at me, from the top
of the ladder, as a parting shot.

I was so happy that I can hardly describe how I felt
when I did get ashore. It was just getting dark, and
the last of those packing-cases was being carried
away by a crowd of men still chanting, ' *Viva los
Inglesas! Viva La Buena Presidente!* ' and the little
messenger who had brought Gerald's letter to
Princes' Town was waiting for me, with a broad
smile on his face. He was dressed very smartly
as a groom, with a clean white shirt and clean white
duck riding breeches. He had one of Gerald's old
polo helmets on his head and a brilliant red sash
twisted round his waist, but his feet and legs below
the breeches were bare. He looked very proud of
his finery, and guided me quickly to the Club, along
dark narrow streets, and across the square, where
hundreds of natives were lighting camp fires.

Gerald was there.

'Come along, the horses will be round in a minute. You will do all right,' he said, glancing at my rig-out. He introduced me to several Englishmen; they all shook hands; we toasted *La Buena Presidente* and Captain Pelayo, the *Hector*, 'Old Tin Eye,' and the King. My head was in a whirl; horses came round; I sprang on one, half-a-dozen chaps were round me making my stirrup-leathers comfortable; Gerald was helped into his saddle (his right arm was still in a sling); some one sang out from the dark Club verandah, 'Three cheers for the two Wilsons,' and off we cantered, the little groom, with his red sash, on ahead, and half-a-dozen natives clattering behind us on more horses.

My horse was one of Gerald's own—Jim—a grand little stallion with a mouth as soft as anything, and he arched his neck, snorted, and danced about like a kitten. 'I wish you'd given me an English saddle,' I told Gerald presently, for this one was a huge native thing with a back to it and a big raised pommel in front. It was impossible to fall out of it, except sideways, and you could not do that very easily, because the stirrups were such a queer shape that your feet couldn't slip out of them. But every other second either the back or the front part thumped against me.

'Lean well back, Billums, you'll find it all right then—you'll be glad of it soon—we've got a twenty-mile ride in front of us.'

I did get used to it in time.

It was absolutely dark now; Jim had stopped cantering and had fallen into an amble; we got into some lanes under trees, and fireflies were darting from side to side ahead of us.   It was simply grand, and I jolly well wished old Ginger was there with us; he would have enjoyed it immensely.   I was so annoyed, and despised myself so much for having quarrelled with him, that it really made me miserable every time I thought of him.   At the top of a ridge we stopped, Gerald wanted to speak to some native soldiers who silently stole past us in the darkness, and got me to fill his pipe for him.   Off we went again, the soldiers cheering my brother and the big ship which was coming to knock the Santa Cruz Navy out of time; down a hill we clattered, splashed through a ford, trotted uphill, and then suddenly plunged into absolute darkness.

'We're in the forest, Billums,' Gerald sang out; 'old Zorilla's in the middle of it.   You'll hear bullets before the sunrise.'

I didn't feel quite so enthusiastic about bullets just then—it was too gloomy under those trees—and it was lucky that the horses could see where they were going, for we ourselves could not.

We kept on meeting long strings of pack mules on their way back from the front, and some of them were carrying wounded men.   It was jolly disconcerting at first, because they came upon you so suddenly, and made so little noise—the men being barefooted and the mules unshod.   On ahead we'd hear our little messenger-groom sing out something, and then we'd come right on the long string of dark shadows, the mules breathing heavily under their creaking packs as they shuffled past.

Gerald told me they were clearing the country of food, and were taking it all into San Fernando.

'How did you learn all this war business?' I asked him, after he had told me his plans.

'Common sense, Billums, common sense!'

There was no need for me to ask him why he'd left his rubber plantation.

'Getting enough excitement?' I asked.

'Not yet,' he said, stopping for me to fill his pipe again.

'Do you know,' he said presently, 'that, nearly three hundred years ago, twenty-two Spanish cavaliers rode along this road, as we are riding to-night, to capture Santa Cruz city. San Fernando was a fortified Spanish settlement then, and a native ruled in Santa Cruz. He'd collared the Governor's daughter; she'd been shipwrecked somewhere up the coast whilst on her way to Spain, and the twenty-two in their armour —fancy armour in this climate — riding their big Spanish horses, with a couple of hundred native bowmen in their quilted cotton armour[1] to help them,

---

[1] In those days the natives wore thick quilted coats, stuffed with cotton fibre, as a defence against sword-cuts.

actually sacked the town. They stopped there, too, and built the fort of San Sebastian.'

'Did they rescue the girl?'

'Yes,' Gerald told me. He was full of such stories —the good news about *La Buena Presidente* had made him quite talkative—and you can imagine how the glamour of the past chivalry excited me. I almost imagined to myself that I was in armour, and should presently have to put lance in rest and charge through crowded ranks of archers and swordsmen.

At about nine o'clock that night we crossed a small stream, and stopped at a *Posada*, or wayside inn— very cheerful it looked under the trees, with a blazing log-fire gleaming through the open windows. People came hurrying out to take our horses, and Gerald and I had a grand feed. They cooked a ripping omelette, and their home-made bread was grand.

'Feeling better now?' Gerald asked me, as I stretched myself and asked for another omelette.

Before we had finished, a lot of officers rode up and came in—all very courteous—and I looked at them curiously; for they had just come back from the firing line, and their white cotton or blue-striped uniforms were covered with mud. When they first came into the room they all stared at the two of us, not quite knowing, for a moment, which was which. One of them, who particularly attracted me, was very short and fat with bandy legs. He had a broad-brimmed, soft felt hat on his head, the front turned up, his face and neck almost hidden by great bushy black whiskers, and he was so stout that his sword-belt wouldn't meet, and was fastened with cord. He had jolly, twinkling eyes, as black as night, and in the flickering shadows of the wood-fire looked like a gnome or goblin under that huge hat. He was very proudly handing round a large revolver for every one to look at, showing grand white teeth as he smiled, and shrugged his shoulders and spread his hands. Gerald handed it to me : 'He captured a cavalry officer this morning, and bagged this.'

The little 'Gnome' drew his stool across and explained its action. It was a Webley-Foster automatic revolver, and as I had not seen one before, I was jolly interested. I liked the little chap very much, and could just imagine him tackling one of those beautifully dressed dandies of cavalry officers we had seen at Santa Cruz.

These officers had come to tell Gerald how everything was progressing at the front, and they seemed to be holding a council of war, or rather listening to what Gerald had to tell them ; for my brother was laying down the law pretty considerably.

At last everything was satisfactorily settled, there was more bowing, and most of them rode off again into the forest.

'Everything going on all right,' Gerald told me. 'Come along ; hope you aren't getting stiff.'

We left the cheerful fire ; the innkeeper refused any

money; my brother sang out, 'José! José!'; the little groom with the red sash brought our horses round, and, with the 'Gnome' and three or four other officers, we were just going to mount when a dozen little *machetos* came up, leading some men.   As they got into the light I saw that these were regular troops, and had yellow and green rosettes on their hats, tall, gaunt, hungry-looking chaps they were, and very much relieved when they saw my brother.   He spoke to them and the excited little chaps guarding them, and then off we started.

'Deserters,' he told me.   'They all have the same tale; not enough food.'

Although 'deserter' has a horrid sound to it, I felt sorry for them, they looked so miserable, and meeting them seemed to make Zorilla's army, of which I had heard so much, much more real.   I watched them being taken away to San Fernando, till they were lost in the darkness.

A full moon had risen whilst we were having our meal, and where the trees did not meet across the road there were patches of very comforting light. However, the moonlight on the road made the forest on either side of us look blacker and more forbidding than ever, and when two of the officers turned into it, by a path their horses seemed to know, I felt jolly glad I wasn't going with them.

'We had a bit of a scrap this afternoon, Billums,' Gerald told me, 'and lost a few people.   Old Zorilla fought his way along to another clearing, but we captured some more of his cavalry, and he's left a field-gun behind him. The horses and rifles will be very useful to us.'

'How far off is he now?' I asked excitedly.

'About eight miles: Zorilla has halted for the night and our people are all round him again. He can't move till daylight. He has only advanced four miles since yesterday; his men are so played out, and his horses too. I can't understand him. It seems absolute folly to do what he is trying to do, especially as his chaps are deserting.'

My supper had made me rather sleepy, but presently, a long way in front of us, I heard the report of a rifle, and sat up so quickly that I bumped my back against that wretched saddle.

'That was a rifle! That's the first I've heard fired in war,' I cried out, and I felt fearfully excited, wondering where the bullet had gone. You bet that my ears were tingling to hear more, but none came for some time, only the crackling and rustling of dead branches snapping in the darkness on either side of us. Then three or four went off, still a long way ahead, and as each one cracked I could not help thinking: 'I wonder what that hit.'

Without meaning to do so, I dug my heels into Jim's ribs and made him go faster, but my brother sang out, 'No hurry, Billums,' and I pulled him back. I believe the little stallion was getting as excited as I was.

Away to the left there were some more shots, and then suddenly, right in our faces, a red glare shone through the trees, coming and going so quickly that I'd only time to say 'Oh!' before it had disappeared, and almost immediately afterwards there was another brighter glare and a tearing bursting noise.   It didn't seem a hundred yards ahead of us, and the little stallion, Jim, began jumping about.

'What was that?' I sang out, though I knew perfectly well that it was a shell, but couldn't help singing out, my nerves were so jumpy.   A scraggy spluttering volley came back from the trees, and then all was still again.

'Zorilla is firing a field-gun down the road,' my brother said; 'I wonder what good he thinks he is doing.'

I heard a crash and a noise of breaking branches. 'What's that, Gerald?'

'My chaps are cutting down trees to haul across the road,' he answered; 'making a barricade.'

That glare—more distinct now, and right in front of us—showed up again, and a shell came tearing and crashing through the trees on one side of us, and we heard a soft 'plump' as it buried itself in the ground without bursting.   There was the crash of another volley, and then nothing but darkness and silence.

'Our chaps see them when they fire that gun, and let "rip" with their rifles,' Gerald told me.   His coolness irritated me, for my nerves were tingling all over with excitement and the funny feeling inside me of being under fire for the first time. I rather wondered whether Ginger would have felt as—well— nervous if he had been here. I'd never known him frightened at anything. A little further along a couple of wagons slowed up in a patch of moonlight at the side of the road, some ragged little natives hovering round them. Gerald stopped a moment to speak to a white-faced officer, and on we went again. 'That's our only doctor, Billums; we keep him pretty busy.' If that was the doctor I knew that we must be close to the firing line, and my heart began thumping very rapidly. We could only go very slowly now, because the road was blocked with wagons and mules jumbled together.

'Jump off, Billums; keep close to me!' Gerald sang out cheerily.

I was jolly glad to be on my feet again, and followed him, José taking the horses. On each side of us I heard axes chipping, a tree fell with a crash quite close to me, and then we got up to the barricade which they were building across the road. Men were swarming here, some dragging more trees out of the forest, others cutting off small branches with their *machetes.*

'The field-gun is right ahead,' my brother said; 'they'll be firing again in a minute or two.' He'd hardly spoken before I saw the glare of it, heard the

dull bang, and a shell burst overhead.   It lighted us
for a second ; I saw hundreds of the little brown chaps
in their white shirts scurrying about among the
trees, and then a regular hail of shrapnel bullets
spattered on the road and against the tree-trunks,
more rifles went off, and bullets sang past.   Behind
me a mule screamed, fell on the ground with a thud,
and began kicking.   I felt myself wriggling up
against the barricade for shelter, but Gerald sang out
for me, and I followed him round it to the road, in
between it and the gun.   I didn't like being there,
in the open, a little bit.

'Must do it, Billums—we're the only Englishmen
here—must go to the outpost lines—they're a hundred
yards ahead of us—come on,' and he began striding
along the road, very conspicuous in his white clothes,
and, as far as I knew, walking straight towards that
field-gun.

I found myself trying to walk *behind* him, but
pulled myself together and walked by his *side*.
'We're at the edge of the clearing now,' he said ;
'bear off to the right,' and you may guess how glad
I was to step off the road.   We wormed our way in
among the trees, and Gerald had just whispered,
'We're right in the skirmishing line,' when a rifle
went off not two yards from me, and I jumped almost
out of my skin.   Rifle firing burst out to right and
left—I could see the little spurts of flame among the
trees—and then a very short way in front and below

hundreds of rifles went off and bullets flew past, branches and leaves falling down behind me.

Gerald pulled me round some thick undergrowth and whispered, 'Look down there.' I peered through and could see nothing at first, but our people fired again, and immediately I saw hundreds of little spurts of fire—a whole line of them. Then that field-gun fired—the flash seemed almost in my face—and for a second I saw the glitter of the gun itself and the dark figures of the men fighting it.

'The whole of Zorilla's army is there,' Gerald was saying, when we heard cheering running far into the woods on each side, down below, and then sweeping far away—it seemed to be running round a huge circle. I could hear '*Viva La Buena Presidente! Viva La Buena Presidente!*'

'They've heard the good news; old Zorilla will pretty well guess what it means. Like a shot, Billums?' and Gerald sang out to the native crouched down beside us. He gave me his rifle with a soft cooing '*Buenos, Señor!*' and I leant it against a branch and tried to see something to shoot at, my fingers trembling with excitement. 'Wait till you see the flashes of their next volley, and try and get your sights on,' Gerald said, and I knew that he was smiling. I didn't wait, I thought I saw something, and fired, the recoil bumping my shoulder because I hadn't held the rifle closely enough. It seemed to start every one else firing, and the regulars began firing volleys ; you could see the ring of rifle spurts below us, thousands of them, and bullets were flying overhead, pit-patting against the trees, and cutting off branches and leaves.

' " Any one assisting the aforesaid Gerald Wilson will be——" ' Gerald chuckled.

' Shut up, you ass,' I sang out. The native gave me another cartridge, and, the field-gun blazing again, I just had time to get my sights more or less ' on ' and fire, which started all our chaps easing off too.

' Can't afford to keep you in the firing line,' Gerald chuckled, and took me back. ' You've made my people waste about two hundred rounds, and I can't afford to waste one. Listen to Zorilla's chaps. You'd imagine they had millions to blaze away.

' Something's wrong, Billums ; I can't make it out. He usually keeps quite quiet, he's too clever at this game to throw away a single round. You'd imagine from that field-gun firing down the road, and from all those volleys he's firing, that he means to advance this way.'

He was talking as coolly as a cucumber ; I was sweating with excitement. ' There's a mule track through the forest from here to El Castellar, and I believe he means to break away there. That's why I came out to-night—to make sure which way he's going. We'll know soon.' We got back behind the barricade, and several hundred of the little brown, whited-coated men began gathering there, gliding noiselessly out from the trees. The moon was hidden now, and it was pitch dark, so that I couldn't see them, except for a moment when the field-gun fired, but only hear them murmuring to each other all round me.

To know that there were four thousand regulars standing by to attack us, in the dark, was anything but comforting, and the bullets whipping past were not any too comforting either. All this while Gerald had been talking to some officers, the 'Gnome' among them, but now they went away, and he came to me.

'This excitement enough?'

'I should think it was,' I told him—rather too much if I had told him the truth. I supposed I should get used to it, but suddenly to find myself in the middle of a fight, in a forest, in the dark, was just a little bit too trying, especially when not a soul, except Gerald, could understand a word I said.

Just then I heard a lot of firing much farther away on our front, and some messengers came dashing up, singing out, '*Yuesencia!*[1] *Don Geraldio!*'

'It's just as I thought, Billums; that firing at us was all a bluff. Zorilla has broken through our chaps on the right and is marching along the track to El Castellar.'

Somebody brought a lantern, and he began

[1] 'Yuesencia' is a contraction for 'excellencia.'

scribbling orders, tearing the pages out of a note book and handing them to messengers, who ran off. He was doing it quite calmly, and was actually smiling. Some officers sitting on the ground, with their swords over their knees, looked absolutely played out, but they roused themselves when Gerald spoke to them, got on their feet, and took their natives into the forest again.

'If these messengers do their work in time,' he said, 'Zorilla will never get through to El Castellar. I've turned on the *machetos*.   We'll go round there and see how things are going.'

I shuddered to think of these little chaps, with their awful-looking *machetes*, gliding among the trees all round them.

He had just sent for our horses, when another bare-footed messenger came panting into the light and was led up to him.

Something glittered in his hand ; he held it out to Gerald, and what do you think it was? My cigarette case !

'It's mine,' I sang out; 'I changed cases with Navarro, Zorilla's fat little A.D.C., when he was decent to me in San Sebastian.'

'Well, he's a prisoner now and badly wounded,' Gerald said, after he'd spoken to the man.   'He's sent it to me hoping I shall recognise it and do something for him. He was in command of a foraging party we cut off this morning, and is lying

with the rest of the wounded in some hut about two
miles away—so this man says.'

Well, it was up to me to do something for him,
and I told Gerald so.

' Right you are,' Gerald nodded.   ' This chap will
show you the way.   You'll be as safe as a house with
your yellow head of hair.   Do what you like.   He's
badly wounded, I fancy.   Get back here by daylight,
and if you don't find me, make your way into San
Fernando.'

I looked at my watch by the lantern light.   It was
ten minutes to one, and there would be another
two hours and a half before daylight.

In five minutes I was on my horse, the man who'd
brought my cigarette case was leading him, and we
had plunged into the forest to the left of the road,
Gerald going away to the right, after Zorilla.   How
the little chap found his way I don't know, but he
did somehow or other, cutting through the brushwood with his *machete*, and jabbering to me in
Spanish all the time.

The bush and the fallen trees were so treacherous
that, after Jim had stumbled badly once or twice, and
was trembling with fright, I got off and helped to
lead him too, and wished I'd left him behind.

Now I had a job of my own to do, I didn't mind
the beastly darkness, and gradually gave up jumping with funk whenever some natives glided past,
speaking softly to my little chap, and then hurry-

ing away to the right. I'd hear, '*Yuesencia!*'
'*Hermano!*' '*Don Geraldio!*' and they'd disappear.

The field-gun had stopped firing, but rifle firing
was continuous, and seemed to be travelling away
towards El Castellar.

Once we met quite a large party, with an officer,
all hurrying after Zorilla, and he would not let us
pass till he'd struck a match and seen my face. That
was enough for him, and he passed on, full of
apologies.

This made me think, more than ever, what a
'boss' old Gerald was, and what a 'boss' I was,
too, simply because I had the same coloured hair.

Somehow or other, after barking my shins and
elbows a dozen times, we got to a small clearing,
where there was a kind of a hut and a jolly welcome
light burning in it.

Some one shouted, '*Quien Vive!*' my guide
answered, '*Paisano! La Buena Presidente!*' and a
score of natives thronged round us, bowing, taking
my horse, and saying, '*Buenas,*[1] *Yuesencia!*' I went
into the hut, and found about fifteen men lying on
the ground or propped up against the wall—cavalry
men all of them—and I spotted my little friend,
although he'd grown a scraggy beard.

He was as white as a sheet, and seemed rather 'off
his head.' '*El Medico,*' he sang out, as I went in

---

[1] Short for 'buenas noches!' = good-evening.

—all of them sang out, '*El Medico,*' holding out their hands to make me notice them.

'William Wilson,' I said, and held out the cigarette case he'd sent me, but he only looked at it vacantly, muttered, '*El Medico!*' again, and his chin dropped on his chest. I thought he was dying, and was in a terrible stew. I couldn't see any wound about him, and felt his arms; they were all right, and I felt his legs. Ugh! then I knew, for half-way above his left knee the bone was sticking through a rent in his breeches and they were sticky with blood. He groaned when I touched it, muttering, '*El Medico*'—'*San Fernando!*' '*Agua! Agua!*'

One of the *machetos* brought him some water.

I scratched my head, I didn't know what to do, and he went on rambling, '*Zorilla,*' '*El Castellar,*' '*William Wilson,*' '*Don Geraldio*'—'*El Medico*'—'*San Fernando.*'

'All right, old chap, I'll get you to San Fernando if I can,' I said to myself.

Well, I knew enough about 'first aid' to lash the two legs firmly together, and somehow managed to make the natives understand that I wanted a stretcher. They made a rough litter out of branches in next to no time. I found a blanket tied to the saddle of a dead horse outside the hut, and covered the litter with it, and then I told off four of the most sturdy of the *machete* men to carry him. They obeyed me like lambs.

I hated to have to leave these other wounded men there—they cried piteously when they saw me going—but there were not enough natives to carry them, so I could not help it. I would try and get Gerald to send for them.

Phew! it was bad enough for me, but poor little Navarro, in his stretcher, had a most awful time as we stumbled back through the forest—he was shrieking with agony,—and when we struck the old Spanish road again, after a most fearful time struggling among trees and brushwood, he was quite delirious. You can imagine how thankful I was to feel it under my feet, and, leaving him on his litter by the roadside, and tying my horse to a tree, I tramped down towards the barricade.

It was just getting light enough for me to see some empty deserted wagons standing at the roadside and the fallen tree-trunks dragged across it, but there was not a single living man there, only one or two dead men hanging across the barricade, with their *machetes* still in their hands.

I had not heard the field-gun firing for at least an hour, the rifle firing had died away almost as long ago, and it was quite plain that every one had followed Zorilla towards El Castellar.

I climbed round the barricade and walked rather nervously down towards where the field-gun had been, and stopped because the weirdest sounds were coming up from below.

CHAPTER VIII

Zorilla loses his Guns

Written by Sub-Lieutenant William Wilson, R.N.

As I stood there, rather nervous and uncertain what to do, listening to the queer noises which were coming up from the clearing, where Zorilla's army had camped the night before, I heard the sound of naked feet, and stepped back among the dark trees. There was just sufficient grey light for me to see the road, and, as I watched it, two natives, breathing very heavily, hurried past me. They were weighed down with all sort of things; one had a saddle over his head and a huge cavalry sword under his arm, and the other had covered himself from head to foot with a blue cavalry cloak.

I guessed now what those noises were, and felt certain that Gerald's people were busy in the clearing looting the camp. I don't quite know why I went down there, but I did, and it was a most extraordinary sight in the uncertain light. First I came to that field-gun which had fired at us, its wheels and small shields white with bullet-marks. An empty am-munition limber was standing behind it, and the naked bodies of two dead men lay close by, mixed up with some dead mules. I stepped across them, and came upon a lot of regulars sitting at each side of the road, quite a couple of hundred of them, with their hands tied behind their backs. Poor wretches, they looked as if they expected death at any moment.

Hundreds of natives were swarming round some wagons, hauling boxes out, forcing them open with their *machetes* and scattering the contents on the ground ; and a dozen of them were fighting over a case of brandy, breaking the necks off the bottles, and cutting their faces and hands in their struggles to drink some of the stuff. Nobody was taking the slightest notice of two field-guns, with their limbers and mule teams, which were standing in the road a few yards further down. The little half-drunken brutes were simply looting as hard as they could, not even troubling to pick up the rifles which lay about in hundreds. I felt sure that Gerald had sent them to take the guns into San Fernando, and, jolly angry, strode down between the two rows of prisoners, who, seeing me, thought I was Gerald, and began singing out a whining ' *Don Geraldio! Don Geraldio!* ' I saw by their uniforms that they belonged to the same regiment as those fellows who had collared me in Santa Cruz, and that didn't make me love them any more, but their mistaking me for Gerald gave me an idea.

Close by, an officer lay drunk as a fiddler, another had broken the neck of a champagne bottle, and was trying to swallow the stuff before it bubbled all away. I seized him by the neck, knocked the bottle out of his hand, and shook him.

He turned round, looked at me, and fell on his knees in absolute terror. I jerked him to his feet, singing out, 'San Fernando!' sweeping my arm round the camp, pointing to the guns, and then along the road towards the barricade.

'San Fernando!' I roared. He had a revolver in his belt, I pulled it out—it was unloaded, but that did not matter—and ran up to the wagons, kicking and cuffing the miserable wretches. They shrieked out, '*Don Geraldio!*' and bolted, but two of them— rather drunk they were—came for me with their *machetes*, and didn't stop when I pointed the revolver at them.

It was a jolly awkward moment, but I gave the first a blow on the point of his jaw, which knocked him flying, and before the second could get at me, there were shouts of '*Yuesencia! Yuesencia!*' and the officer from whom I had taken the champagne bottle cut him down, clean from the top of his skull to his mouth. He did it with a *machete*. More officers— half fuddled—came running up, and whether they thought I was Gerald or not, they were in a hopeless fright, and began to lay about them with the flat of their swords, and soon got their natives into order, although I saw a good many of them stealing away among the trees, laden with spoil.

Ugh! the brutes had evidently killed all the
wounded. It was a perfectly sickening sight. I was
beside myself with rage.

Then just as some mules were being hitched to
that first field-gun, I saw a native trying to lead away
a big black horse. The poor beast was limping
badly every step he took, and the man was beating
him cruelly. I rushed across, and the man saw me
coming, and ran off. The horse had a very elaborate
head-stall and blue saddle-cloth, and I felt certain
that I had seen him somewhere before. 'Poor old
fellow,' I said, stroking his nose. He was simply sweating with pain, and seemed to know I was a friend. I
rubbed my hand down his legs, and looked at his
feet, and soon found what the mischief was. One of
his rear shoes was half off, and a projecting nail had
made a gash in his frog, so no wonder the poor old
chap was in such pain.

I found a bayonet and managed to lever the shoe
off altogether, and then led him up to the field-gun.
He came along as gently as a lamb, still limping a
bit, but I do believe he was grateful, and as I led
him between the lines of prisoners, one of them got
quite excited, struggling to his knees, then to his
feet, singing out, '*Yuesencia! El General! General
Zorilla! Caballo del General Zorilla.*'

Ah! now I knew. He was the very horse on
which Bob, the 'Angel,' and I had seen Zorilla ride
across the square at Santa Cruz. He seemed to

know the prisoner, so I thought he might have been his groom, and undid the cord round his arms. Directly they were free, he threw them round the horse's neck and loved him.

'*San Fernando!*' I said, pointing up the road, and he nodded, '*Bueno, Señor! Bueno, Yuesencia!*' and was as pleased as Punch.

The officers had, meanwhile, found enough mules for all three guns, and I sent them rumbling and rattling up towards the barricade, which the natives were already hauling away. You may bet your life I was jolly glad to see them make a start, for I knew that they were worth all the world to Gerald, and there was always the chance of some of Zorilla's regulars turning up and recapturing them.

There were not mules enough for all the wagons— I felt perfectly certain that the natives had simply bolted into the forest with a lot of them—but there were sufficient for four, and I chose two, full of field-gun ammunition, and sent them up the road, and then we set about and collected all the rifles lying on the ground, and as many boxes of rifle ammunition as we could stow on another two, and I felt jolly pleased with myself when all four were jolting on their way to San Fernando. I made the officers understand that the prisoners' arms were to be untied, but it wasn't till I began cutting the cords adrift myself that they, rather sullenly, ordered their men to release the others. You can just imagine how gratefully they looked at me, and I felt certain that they wouldn't be such fools as to try and escape, with five hundred fierce little *machetos* all round them, and thousands more in the forest. It was quite light by the time every one was under way, and I began to feel most horribly hungry and tired. Up above in the clear sky a number of vultures were slowly circling round and round with their long necks stretching downwards, waiting till we went away before they came down for their horrible feast, and as I left the clearing, and looked back, I saw any number of the little brown men sneaking out of the woods again to carry on looting, but I couldn't be bothered with them, and they would keep those vultures away. I had rescued all that was most valuable, and wanted to get back to San Fernando as quickly as possible.

When we got up to where poor little Navarro was lying, by the roadside, I gave him some brandy from a bottle I'd stowed away in a wagon ; it did him a power of good, and he now seemed quite sensible, looking very miserable when he saw the guns coming along.

'The horse of *El General*,' he said sadly, as the black horse limped past with the groom.

I put him on top of one of the wagons, but the jolting was so painful that he had to be carried on the litter again. He knew me all right now, and I gave him back my cigarette case, pulling his own out of my pocket to show him.

'San Sebastian,' he said, smiling; 'I remember always.'

Well, off we went, the three guns and the four wagons on ahead, the two hundred prisoners, surrounded by the little *machetos*, marching behind them, and Navarro, on his litter, the groom with Zorilla's black horse, and myself, on my little stallion, 'Jim,' bringing up the rear. I'd found some ammunition for that revolver, and had loaded it, but my face and yellowish hair was all that was wanted to make any one obey me, and I rode along on my tired little horse, absolutely bossing the show.

You may laugh if you like, but there I was in charge of the whole blooming crowd, feeling simply dead tired, but kept awake by the excitement of it.

'Any one assisting the aforesaid Gerald Wilson ——' kept running through my head, and I grinned every time I thought of it.

At about ten or half-past we came to that wayside inn where Gerald and I had had those omelettes last night. It was most appallingly hot, and, though there was no food there, I determined to halt for an hour to rest the mules and men.

The prisoners lay down at the sides of the roads, under the shade, the little *machetos* curled up under the trees, and went to sleep in a twinkling, the officers went into the inn, and Navarro's stretcher was laid down outside it, in the shade of the projecting roof. I could hardly keep my eyes open, and dare not even

"I GAVE THE FIRST A BLOW ON THE POINT OF HIS JAW"

II

sit down for fear of falling asleep, because I wasn't going to trust those officers again. They didn't look in the least pleased (of course by this time they knew that I wasn't Gerald), and a good many of their men had a sullen look on their faces, which I didn't like a little bit. Still, so long as I kept my eye on them I wasn't afraid of them playing the fool, and I spent that hour walking up and down the line of guns and wagons with their dejected mule teams, passing a word or two occasionally with Navarro, who was much brighter now, sitting up on his litter smoking a cigarette.

I thanked him for the letter which he had written to me from Santa Cruz, warning me about that ex-police agent. 'Very bad man—he will never cease from revenge—next time you see him kill him,' he said; and I rather wish that I hadn't mentioned it, because I hated thinking of the little brute. Of course he was as anxious to get to San Fernando as I was; he wanted to see a doctor as soon as possible, and have his broken leg looked after.

At the end of the hour I tried to push on again, but I'm hanged if I could. I walked up to the inn and sang out, 'San Fernando!' to the officers sitting inside it, with half-empty bottles of wine in front of them, but they shook their heads and didn't even stand up. This, I knew well enough, was meant to be rude. Only the chap who had killed the native as he was going for me, the one whom I had prevented drink-

ing that champagne, stood up and came out, shaking
his head, and jabbering Spanish.   ' *Mucho caliente!*
Mucho caliente! '

'He say no go San Fernando till night,' Navarro
explained.   'Too hot.'

Well, as I've told you before, I've got a beastly
bad temper: I wasn't going to stand any nonsense,
and I was inside that place in a twinkling.

'San Fernando!' I shouted, pointed to the blazing
white road, where the mules were lying panting in
the glare.

They only smiled.

I pulled my revolver out and roared again, but
they only pulled theirs out and shook their heads.

I knew that I was up against something 'tough,'
and I don't know what would have happened if I
hadn't heard my name called.

Navarro was beckoning to me, and I went out, the
officers laughing, and only that one following me.

'Prisoners obey me—give them rifles—I want
El Medico—San Fernando—quick,' and he pointed
to where the regulars were all lying asleep.

I knew well enough what he meant, and was in
such a towering rage that I'd have taken any risk.
I held out my hand, he held out his, and we shook.

'Right you are, old chap, I'll trust them.'

He jabbered to the officer who had followed me,
and then said, 'Take me to prisoners,' so we picked
up the litter and carried him to where they were, the

other officers laughing, and not even getting up from their benches to see what was going to happen.

Then he introduced the officer to me. 'Don Pedro de Castilio—Señor William Wilson,' and we bowed to each other. I thought it an awful waste of time when every second mattered, and what we had to do had to be done quickly.

He went among the regulars, waking them, and half-a-dozen glided to a wagon and came back with rifles. Don Pedro took four of them along to the inn, and I saw them pointing their rifles through the windows.

'Don Pedro make them prisoners,' Navarro whispered, with his eyes gleaming.

That was a jolly smart move, and the officers never made a sound. If they'd sung out or fired a shot, we should have had the *machetos* round us in a second.

As fast as the other two woke their comrades, they stole away and got rifles, some of them bringing back a box of ammunition.

Not a *macheto* moved, and you bet I kept my eyes skinned lest they should wake, handing out ammunition as fast as the regulars came up for it. By the time I had seventy or eighty armed, I made them climb on top of the four wagons, so that they could defend themselves better in case the little forest-men tried to rush us with their *machetes* ; I lifted Navarro on top of one of them too.

One of these wagons was right in front of the

inn, so that my five young friends inside it had about twenty rifle-muzzles to look at. Still not a *macheto* stirred—they seemed dead to the world—so I went across to the inn.

It was they who were up against something 'tough' now, and they knew it, stood up, began unbuckling their sword-belts, and were just going to hand them to me, when I heard cries of '*Señor! Señor!*' heard men running, and, looking over my shoulder, saw the rest of the regulars swarming round the wagon with the rifles in it, making a tremendous noise as they pulled them out. I ran along the road, and, as I ran, I saw the *machetos*, under the trees, all rising to their feet, gripping those horrid *machetes*.

I pointed to the wagons, there was no need for orders, the regulars simply scrambled on top of them like drowning rats on a log, running from wagon to wagon to find room, and crawling underneath them when they couldn't. I jumped across to where Jim, my horse, was standing, got on him, and pulled him into the middle of the road.

The little *machetos* hadn't quite got the hang of affairs, and looked half-dazed to see the regulars on top of the wagons and the rifles pointing at them.

I roared out, 'San Fernando! San Fernando!' but they were too startled to obey; and Don Pedro and his four men, too frightened to stay where they were any longer, bolted for the nearest wagon, the

officers bursting out after them, and plunging into the
forest among their own men.

'San Fernando!' I shouted, pointing down the
road, and some of the little forest-men seemed to
want to obey, but I saw those contemptible officers
going in among them and dragging them back.

My aunt! I was in a jolly awkward fix. If they
only made a rush, my chaps would simply be eaten
up. I dare not get them down from the wagons to
stir up the mules, for I felt absolutely certain that
that would only be the signal for a massacre. We
couldn't move the wagons till the guns went on—
the road was not broad enough to pass them—and
the leading one was at least a couple of hundred
yards away. I saw a lot of the *machetos* dart across
the road ahead of us, and my heart went thump, for
I thought they were making ready for a rush, but the
little brutes simply unhitched the leading gun's mule
teams and led them into the forest.

Well, that was checkmate with a vengeance.

One of the officers now came up to the wagon on
which Navarro was sitting and spoke to him. He
sang out to me, and I went across.

'He say, "No go San Fernando till night; if
soldiers no give up rifles, *machetos* kill them. Officers
tell *machetos*, soldiers take guns to Zorilla."'

He was in a funk himself; the trees on both sides
of us were simply swarming with the fierce little men,
and I didn't know what to do, my brain seemed all

woolly, but I dare not let the regulars throw their rifles down.

'Oh! that I knew Spanish and could talk to the little chaps and explain things,' I was thinking, when there was the sound of a horse galloping along the road, behind us, and the 'Gnome' dashed up. I *was* glad to see him, if you like.

He looked at the regulars on top of the wagons, timidly pointing their rifles across the road, and at the crowds of *machetos* in the woods, and didn't know what to think of it. Before he'd caught sight of me, I saw one of the officers running to him. I knew he'd tell him lies, so I cantered up to him too. He looked startled to see me, but quite pleased, and I made him come to the wagon where Navarro sat. 'Tell him—ex-plain,' I sang out. They seemed to know each other very well.

You should have seen him after he and Navarro had talked for a few seconds. He was in a towering rage, and he rode backwards and forwards along the edge of the road, evidently telling the officers exactly what he thought of them, and I knew that things were going right, because Navarro looked so chirpy and the officers so ashamed of themselves. The regulars, too, began to put up their rifles, and those who had crawled under the wagons crawled out again. Then, at last, the little forest-men stuck their *machetes* back into their belts, and a couple of hundred of them came along, looking like naughty children, and took charge of the mule teams. My aunt! I was so relieved and thankful and tired and hungry and hot all at the same time that I would have done any mortal thing for my fat little 'Gnome.'

He sent the officers and the rest of their men away into the forest—to rejoin Gerald, I suppose—and jolly glad I was to see the last of them. Then we shoved off, rattling down the road, and you may guess that I never wanted to see that inn again. The 'Gnome' stopped with us for about a mile, and then, taking off his hat to me, galloped on ahead, leaving me with no one to question my authority any more.

Still, I didn't feel in the least sure that those other fellows wouldn't come back, so, with help from Navarro and Don Pedro, I got the two hundred regulars into some sort of order, fifty of them well in front of the guns as an advance guard, fifty between the guns and the wagons, fifty as a rear guard, and the remainder riding on the wagons themselves.

I wanted to make the little forest-men, who were leading the mules, give up their *machetes*, and explained that to Navarro, but he smiled, shook his head, and said, '*Machetos* good men now,' so I had to be satisfied.

We tramped along like this, the mules getting slower and slower, till half-past one, when a violent thunderstorm made it almost as dark as night, and wetted us to the skin. It was jolly refreshing whilst it lasted, cooled the air splendidly, and afterwards we

got along much faster. By three o'clock we were out
of the forest; I had nothing to fear from the forest-
men, and was as happy as a king. We rumbled
down to the stream, splashed through the ford, after
a lot of trouble with the mules, who would fill themselves with water before they'd come on, breasted the
slope again, and got on top of the ridge looking
down over San Fernando.

You can jolly well imagine how glad I was to see
it, and the old *Hector* lying offshore. From here it
was simply a triumphal procession. The 'Gnome'
must have let the people know what had happened,
for they met us in hundreds, flocking round me,
trying to lead my horse, even to kiss my gaiters,
dancing and shouting and clapping their hands, and
fighting for the honour of holding on to the gun
traces. '*Viva los canones! Viva los Inglesas!*' they
shouted, and dragged the guns along, much to the
relief of the mules.

The cathedral bells were clanging joyously when
we marched into the square, I in front, Navarro on
his litter beside me, Zorilla's charger behind us, then
the two hundred regulars walking in front of the
leading gun. You can guess how jolly important
I felt, for the whole population had turned out,
huzzahing and throwing their hats in the air, and on
the steps and verandah of the Club were a lot of the
Hector chaps and the Skipper himself.

As I took off my panama hat to salute him, he

sang out, 'Good lad! Good lad!' and Navarro, seeing them, called out, '*El Medico!*'

Clegg, our Surgeon, was leaning over the verandah, so I stopped and had him taken in there. 'Look after him, will you?' I called out to Clegg; 'his leg's badly broken,' and on we went again.

The regulars, in their hated uniforms, were a bit of a puzzle to the crowd, but they thought they had deserted to the insurgents, and soon swarmed round them, shouting, '*Viva los cazedores!*' tearing off their own green and black rosettes and pinning them on the soldiers' sleeves. Many of them had already got rid of their green and yellow badges, and you may bet your life they didn't object to the black and green ones, so long as their skins were safe.

Ever since I had been stabbed by that wretched little ex-policeman, and whenever I got in among a crowd of natives, I found myself looking round to see if I could recognise him. I was doing so now without knowing it, looking from face to face all round me. Perhaps it was because of what Navarro had said, 'He will never cease revenge,' but I had the most extraordinary feeling that he was there, somewhere, and had his cunning little eyes fixed on me. I couldn't see him anywhere, and thought the strange fancy was probably due to my being so sleepy. I pulled myself together, because we were now abreast the cathedral, the front of which had been hung with black and green flags, and, on the steps, the whole

of the Provisional Government was waiting for me,
bowing and taking off their top-hats. It was all I
could do to keep from laughing, although I was so
tired and sleepy and hungry that I could hardly sit
in my saddle. They made me dismount, and would
have kept me there for ages, but I seized hold of
Mr. Don Pedro, pushed him forward, took my hat
off, bowed, and led my plucky little stallion back to
the Club. I knew that he would explain everything,
and I always hate being fussed over. The crowd
made way for me as if I'd been a blooming emperor ;
but I felt a touch on my shoulder and jumped, for I
was still thinking of the little brute.

'Beg parding, sir,' I heard some one say, and
there was O'Leary, his funny old face simply as
excited as a child's. 'We'd just like you to see that
'ere bit of 'ydraulic machinery what we brought along
with us, sir.'

'Right you are,' I sang out—I know I yawned, I
couldn't help it—and he took me through a side street
to the water front and a long low building, which ran
along the shore, with a tumble-down 'yard' in front
of it.   Inside the tumble-down gates there were thirty
or forty of our petty officers, with their jumpers off,
digging out like pepper among a crowd of half-naked
natives.

'Look what we've done, sir,' O'Leary grinned,
and there I saw the long chases of two 4.7's sticking
up from their field carriages.

'Pretty good work that,' I said, yawning again.

'They didn't know nothink about 'em, sir, but for us, sir,' he grinned; they were all grinning with delight, and the armourer's crew, as black as paint, came across from a forge, in a shed beyond, stood by the guns, and grinned too.

'Your brother's done a good day's work, we hear, sir,' Griffiths, the boatswain's mate, said, saluting me; 'these 'ere guns'll be a pleasant sur—prise to him when he gets back.'

Then Bob and the 'Angel,' Barton, the senior mid., Blotchy Smith, half-a-dozen more mids., and Marchant, the 'Inkslinger,' with their coats off, and covered with grease and dirt, came running across.

'What are you up to?' I asked, and they dragged me to another corner of the yard, and I found they'd been 'assembling' the pom-poms.

'We've just been giving the chaps a bit of drill,' Bob squeaked. 'We're having a glorious time. I wish we could stay on shore till the morning. We'd have everything finished by then. Won't Cousin Gerald be pleased?'

Well, I was much too tired to stay any longer, and shoved off, all of them hurrying back to finish their job.

O'Leary followed me out. 'They don't know how they came 'ere, sir. I gave them English gents the "tip," and they were all out of their packin'-cases when I comes along, innercent like, with all these chaps. We just looks in at the gateway, and sees 'em all lying "'iggle de piggledy" like, a-lying on the ground, and, well, I says to 'em, "Mr. Wilson, our Sub, what the Commander bullies, 'as a brother fighting for these 'ere niggers, so one good turn deserves another, so 'wot oh!'" and we just 'as a quiet arternoon's fun, and you sees what we've done, sir.'

'He'll be awfully pleased. Thank you very much indeed,' I said, and tramped back to the Club, more dead than alive, looking from side to side all the time, in case that little brute was lurking about anywhere with his knife. I was so stiff that I could hardly move one leg in front of the other, and my back aches now when I think of it.

Zorilla's black charger was tied up to the Club railings, the groom apparently waiting for me, and I handed over both of the tired horses to one of the Englishmen who was there, stumbled up the steps, and fell back in one of those easy-chairs on the verandah, pretty well played out. Dr. Clegg came along.

'What do you think of my pal?' I asked him.

'He won't be on his legs again for six months,' he told me, 'I'm going to take him on board the *Hector* for the Fleet Surgeon to see.'

I was absolutely too weary just then to worry about anything, but I know that there were a lot of formalities to go through before he could be taken aboard, and that the Skipper and one of the San Fernando Englishmen bustled about and managed it all right. The Provisional Government would have done anything for us just then. I was jolly glad, because I owed a great deal more to little Navarro than I could repay.

I don't know when I had felt so tired, and though any number of our chaps were crowding round me wanting me to talk, and the townspeople were thronging against the Club railings to see me, I hardly noticed them, and just wanted something to drink and then go to sleep. I really couldn't keep my eyes open.

CHAPTER IX

Zorilla attacks

Written by Sub-Lieutenant William Wilson, R.N.

I SLEPT like a top for an hour, and woke up in a fright; I thought that little brute was trying to stab me, but it was only one of the local Englishmen, a man named Seymour, shaking me.

'I'll be more careful next time,' he said, smiling and rubbing his shoulder where I'd caught him 'one' as he bent over me. 'You yelled as if you were being murdered.'

'I thought I was,' I said, waking up.

He had just come back from Gerald, and had a message for me. Gerald wanted me to go out to him again. He was at a place called Marina, about eight miles along the coast-line, half-way to El Castellar, and was making it his headquarters for the night.

'You'll see lots of fun if you go out there,' Seymour told me, 'he has Zorilla's army surrounded just above Alvarez's farm, not two miles from Marina, and expects to collar the whole lot to-night or to-morrow morning. He's done a great day's work and has captured the last gun they have.'

He was sending his own buggy to Marina with Gerald's bag, and offered me a lift.

You may bet I jumped at the offer; there was just time for me to have a wash and some tea; along came the carriage with two jolly smart ponies in it; one of the Club servants brought down Gerald's kit-bag—one of the last presents the mater had given him before he left home—in I jumped, and away those ponies flew, bumping the carriage along at a fine rate.

There was no more going to sleep then—it was as much as I could do to hold on to my seat, and prevent myself being chucked out.

We rattled down to the foreshore and turned along the coast road, bowling along it at a great pace, every now and then meeting wounded men limping wearily towards San Fernando. Some of our own ward-room officers were tramping back to catch the 'dinner' boat off to the ship, and they must have envied me pretty considerably. Thank goodness, the Skipper had given me forty-eight hours' leave, and I hadn't to get aboard till to-morrow at noon. I was so jolly keen to see some more fun, and to tell Gerald how I'd managed to bring those guns back to San Fernando, that I forgot all about being so sleepy.

The road ran along the top of the beach, skirting the shore all the way, and the forest came right up to the side of it, and made it beautifully shady, but it was in such a terrible state of holes and ruts, crumbling down here and there on the beach side, and overgrown with bushes on the forest side, that it looked as if the sea and the forest between them would swallow it up pretty soon.

Four miles out from the town there were two poor chaps lying by the roadside; I expect they had been wounded during the night, and had tried to make their way into San Fernando, but died before they could do so. Horrid-looking crows, something like vultures, were hopping about round them. I hated the brutes—they hardly got out of the way of the wheels.

Just as it was getting dusk we passed some bungalows, and the native driver shouted, ' *Marina! El Casino!*' pointing ahead to a large building in front of us standing close to the beach.

'*Don Geraldio!*' he nodded.

Then we splashed through a stream, and it wasn't too dark for me to see a little native chap squatting by the side of a low garden wall there, or to recognise him. It *was* that ex-policeman—I could see the scar on his forehead—somehow or other I was expecting to see him—and, without thinking, I jumped out of the carriage, stumbled for an instant, and then sprang at him, but he'd seen me too, and fled. I had Don Pedro's revolver with me, and fired as he jumped the low wall and darted among some trees. I was after him in a second—of course I had missed him, I always was a rotten shot with a revolver at any time—and then he fired back, and a bullet sung past my elbow. I caught sight of his white shirt among the trees, and fired at him again, and he bolted out of the garden, across the road, and into the forest.

It was hopeless to follow him there.

The pistol-shots had frightened the ponies, and they were dashing madly along the road, Gerald's kit-bag flying out. I picked it up, and lugged it along to the front of that big building—a gaudy-looking kind of place, nearly all windows, with a flat roof, verandahs and balconies all round it, and '*El Casino*,' in big gilt letters over the door, half-hidden by a huge black and green flag which hung down over the entrance.

Gerald, surrounded by officers, was standing at the top of the steps, and I was only thankful that that little brute had not gone on another hundred yards.

'Hello, Billums!' Gerald sang out. 'Got my bag all right? I thought, when the buggy dashed past a moment ago, that old Zorilla would get it. Come along with me, I'm going to have a shave and get into clean things.'

He took me along with him, and whilst he was shaving himself, and his little groom, José, was unpacking his bag, I told him about the ex-policeman.

'For goodness' sake, take care of yourself, Gerald,' I said; 'he'll get you if he dies for it,' but 'Don't worry,' was all I could get out of him, as he scraped his face. I don't mind telling you that I was thoroughly frightened—much more for Gerald than myself, though the more I bothered him to take some precautions, the more angry he got.

'Blow it!' he said; 'you've made me cut myself. Confound these safety razors. My dear Billums, if he's going to get me, he will. I'll keep my eye skinned for the beast, but they're all so much alike that you can't tell t'other from which — scar or no scar. Nobody's life is worth a cent in this country unless you trust to luck.'

'But why don't you have an escort?' I pleaded.

'Have an escort? My dear Billums, if I had an escort, they'd think I was afraid.'

I gave it up, and told him all about bringing those guns and ammunition-wagons back into San Fernando, and all the troubles I'd had with the officers and their men; I didn't forget to tell him about the 'Gnome' coming up in the nick of time.

He was jolly pleased, though he didn't say much. 'That chap you call the 'Gnome' is one of the best people I've got, I don't know what I should do without him.'

All this time orderlies came in and out, and Gerald did not seem to have a moment's peace. Then a man came in with a note.

'It's from Zorilla,' Gerald said. 'He wants to know what's become of Navarro, his fat little A.D.C. You ought to know—that chap with the cigarette case.'

I told him he had been taken on board the *Hector*.

'Jolly glad,' he said, sent for some paper, sat down

with the soap lather on his face and a towel round his waist, and wrote a reply. 'Wouldn't be the proper thing not to write it myself.'

'Tell Zorilla we found his horse, and have brought him into San Fernando,' I sang out.

'Good stroke, Billums, good stroke. We'll send him back when he's fit—always make friends of an enemy, especially if he's a good chap like Zorilla,' and he added a postscript.

'Where is he?' I asked, as the messenger darted away.

'About three miles off—in another clearing, for the night.'

'But the horse won't be much good to him,' I said, remembering what the Englishman had told me. 'You've got him surrounded, and he must surrender, mustn't he?'

'Yes, I have,' Gerald smiled, 'three thousand men round about the same number. I don't believe I have more—hundreds have gone off to their homes with loot. I tell you what. Old Zorilla isn't beaten till he's dead, and he may be up to any tricks to-night. It's seven miles to El Castellar and it's eight to San Fernando, and he'll lose his job and his reputation if he falls back on the fort. He's lost his guns, and he'll get 'em back, and San Fernando too, if he dies for it. I know the dear old chap.'

'I thought you'd won.' I said, feeling very worried.

'Oh, bother! You've never won in this country. The more you win, the more enemies you make—there are plenty of people, on our side, who want me out of it. That is why those chaps wouldn't obey you this morning—they're as jealous as thieves. I run the show, and they don't like it—a good many of them don't—not the men, the officers. They want their siesta in the middle of the day, and eight hours' sleep besides—it's the custom of the country—they don't get it. They've always run revolutions on those lines, and I don't.'

He'd dressed himself now and brushed his yellow hair well back. 'That's better; come along and have some grub.'

Well, I hadn't any appetite, but he had—and ate a jolly good meal in spite of all the orderlies and officers coming and going. He did want to dine on the open verandah, close to the road, but I thought of that little beast creeping up with the revolver, and managed to get him into an inside room, by complaining of the cold. The air was so still that all the time he was eating we could hear firing going on far away in the forest, but that didn't interfere with his appetite in the least. 'Zorilla's not made a move yet,' he said at last. 'Come and have a game of billiards,' and we did actually play on a French table with balls as big as oranges, in a room overlooking the sea, the cool breeze blowing through wide-open windows, and the noise of rifle-shots almost drowned by the lazy noise of the water on the beach. José, who seemed to follow Gerald about like a dog, squatted in a corner, a young insurgent officer scored for us, and Gerald, playing stiffly with his bad arm, was as keen on beating me as if we had been in the pater's billiard-room at home. We were half-way through the game, and he was piling up cannon after cannon, sprawling over the table to make his strokes, and I was standing at his side, when I suddenly heard something snap outside, saw the insurgent officer look out—fright on his face—turned my head, and there was that little beast, with a joyful smile on his ugly face, pointing a revolver straight through the window at Gerald.

I don't know how I did it, but I'd pulled Gerald off the table, and he was sprawling on the floor, before the room filled with smoke and noise, and a bullet had cut clean across the green cloth. I saw the insurgent officer whip out a revolver and fire, I sprang out into the dark with mine, and José, with a yell, a *machete* in his hand, dashed past me, down on to the beach. But there wasn't a sign of any one.

People rushed into the room, the lights were knocked out, and then Gerald sang out, asking what was the matter.

'My dear Billums, I wouldn't have had that happen for worlds,' he said, when the lamps had been relighted, and I'd shown him where the bullet had ripped across the table.

'What happen?' I asked.

'Why, you knocking me down, of course.'

He was quite hurt about it, and wanted to finish the game, said the cut across the cloth would make it all the more 'sporting,' but the noise of firing in the forest became more furious, and orderlies came in with news that Zorilla was on the move at last.

Gerald wrote out more orders and shrugged his shoulders. 'He's marching towards El Castellar. I suppose he thinks I shall try and prevent him.'

'But won't you?' I asked.

'My dear Billums, of course not; he can go there as fast as he likes. He thinks I shall try and get in front of him, and then he'll double back to San Fernando. Not much! Come along and we'll have a look round.'

I followed him out of the Casino—it was quite dark, the forest absolutely black—we mounted horses, and, with a lot of officers, trotted down the road. I was so nervous and overwrought in the dark lanes, which we presently rode through, that my heart thumped every time I heard '*Quien Vive!*' or '*Que Gente!*' called out by sentries or pickets we couldn't see, and the murmurs of '*Yuesencia!*' or '*Don Geraldio!*' from hundreds of unseen mouths. Gerald found some officers and seemed satisfied; somehow or other we got back, and the night was so still, except for the distant firing, the rustling trees, and the very faint noise of the sea, and the darkness was so intense, that I was jolly glad to be inside the Casino again.

More orderlies were waiting for Gerald here, and a prisoner was dragged into the light.

'That settles it,' he said decisively, looking at the poor, miserable, frightened, whining brute. 'He's been caught in the El Castellar direction—where they are advancing. He belongs to the 5th Santa Cruz *Cazedores*—the worst fighters in the army. Old Zorilla wouldn't put them there if he was in earnest. I'm going to bring back every man I can get hold of, place them the other side of that stream—down the road there—it runs nearly straight inland for four or five miles, and I wish to goodness the moon would come out.'

Whilst he was speaking, a whole crowd of bare-footed riflemen and *machetos* went silently past, going back towards San Fernando, the officers, haggard and dirty, stopping to salute Gerald and ask for orders before disappearing after them. It was the noiselessness of them all that was getting on my nerves, and the feeling of hopelessness at not being able to speak to any one except Gerald. All this time, too, I kept looking out for that ex-policeman, expecting him to spring out at any moment.

Every one who came along I half expected to be he, and little José, I think, did so too, standing close to Gerald, just like a cat, with a *machete* in his hand. Gerald saw it once, and made him throw it away, but he picked it up again when Gerald wasn't looking.

The 'Gnome' appeared from somewhere, and I saw that my brother was very glad to see him—he came across to me, and we bowed, and I squeezed his hand. He was sent away along that stream with some men he'd brought. 'Come and finish our game of billiards, Billums,' Gerald sang out. Honestly I don't know whether he was showing off, or was nervous, or whether he did really want to finish it, but we heard a heavy carriage splashing through that stream, and the new President—de Costa himself—appeared. They both went into the Casino and, I was thankful to see, into an upstairs room, where they couldn't be shot at. I went with them and sat down in a chair—their voices seemed to be floating away somewhere—and the next I know was that little José was pulling at my sleeve, it was just getting light, very heavy firing was going on close by, yells and shrieks were coming from the forest, and men were running noisily along the road beneath the window. Gerald wasn't there.

I sprang up and followed José. The Casino was empty, and, as I dashed out, a window, above me, broke and fell in little pieces at my feet. I heard bullets flying everywhere.

I looked down towards the stream, and people were lying on the road, beyond the ford, firing in our direction. José pulled me back behind the

Casino, and we ran along the shore, waded through the stream as it flowed over the sands, and got behind our people.   Gerald wasn't there either, only the 'Gnome,' in his big hat, waddling backwards and forwards.

'Geraldio? Don Geraldio?' I asked, and he stopped a moment to point away up stream.

He was trying to stop the shooting, because there was nobody in sight, although bullets were flying past all the time, and very heavy firing was going on further inland.   He managed to stop it presently, and then I had time to look round.

Just across the stream was the little wall under

which the ex-policeman had been sitting last night. It enclosed the garden of a small bungalow, and one side of it ran along the road, and the other along the stream. It was light enough for me to see the road running up to the Casino, about a hundred and fifty yards further on—the black and green flag was still hanging there — and about three hundred yards beyond this it turned away to the left, and we could only see the glimmer of light on the water. As far as I could tell, we had none of our people in front of us, but it was impossible to make out anything in the forest, on the left of the road, and it turned out that we still had a lot of chaps there.

The 'Gnome' was extending his people down the beach, making them scrape up a kind of breast-work in the sand, right down to the edge of the sea. They began digging away like a lot of hungry wolves, and some of them had found fishing nets, and were laying them down on the far side of the stream. I suppose one always thinks the position one happens to be in must be the main point of attack, and I wished to goodness that Gerald would come along, for I didn't like the way the chaps lying in the road kept looking back. I guessed that what Gerald had expected last night had happened, and that Zorilla had turned at last, and thought what a grand old chap he must be, after all his bad luck, to be able to make his disheartened, half-starved troops attack us.

CHAPTER X

The Fight round the Casino

Written by Sub-Lieutenant William Wilson, R.N.

WELL, if Zorilla intended to try and cut his way past us into San Fernando, I'd learnt enough about the old man to know that it would be jolly hard work to stop him, and it struck me that the little chaps, on each side of me, were not placed in a very good position to defend the road and the beach, and that the 'Gnome,' however plucky a chap he was, did not seem at all certain what to do.

The good sleep which I had had must have cleared my brain. Whatever was the cause, I seemed to realise, all at once, exactly what ought to be done. Of course I was tremendously excited, but I tried to calm myself by imagining that this was only a sham-fight, and to think what would be the natural thing to do.

It was all very well to make our little chaps lie down behind the ford and behind the stream where it trickled down the beach, but, however deep it was farther inland, it was so shallow here that it hardly covered one's boots and wouldn't stop a cat. To stop where we were, and leave that bungalow garden wall, on the enemy's side, unoccupied, was perfectly silly, and I looked about to see if there was not something we could use to barricade the road itself.

I saw those empty wagons standing in front of the Casino, and knew that if we only pulled them across the road and put some of our chaps behind them, it would be grand.

First of all, for that bungalow wall, I thought, and, almost before I knew what I was doing, I found myself dashing across the stream, and looking over it to see if it would be any use to make the little chaps fire over it. But for the giant palms and ferns, in the garden, I could see right along the road, and fellows behind it could easily sweep the road with rifle-fire. I called José, and he came, then the 'Gnome' came, stood on tip-toe, looked over, and knew exactly what I meant. I seized a *machete*, jumped over the wall, and began lopping down the palms, and in a minute he'd sent thirty or forty chaps to help me, and began bringing riflemen over to line the wall—he made some climb on the roof of the bungalow, too, where they could get even a better field of fire.

Now for those wagons, I thought, and began trotting down the road towards the Casino, hoping that the others would come along as well, but only José panted after me, singing out 'No, no!'

'*No, Señor, no!*' the Gnome shouted, but I wasn't going back, for another idea came to me. How about the top of the Casino itself?

I got up to the Casino, dashed in, and ran upstairs
—I knew that there must be a way to the roof, as
there were railings all round it, and it was flat. I
found a staircase leading up there, and was on top in
a jiffy, José following me and pulling me down to my
knees, because, directly my head had shown above
the railings, there were yells from the edge of the
forest, and bullets came splattering against the house.
I wriggled myself to the edge and looked down,
really only wanting to see whether it commanded the
road properly, but—my eye!—beyond that corner,
three hundred yards further along, collecting there,
as far back as I could see, were hundreds of cavalry,
and the woods were thick with infantry.

I beckoned to José, and he crawled across and
looked too; his face got almost white when he saw
what I had seen.

I heard the people at the ford opening fire.
'*Señor! Señor!*' José cried, and pointed down into the
road at our feet, and I saw there, right below us,
twenty or thirty regulars streaming across the road
from the forest to the front of the Casino—the leading
ones were already springing up the steps.

We were down off that roof like redshanks, and as
we got down to the first floor we heard them clambering up the main staircase. We raced down the
corridor and saw the first of them. They saw us and
yelled. I fired my revolver in their faces and dashed
into a back bedroom, José slamming the door behind

us. I knew there was a verandah outside, and we jumped out, swarmed down a supporting pillar—like monkeys—and swung off back along the beach, the soldiers firing at us from the verandah we'd just left. I split one of the knees of my riding breeches, I ran so fast.

I didn't run so fast entirely on account of those bullets, but because I wanted to let the 'Gnome' know what I had seen round that corner. José told him, pointing up the road.

They had commenced firing at us now from the Casino ; one of our chaps kneeling in the road dropped his rifle and fell backwards, the 'Gnome's' big hat spun round and fell on the ground. He picked it up, put a finger through a bullet-hole, and stuck it on again. He didn't look frightened, but muddled—he didn't seem to know what to do.

My aunt ! it was all clear enough to me—now.

All that heavy firing, away on the left, where my brother had gone, was merely Zorilla's bluff, just a piece with his pretending to fall back on El Castellar, in the night, and he meant to make his real attack along the road. As soon as his cavalry were ready he'd launch them along the beach and across the ford, and simply gallop into San Fernando, clearing the way for his infantry.

Oh, why wouldn't Gerald come and tell us what to do !

'Geraldio! Don Geraldio!' I shouted to José,

pushing him to the left, and he understood, and bolted along the edge of the stream in among the trees where our little men were swarming.

We couldn't stay where we were, for the regulars simply rested their rifles on the verandah and the window ledges and fired point-blank at us. Several of our chaps, lying across the road, had been hit already, and although the 'Gnome' brought more men and made them form a double line, with fixed bayonets, ready to spring to their knees directly they were wanted, they were terrified and kept turning to look backwards. Every second I expected to see the cavalry come thundering round that bend in the road, and I knew that we couldn't possibly stop them. Our own chaps behind the low wall were certainly potting at the regulars in the Casino, but they didn't even aim properly, they were too frightened, simply popping up over the wall and firing haphazard.

Three more of our men were hit, the 'Gnome' couldn't make any more fill their places, and I knew that, in a few minutes, those who were there would creep back among the trees. The 'Gnome' stood in the middle of the road, behind them, one hand on his sword-hilt and the other on his revolver holster, as brave as a lion, but I could see that he hadn't an idea what to do.

I knew, I knew well enough, that we couldn't stop the cavalry, but if we could only capture the Casino and occupy that flat roof before they charged, we might possibly check the advance of his infantry till Gerald came back. I couldn't explain all this to the 'Gnome,' who stood there looking stupid, with bullets flicking all round him.

Oh, why wouldn't Gerald come and lead them!— I couldn't.

I heard the sound of a horse galloping towards us —from behind—from San Fernando way. Some one in white was coming along as hard as his horse could go. Gerald at last, I thought, and my heart thumped with joy, but it wasn't, it was Seymour. As he leapt off his horse it fell in the road, dead, and before it had finished shuddering, half-a-dozen chaps were fighting to take cover behind it.

'For God's sake, help!' I said jumping towards him. 'Zorilla's cavalry is all round that bend—the woods are full of his infantry—they're firing at us from the windows of the Casino, and I can't make a soul understand.'

'Where's your brother?' he said, out of breath.

'Over to the left—there's been very heavy firing there—I've sent to tell him.'

'I've come on to tell him there's a pom-pom coming along the road—Jones and Richardson are bringing it—it will be here in half an hour.'

Half an hour! Good God! In half an hour all would be over.

'We must capture the Casino,' I said, trembling with despair. 'They've only about twenty men there

"I DODGED TO THE REAR OF THE FIRST WAGON"

at present. Tell him—tell that chap,' pointing to the 'Gnome', who was kicking and cuffing some of the little men, squirming on their bellies and fighting each other to get behind two dead men who lay in the road.

'Right you are, old chap,' and Seymour shouted to him.

I saw his face clear, he dashed off, and in a couple of minutes had got hold of some men—those who were lining the beach—harangued them, and then we all rushed along the shore to the Casino. We were hidden, a little, by that bungalow and the garden, but I saw several hit before we got into the open, and then a dozen fell. Seymour was in front of me with a *machete* in his hand, I was a good second, and the 'Gnome' and thirty or forty natives were close behind us. We poured over the verandah into the billiard-room, but not a sign of any one was there, and all the regulars were upstairs. Seymour yelled something, and some of our fellows began firing up through the ceiling, bringing the plaster down in clouds. I and some others dashed for the main staircase, but, at the top, the regulars were gathered, and were firing down.

It was the most appalling din—rifles firing, mirrors and glasses smashing, and wood-work splintering all round us. Our men wouldn't face the stairs.

'There's a back staircase,' I heard Seymour yell, and I went after him. We clattered up and burst on

those chaps from the rear. There was a scuffle,
Seymour shouted down for our people to stop firing,
and in five minutes there wasn't a living regular in
the house. Most of them had escaped by sliding
down from the verandah, and had run back into the
forest again, shooting at any one who went near a
window.

'On the roof!' I heard Seymour shouting, and
rushed back to find him leaning on the banisters—
the excited little brown men, thirsting for more blood,
crowding up the stairs, past him. He looked awfully
white.

'What's the matter?' I yelled.

'Shot through the stomach—make these chaps
line the roof.'

I saw the 'Gnome' dashing from room to room,
placing his men at the windows, and I rushed up to
the roof, pushing all the chaps in front of me, and
made them lie down along the four edges, shoulder
to shoulder with their rifles pointing over the
concrete ledge—across the beach at the rear of the
house, back towards the stream where Seymour's
dead horse was lying, across the road in front of the
Casino, and, on the fourth side, right along the road
and round that bend in it. The cavalry men were
still clustered there, and they were so numerous that I
couldn't see the end of them among the trees; some
were dismounted, so that Zorilla evidently was not
ready yet,

'Fire! Fire!' I yelled, pointing towards them, but the little chaps seemed numbed and frightened at the sight of them and wouldn't fire. I suppose they were overawed by the sight of the cavalry, or perhaps they knew there would be no escape from that house if Zorilla's people won, and feared to anger them. Perhaps, too, as no bullets were coming at them they didn't want to draw their fire. Whatever it was I couldn't get them to shoot, so I seized a man's rifle, kicked him out of the way—pulled back the bolt to see if it was loaded—leant it against the edge, aimed right in among the cavalry, and fired. I saw a horse fall down in a heap, and his rider extricate himself, looking this way and that to see where the bullet had come from. I fired again and again—there was a stir among them—the little chaps on either side of me bucked up and began to let off their rifles—the cavalry began fidgeting, crowding and jostling together—more horses fell—there was a sudden turning of the horses' heads, and they all began to retire. My little chaps squealed with delight, the little fellow whose rifle I'd bagged, seized it, imploring me with his black eyes to let him have a turn, and I crawled away, breathing freely again, for the cavalry had all retired behind the next bend in the road, and I knew that they were not yet ready to charge. But we had drawn a tremendous fire from the infantry in the woods, and we could not see any one to aim at.

Then I thought of Seymour, and jumped down the stairs to see what I could do for him. He was still leaning on the banisters—deadly pale. 'The cavalry have retired. We've time for a breather. Show me where you are hit.'

He pointed just below the middle of his stomach, and I knew what was the only thing I could do, for Dr. Clegg had been teaching us 'first aid' ever since we left Gibraltar. I tore a sheet off a bed, tore it in strips, and wound them round his stomach as tightly as I could. 'For God's sake, fetch me a drink,' he gasped, but Dr. Clegg had said: 'If any of you get shot through the stomach, throw your water-bottle and biscuits away and lie down. It's your only chance.'

'No, not a drop!' I said, and wanted him to lie down—he wouldn't. 'I'll go on the roof. I can help there.'

I carried him up, very gently, and laid him down in the middle—with the little men's naked feet and their yellow soles and toes all round him. I got a mattress, too, and made him lie on it.

' I can just see that bend in the road,' he said; ' I can manage all right; get those wagons across the road.'

I had forgotten them. I ran below, slipped on the stairs—they were wet with blood—steadied myself, and got down to the ground floor. The 'Gnome' was there, tying a table-napkin round the arm of a native. He smiled at me.

'Wagons!' I shouted, pointing through the door-way to where they stood. He knew what I meant, dropped the napkin, roared to his men, and they began pouring out from the lower rooms. We ran across the road under a very heavy fire, got hold of the wheels of one, and, shoving for all we were worth, pushed it into the middle of the road. The man next me fell, shrieking, and clutched my feet; I shook him off, and we rushed back for another wagon, and were just getting a 'move' on it when I heard yells of '*Yuesencia! Yuesencia!*' The little chaps on the roof who were lining that side of the Casino began shouting, '*Don Geraldio! Don Geraldio!*' and I saw Gerald galloping up to the ford and the few men who still lined that garden wall. I shouted out 'Hurrah!' we all shouted, and then came a roaring noise from the road, the clatter of horses' hoofs, and round the bend thundered the cavalry. They were coming along the beach too, their lances and pennons lowered—and my fellows on the roof began firing like 'billy loo.'

'One more push—shove altogether!' I yelled. The front wheels were on the road, but the rear ones stuck fast, and the 'Gnome' and his men dashed back to the Casino.

Before I could follow them, Zorilla's cavalry were on top of me. I dodged to the rear of the first wagon as they swept round it. Over it went, there was a jumble of horses and men, and I was dashed to the ground, my right leg jammed down by a horse. Troopers tried to cut at me or get me with their lances, but they were swept along by those coming behind them. The horse which was pinning me down half struggled to its feet, I drew my leg away, and huddled under the wagon as they thundered along the road to the ford.

I'd been knocked a bit 'silly,' and the next I know I was hobbling up the stairs to the roof with my right leg giving me 'gyp,' and the little brown chaps firing like mad.

'Look! Look!' Seymour cried, leaning on his elbows and pointing towards San Fernando.

Oh! My God! The cavalry had swept clean across the stream and were dashing madly along the road and beach, but behind them they left a trail of dead and wounded men and horses. I saw some riderless horses dashing backwards and forwards, and then had to lie down because the firing was so heavy. I hadn't seen Gerald, and there seemed to be no one alive at the ford.

'The infantry are advancing now,' Seymour told me, but it was that cloud of cavalry galloping towards San Fernando that I couldn't take my eyes off—there must have been five hundred of them, and we could hear the noise they made though they were a mile away.

'D'you hear that?' Seymour cried; 'Jones and Richardson have started firing.'

Hear! Why, I jumped to my feet and yelled with delight, for the 'pom—pom—pom—pom,' 'pom pom—pom,' 'pom—pom—pom' and the 'crack—crack—crack' of the little one-pound shells bursting, told me what had happened.

'Keep down, you fool!' Seymour shouted. Bullets were shrieking past, chipping against the concrete every second, and Zorilla's infantry were coming down the road and through the trees, in close order, sweeping past the Casino towards the ford.

My aunt! how we shot! I'd never heard any noise like the noise of the firing that went on then, and I wonder, now, how many of those rifles were properly aimed.

The Casino seemed to be trembling and shaking, my little chaps began scrambling in the bottom of their bags for cartridges, and I knew that they were running short of ammunition, but then they began shrieking with joy, because the infantry couldn't stand the fire from Gerald's chaps along the stream, and we saw them dodging back again from tree to tree, and clearing away from the road—a tall gaunt officer, on horseback, trying to stem the retreat and turn them round again.

Even at that distance I recognised him. It was General Zorilla, but he couldn't make them face the stream again, and they swept past him out of sight.

'The cavalry are broken!' Seymour cried

joyfully, and, turning my head, I saw them coming
back again, the pom-pom shells knocking up little
spurts of dust and smoke among them, and some of
Gerald's people at the side of the road firing point-
blank at them.   They were having an awful time,
horses and men coming down every second, and as a
horse fell, it brought down others behind it, in a
heap of struggling bodies and legs, the little white-
shirted men darting out from the trees with their
machetes to kill the wretched troopers before they
could get to their feet.

Those still on horseback came nearer and nearer,
the leading ones were almost up to the ford, and I
could see them lying down on their horses' necks,
their arms raised in front of their heads, as Gerald's
people crowded to the side of the road to fire at them ;
they burst through the stream and came flying past
the front of the Casino, many horses riderless, their
flanks streaming with blood from sharp spurs, and
their blood-shot eyes almost sticking out of their
heads.   We could hear the sobbing noise they made
in their distress—poor brutes, they were absolutely
foundered.

Those of my chaps, on the roof, who had any
cartridges left let off their rifles at them again, and
at others who were lashing their poor tired brutes
through the sand, along the beach, at the ˙back of
the house. I don't think that more than a couple
of hundred got back beyond that bend in safety.

Forest
Clearing

Forest track followed by General Zorilla

FOREST

FOREST

QUEEN ISABELLA'S ROAD to SANTA CRUZ

FOREST

Stream

Posada

FOREST

EL
CASTELLAR

FORT

FOREST

MARINA Road to El Castellar

Lighthouse

EL CASINO

Road to Marina

LAGUNA

RIVER

SAN
FERNANDO

FOREST

FOREST

FOREST

PLAN
OF
OPERATIONS
ROUND
SAN FERNANDO.

TO
SANTA
CRUZ

One, a powerful-looking native, half-nigger, was the last to come struggling along the beach. Hundreds of bullets were hitting the sand all round him and splashing in the water beyond, but he seemed to bear a charmed life. He'd thrown away his rifle and his lance, and as he came to that line of Gerald's people across the beach, he put his hand in front of his face, bent low over his horse's neck, and charged right through them. I felt jolly glad to see him safe and coming towards us, but then one of my own little chaps ran out from the Casino, down the beach, knelt down, raised his rifle, and waited for him.

The trooper saw him, struck his poor beast with the flat of his sword, and made one gallant effort to ride him down, but the horse was so exhausted that he could hardly raise a trot in that loose sand. The little kneeling man fired, and the horse plunged on to its head and rolled over, the trooper slipping to his feet and jumping clear. With a yell he grabbed his sword and rushed at the little man, and I thought my chap was finished, but he had another cartridge in his rifle, fired again, and the big trooper slithered forward, clawed at the sand, and was dead. I felt jolly sorry, but the men on the roof, watching with bloodthirsty eyes, jumped to their feet and yelled, and the little man, bending over the body, pulled off the big trooper's boots, stuck them on his own feet, and came awkwardly up to the Casino again, his face beaming with pride.

I felt rather sick, and looked round.   Seymour was on his knees.

'We've won,' he cried, with a wild look in his eyes. 'I've done my bit, too.' He raised himself to his feet, and would have fallen if I hadn't caught him and lowered him on his mattress.

I heard shouts of '*Don Geraldio!*' '*Viva los Horizontales!*' and looking over into the road, saw dear old Gerald stalking along smoking his pipe, making big strides over dead men and horses, and José, in his red sash, leading his horse behind him. I ran down to meet him as he came up the steps.

'We've won, Gerald!' I sang out.

'You've made a beastly mess of the Casino, Billums; I hope no one has collared the mater's bag,' was the only thing he said.

Well, that finished the 'Two Days' Fight' as it was called; Gerald's chaps were too worn out and too short of ammunition to follow Zorilla immediately, and gave him time to withdraw, with the remnant of his people, along the road to El Castellar.

Jones and Richardson came along presently with their two pom-poms and five or six hundred riflemen they had brought from San Fernando. They were awfully full of 'buck.'

'We frightened those cavalry chaps with our shells, and these little brownies stopped them with their rifles,' they told us, as we all carried Seymour down from the roof and put him in his buggy, which turned up from somewhere or other.

They took him back—very slowly and gently—to San Fernando, and intended to take him on board the *Hector*.

'Thank God, you came!' I said. 'You were just in time.'

He smiled wildly, wanted to say something, but didn't, and was taken away.

And now came the saddest of all things, for the wounded began to creep out of the forest and make their way to the Casino or be carried there—hundreds of them—and there wasn't a piece of lint or a bandage in the place. They simply squatted down and waited —for what I don't know. I got a good many of them water from the Casino well, and they were very grateful, but I couldn't do anything else.

I missed Gerald, went in search of him in the Casino, heard the noise of splashing water, and found him having a cold bath, José standing by to rub him down.

'Only thing which keeps me awake, Billums,' he laughed. 'I've given my chaps a couple of hours' sleep, and shall follow Zorilla as soon as those field-guns you took into San Fernando come along. I've sent for them.'

'They don't seem to be going to sleep yet,' I said, for there was any amount of noise outside and shouting of ' *Viva Don Geraldio! Viva los Inglesas!* '

'They want me, I expect,' he said; 'chuck us a

towel, Billums,' and, winding it round him, he went
out. He still had a nasty scar on the right arm—
where that bit of shell had hit him a month ago.

'Tidy your yellow mop a bit,' I sang out, 'it's all
over your eyes,' so he smoothed it back and went
out on the balcony overlooking the road.

My aunt! there must have been thousands of the
little brown men and their black-bearded officers there,
and they made a tremendous noise, shouting, '*Viva
Yuesencia Don Geraldio!*'

I was looking out from behind a door, and you bet
I was proud of old Gerald. Wouldn't the mater have
just loved to see him there, the only white-skinned
chap among them, and wouldn't the old pater have
grinned and chuckled to think he'd been the father
of him. I could just imagine him patting Gerald's
naked shoulder and tipping him a sovereign.

There were more yells.

'Come out, Billums, they want you!'

I went cold all over.

'Come out, you ass! Take your hat off too—let
'em see your straw thatching.'

I went and stood beside him, and it was the
proudest thing that ever happened to me; it was
nothing but a sea of brown heads and white hats,
rifles and bayonets, and then they yelled and waved
their hats—even those of the wounded who could
stand, stood up and shouted, '*Viva los Hermanos!*' [1]

---

[1] Hermanos = brothers.

When the noises stopped a bit, I sang out, '*Gracias! Gracias! Muchas Gracias!*'—about the only Spanish words I knew. They cheered more than ever.

'Quite effective show, that,' Gerald smiled cynically, as he went back to dress, 'you and I standing there by the side of the insurgent flag. They love anything like that.'

I hadn't really noticed the flag—I'd been much too nervous.

'That little fiend of yours tried his tricks on again last night, tried to knife me,' he said presently.

'And you killed him?'

'I took away his knife and boxed his ears,' he told me, lighting his pipe with one of my last matches. 'It's a treat to get a decent match, Billums, I hate those "stinkerados"[1] we get in this confounded country.'

'Confounded country!' I answered angrily. 'You seem to be risking a good deal for it. I wished to goodness you'd killed the beast.'

'My dear Billums, I'd fight on either side so long as I could get a bit of excitement—so long as I could boss the show.'

'I wish to goodness I could chip in with you,' I told him. 'I don't even boss the gun-room—not properly, the Commander thinks.' Oh, bother the

---

[1] 'Stinkerados' is a term applied to the ordinary foul-smelling Spanish sulphur matches.

Hector! I remembered that my leave was up at noon. 'Bother it all, Gerald, I've got to keep the "afternoon" watch, and see that a boat doesn't shove off with the fenders over its side, and listen respectfully whilst the Commander bellows at me that a man hasn't got his chin-stay down, and that I'm an incompetent, useless fool. It's nearly ten o'clock now and I must be off.'

He got me a horse, and I left him, his worn-out little brown chaps, and his wounded, and shoved off back to San Fernando, galloping along the beach, and learnt then what an unsuccessful cavalry charge meant; for the shore was strewn with dead and dying horses, dead men, rifles, swords, lances, and, more conspicuous than anything else, the red blankets they'd thrown away in their retreat. The tide, too, had risen and was half covering some of the bodies with sand, as if it wanted to hide the horrid sight and wipe out all traces of that awful morning's work.

I was looking about me for something to take back for the mater, and had passed any number of ordinary swords, which were not worth the trouble of dismounting, but at last saw one with a very elaborate hilt and sword-knot, lying close to a body stretched face downwards in the sand, so jumped off and picked it up. The uniform on the body was that of an officer, and out of curiosity I turned the head round with my foot. Ugh! It was Zorilla's black A.D.C., the chap who had been so impressed with our after

9.2 gun that day we anchored off Los Angelos. I scrambled back into the saddle with his sword and rode on, shuddering and thinking a lot of things which I couldn't write down, without you laughing at me.

Presently, as I got a bit more chirpy, and began looking round again, I saw a little chap trudging along ahead of me, splashing through the edge of the sea where the sand was firmer. Something about him seemed familiar, and as I overtook him he looked round, gave a yelp of fright, and bolted, drawing a *machete* out of his belt. It *was* the little brute, and I dug my heels into the horse and was after him like a shot. I simply rode him down—he couldn't run fast in the loose sand—and at last turned, holding up the *machete* to protect himself. I was jolly glad that he'd lost his revolver, for I had lost mine somewhere. I meant to kill him, and I saw that he knew it, and that he couldn't be springy on his feet in the sand, and struck at him for all I was worth with the A.D.C.'s sword, meaning to beat down his guard and get at his head, but the horse swerved when he saw the sword flash, and the blade only came down on the back of the hand which held the *machete* and lopped the fingers clean off, the *machete* falling down. I wrenched the horse round and went at him again, and was just going to finish him when, I'm sorry to say, something inside me wouldn't let me kill him now that he couldn't defend himself, and, like

the ass I am,—how I cursed myself for it afterwards
—I jumped off and tried to stop the bleeding.   He
thought me a fool, I know, and so I was.

Then I made him step out alongside me, and was
so angry with myself for being so soft-hearted that
I prodded him in the back when he wouldn't go
fast enough.

But the miserable brute, with his bleeding stumps,
was nearly dead with fright and could hardly put one
foot in front of another, so at last I swung him up
in front of me, and took him into San Fernando like
that, riding up to the *Cuartel de Infanteria*, where
a 'red-cross' flag was flying, and handing him over
to the people there, trying to explain that he was a
prisoner.

My Christopher ! the look he gave me when I
went away !

I left my horse at the barracks, walked down to
the shore, stood on that jetty, and waved my arms
about till one of the *Hector's* signalmen spotted me,
and the skiff was sent in to take me off.

I had just time to change into uniform, and get
a bit of grub in the gun-room, before the 'Forlorn
Hope,' who'd kept the 'Forenoon' watch and wanted
his lunch, sent down an indignant message to know
when I was going to relieve him, so up I went, buck-
ling on my sword-belt, and tramped up and down
the quarterdeck for four hours.   I'm certain that I
could never have stopped awake had not Cousin

Bob, the 'Angel,' and young Marchant walked alongside me and made me tell them all that had happened ashore.

When I went down below again, I showed the black A.D.C.'s sword to Navarro, and told him, as well as I could, all that had happened. He was very depressed, chiefly because he was so fond of old Zorilla, but didn't seem to worry in the least about the black A.D.C., and made me keep the sword.

He shrugged his shoulders when I told him about not killing that little ex-policeman, and said, 'Till he die he always make revenge,' which made me think myself more of an ass than ever for not having killed him when I had the chance.

CHAPTER XI

San Fernando attacked from the Sea

Written by Captain Grattan, R.N.

MUCH to my relief, young Wilson came off in time to keep his afternoon watch, none the worse for his extremely exciting forty-eight hours' leave, and directly he had told me that all fighting had ceased, I sent Watson, my Fleet Surgeon, and my young Surgeon, Clegg, ashore to help patch up the wounded, giving them as many chaps as they wanted to take to help them, and writing a polite note to the New President's Secretary informing him of the fact. I knew that every doctor would be wanted, because the fighting had been very severe and all that morning we had seen streams of wounded men dragging themselves back from Marina along the road by the sea. Already one Englishman, a man named Seymour, had been brought off to the ship, badly wounded, but he died as he was being hoisted on board, so his friends took the body ashore again.

I went ashore, myself, soon afterwards, and found everybody at the Club. A cheery lot of chaps they were, in spite of their pal's death, and when the little

235

Secretary, who had heard that I had come ashore and
followed me there, bowed himself in half and said,
'The President is much gratitude for the guns,' they
yelled with delight.

'The hydraulic machinery you brought from
Princes' Town,' they roared. 'We couldn't have
managed without it—just came in the nick of time,'
and then bundled my little friend into the next room.

They told me that the whole of General Zorilla's
artillery had been captured, and, before I went back to
the ship, drove me down to have a look at it—four
field-guns of French manufacture, four English field-
guns, and two 4.7's on field carriages.

'Those English guns don't seem to have done
much work,' I suggested, screwing my eyeglass
in very hard, 'do they?' and they explained that
they'd been busy polishing them up ever since they'd
been brought in—that was why they looked so new.

It struck me that, now the insurgents—or I suppose
I should say Gerald Wilson—possessed all these guns
and had knocked Zorilla so hopelessly, they had only
to capture El Castellar to make themselves safe from
the Santa Cruz Navy. Once they had captured it,
the guns there would prevent any cruisers passing
through the narrow entrance, and they could sit still
and wait till that big cruiser, *La Buena Presidente*,
came along and made them masters of the sea.

I told my friends, the Englishmen, about that
little 'accident' down at El Castellar with our 9.2,

and they were highly amused—everything seemed to amuse them that day. A most cheery lot they were, and when I wished them good-bye, before getting into my boat, and asked them what they actually had done with the hydraulic machinery I had brought them, they were more amused than ever, and I left them enjoying some little joke they had.

Old 'Spats' sent me a wireless signal from the *Hercules* next day to tell me that *La Buena Presidente*, flying the black and green flag, had put into Madeira to coal, but had been refused permission. If that was the case, she'd have a good deal of trouble to arrange for colliers to meet her at sea, and it might be many weeks before she arrived here.

Things went along remarkably peaceably for the next few days, my two doctors were up to their necks in work ashore, and hardly had time to come aboard and ask after my gout, and we heard that Gerald Wilson had driven Zorilla and his army into El Castellar and was investing it.

Then, one fine morning, along came the whole of the Santa Cruz fleet, cruisers, gunboats, and torpedo-boats, escorting half-a-dozen tramp-steamers filled with troops.

They anchored close to El Castellar—we could see their smoke plainly enough—and began firing—shelling Wilson's trenches, we presumed. Of course we all thought they'd do the natural thing—land their troops there, drive off the insurgents, join hands with all that was left of Zorilla's army—about two thousand infantry—and come marching along the seashore under cover of the ships' guns. This was evidently what Wilson's brother thought, for we could see his people streaming out from San Fernando, along the road to Marina, towards El Castellar.

Well, I suppose I'm a bit of a fool, but when I was a youngster I should have been mad to have missed anything like that, so I sent for the Commander, and told him he could give leave to the mids. and as many of the officers as he could spare. Most of them were already crowding on the fore bridge and up in the fore fire-control position, trying to see the Santa Cruz ships through their telescopes, but they clambered down in a twinkling, and cleared ashore in less than half an hour.

'Don't get into mischief or there'll be the dickens to pay,' I sang out to them, and, of course, immediately afterwards regretted letting them go.

They had been gone about two hours, and we'd seen them driving or walking out towards El Castellar, when the firing ceased, and it was reported to me that the fleet and transports were standing towards us.

I went along to my spare cabin, which I had given up to fat little Navarro (Zorilla's A.D.C.) whilst he was aboard, with his broken thigh, and told him what was happening. He was very excited, and

craned his neck out of his scuttle to see the advancing
ships.

In an hour they were abreast the *Hector*, and
steamed slowly past.   First their flagship, the
Presidente Canilla, then the still smaller cruiser,
San Josef, the old-fashioned torpedo gunboat,
Salvador, the rakish *Estremadura*, an armed steam
yacht, and the *Primero de Maie*, looking like a
Gosport ferry steamer.   They were steaming at
about seven knots, but even at that speed the *Primero
de Maie* and the *Salvador* could not keep station.
Although I had a marine guard on the quarterdeck,
my fat Subaltern of Blue Marines—the Forlorn Hope
—flourishing his sword, and the bugler sounding an
Admiral's salute, as the flagship crawled past, she
took not the slightest notice of us, and we were all
intensely amused to see the officers on her fore bridge
gazing everywhere except in our direction, absolutely
pretending to ignore the fact that we were there at all.

When you remember that barely seven weeks ago
my ship had towed the whole five of them out from
behind the breakwater of Los Angelos, it was all the
more funny.

They fired a few shells into the town as they went
past it, not more than three hundred yards from the
shore, and I wondered whether my humorous friends
at the Club were laughing quite so heartily.   Half a
mile astern of them came the two old-fashioned French
torpedo-boats and the first of the transports, crowded

with blackamoors, with yellow and green stripes in
their hats, hooting and hissing as they passed close to
us, though their officers, standing up amidships, took
off their hats and bowed to make up for their men's
rudeness. I took off mine and swept it to the deck
in the most approved Spanish fashion.

Three more little transports lumbered by chock-a-
block with troops, and the whole armada anchored
at the head of the bay, about two miles beyond the
town, and immediately began lowering their boats.
My Sub was terribly put out. 'I'm afraid they've
caught my brother napping this time, sir,' he said
to me. 'He must have rushed all his troops out
there early this morning, and look, sir, you can see
them hurrying back again. They'll be too late.'
I proceeded to give him a little lecture on the advan-
tages of possessing the 'Command of the Sea.' 'A
very neat illustration, my boy, right in front of your
eyes. Canilla moves his troops about by sea—dumps
them here and there, wherever he likes, whilst your
brother, uncertain where he's going to land 'em,
runs his chaps off their legs, backwards and forwards.'

'It's jolly hard luck, sir,' he answered, not relish-
ing my short course of instruction on strategy.

In half an hour we saw three or four boats crowded
with troops make for the shore, saw the black ragamuffins jumping into the shallow water, scrambling
up the beach and lining the top of it, whilst more
boats came along from the transports. They went

to and fro so rapidly that, before the insurgents could get back to San Fernando, they must have had nearly a thousand men ashore. At last some insurgents began to pour out of the town along the beach, but directly they came in view, the cruisers began to fire at them, their shells bursting right among them on the beach, and the road, and among the trees behind it. The insurgents scattered like smoke.

Presently we heard a good deal of rifle firing from the same spot, and Wilson sang out, very excitedly, 'They're still there, sir; I can see them crawling along the beach, and there are others in the woods. The regulars are firing rifles at them now, sir.'

However, regular troops were being landed in such numbers, and we could see that they had already begun to push their way towards the town so determinedly, that I thought there was every likelihood of San Fernando being captured within an hour or two, and wished to goodness I had not allowed all those officers of mine to go ashore.

I had just sent for the Commander, to see what could be done about recalling them, when suddenly two loud reports of guns fired from somewhere behind the town made me jump—they sounded so close, and were so unexpected—and two spouts of water leapt up among the anchored ships close under the bows of the *Presidente Canilla*. I guessed at once that they came from those two 4.7 guns I had seen ashore, and smiled to see my Sub's face brighten. We all looked through our telescopes again to see what would happen. 'Bang! Bang!' the reports knocked against our ears, the two guns had fired again, and two more water-spouts sprang up just beyond the flagship. The noise came from the back of the town, but I'm hanged if I could see the guns, though I searched the whole of that tree-covered ridge most carefully.

I turned my glass on the ships and saw that they were all in confusion, their crews running about like ants, and then a spurt of flame shot out from the fo'c'stle of the flagship, and a large shell screamed and shrieked over the town. The other cruisers began firing too, their shells dropping all over the place, but very seldom bursting. One struck a patch of swamp, and sent the mud flying up in fine style.

The two shore guns fired again, and this time I did see the thin brownish smoke for a second, but a moment later couldn't see the guns themselves.

'The flagship's got one aboard, sir!' several people shouted. She was covered with smoke for twenty or thirty seconds, but when it cleared away we could not see what damage had been done, and she still fired the big gun on her fo'c'stle and the little ones on one side of her battery. She was searching that ridge, trying to find those guns, but was making execrable shooting.

'They're going back to their boats, sir!' Wilson

shouted, and turning my glass on the shore, I saw
the ragamuffins hurrying down as fast as they'd
scampered up half an hour ago, clustering at the
edge of the water, and wading out towards the boats.
I watched one boat-load pulling like blazes back to
its transport, and, just as it got alongside, these two
guns fired again and, simultaneously, I saw two
black gaps appear in the transport's side. One
spout of water sprang up on the lee side, so I knew
that one shell must have gone clean through her,
but the other evidently burst aboard, for smoke
poured up from amidships.

These transports didn't do much waiting for boats
then, they simply slipped their cables and got under
way, steaming farther out from the shore—the boats
pulling frantically after them.

The cruisers, too, weighed their anchors and hauled
off in a hurry. In fact, they were in so much confusion, and in such a hurry, that the *Estremadura*,
whilst trying to avoid being rammed by the flagship,
ran 'slap' into the little *Primero de Maie*, and when
they separated, we saw that her stem was twisted, and
that the little gunboat had a big gap in her side.
She suddenly fell over to starboard, and was so
evidently sinking that I sent the Commander away
in the picket-boat to help save life. By the time he'd
reached her, only her one mast and the top of her
funnel could be seen, and the water was thick with
little black heads.

The otner ships left most of the 'save life business to the picket-boat, and steamed off, firing wildly all the time, though as we who were near could not see those two shore guns, *they* certainly couldn't, and hadn't a chance of hitting them.

The whole flotilla steamed very slowly along the opposite shore, waiting there a little while for their boats, but those two guns soon picked up the range again, and quickened their retreat, actually having the cheek to fire once or twice at them when the *Hector* was in the direct line of fire, the shells going right over my ship.

The cruisers and transports got out of range presently, and again waited for those of their boats which were still pulling desperately after them.

One wretched boat, crowded with soldiers, had taken a short cut past the town, and as it came towards us, we saw that it was under a heavy rifle-fire from the shore, bullet splashes jumping up all round it.

The men were pulling frantically, ran the boat under our side—the side away from the town—where they were safe—and stopped to take breath. I recognised the officer standing in the stern-sheets—the smart chap who had put old 'Spats' and myself into our seats in Santa Cruz Cathedral. He recognised me too, and, taking off his hat, sung out, ' *Permis— sion, Yuesencia*, to stay.'

'Tut! tut! boy! Stay as long as you like,' I

called down, and pointed to the gangway. 'Come on board and have a drink.'

He got his boat alongside, and was up the ladder in a twinkling. I took him down below. He was very excited, and kept shrugging his shoulders and spreading out his hands.

'*Nous sommes trahis—trahis!* Before that we depart from Los Angelos, ze guns of ze forts make *plusieurs coups*—bang!—bang!—bang! We all up jump—we ask *pourquoi* they do so? They tell us General Zorilla has won *une grande bataille—los insurrectos sont vaincus complètement—allez!—allez!— San Fernando est le vôtre. Nous sommes trahis— trahis! Nous arrivons à El Castellar*—what we find? *El General? Oui! Mais l'armée?* — where is it? *L'artillerie*—all gone—*peuf!* We are brave—we advance—*et quoi!*' he shrugged his shoulders till I thought he'd dislocate them. 'You see what arrive— and they leave me *en arrière*—behind. *Peuf! Nous sommes trahis!*'

I tried to soothe him, praised his great courage, and sent the picket-boat, which had already brought back the few people from the sunken gunboat who had not got aboard their own ships, to tow him and his boats down to the transports. I knew that the insurgents would not fire on her when she was protected by the steamboat's White Ensign, and as we had helped them several times, we might as well do the Government troops a good turn—once in a way.

Then I went ashore myself—the smoke of the gallant armada smudging the opposite side of the bay as it steamed back to El Castellar. I went ashore in uniform, too—Perkins, my First Lieutenant, coming with me, and the Comfort, my coxswain, following at a respectful distance behind.

I was doing my best to work myself into a temper, for I wanted to know what the dickens the Provisional Government and Mr. Gerald Wilson meant by firing over my ship, but I'd hardly got ashore, before Mr. Gerald Wilson came galloping past—on his way back along the coast—and I forgot about the shells over my ship, and sung out, 'Beaten 'em again! Good lad! Good lad!'

'I hope he didn't hear the "good lad" part,' I said to Perkins, as Wilson galloped on. 'Afraid I wasn't *very* angry with him.'

'I don't think you were,' he said, smiling.

I really don't think I was.

We met hundreds of the insurgents pouring back through the town, sweating like pigs, but wild with enthusiasm at the defeat of the Government troops, shouting '*Viva los Inglesas*' as they passed us on their long march back to El Castellar.

'I don't see how we helped 'em to-day,' I said to Perkins, who was hobbling along on his game leg beside me.

'Nor do I, sir, but they seem jolly pleased.'

I found de Costa and his blooming Provisional

Government—they were all bows and scrapes and hand-spreading.

'I want to know how you had the confounded impertinence to fire over my ship?' was what I said to the little Secretary.

I don't know what he repeated, and for a minute there was terrible consternation among them. They all—theoretically—grovelled in the dust before me. But then they began to smile.

'His Excellency the Presidente will take you to see ze two gons,' the Secretary told me, and I think there was a twinkle in his eye.

He did take us, I, de Costa, and his Secretary driving solemnly in one carriage, Perkins and the rest of the Provisional Government crowding into another. We rattled through the lanes, along which Gerald Wilson had driven me, and stopped on top of the ridge. Here we got out, and had to tramp along it.

'You will see a sur-prise,' the Secretary bowed— I'm certain that now there was a twinkle in his eye.

We tramped along for a hundred yards or so, turned round a bit of a cocoa plantation, and there, behind a slope, was the first gun, and sitting on the top of one wheel was Bob Temple, and on the other, young Sparks—the 'Angel' they called him—both as black as my hat, swilling kola bitters,[1] whilst my young clerk, Marchant, with his hand bound up

---

[1] Kola bitters is a sweetish pink aerated water.

in a blood-stained handkerchief, and half-a-dozen other mids. were lying on the slope, most of them doing the same. Twenty or more ragamuffins were standing by with baskets full of more bottles of kola, and trays of pastry, and the ground was littered with empty brass cylinder cases.

So it was they who'd fired over the *Hector*, was it! and I wished to goodness that I could look impressive and angry when I wanted to.

They'd sprung to attention when they saw me, and the only thing I could say was, 'Tut! tut! disgraceful!—go on board at once—your leave's stopped for *ever*—tut! tut!' and as they picked up their coats and obeyed me, I stalked away to the other gun, fifty yards farther along.

Well, the rest of my beauties were there, but I'd had time to fix my eyeglass, and had worked up a fierce glare—I can glare much more successfully behind an eyeglass.

Mr. Bostock, my Gunner, was with them, too, in plain clothes, looking very sheepish, and trying to put one foot on the ground between two brass cylinders which would roll together.

'You ought to have known better, Mr. Bostock,' I said.

'Beg you pardon, sir,' he muttered humbly, 'but it was like this. I 'appened to stroll up 'ere, arter the firing began—just to 'ave a look, sir—and I sees the young gen'l'men 'aving a bit of a spree.'

'And you helped them—you ought to be ashamed of yourself.'

'Well, sir, it was like this, sir, I didn't want the young gen'l'men to disgrace 'emselves in front of all this kittle cattle, so I just stays 'ere, sir, to see they do the drill proper, sir.'

'Well, go aboard and report yourself to the Commander. I'll see you to-morrow.'

'*Viva los Inglesas! Viva la Marina Inglesa!*'[1] yelled the ragamuffins, as I solemnly marched back to the carriage, and drove back, trying to avoid the eyes of de Costa and his Secretary, who were tittering and grinning delightedly.

'Hi, lad! Get in here,' I called to Marchant, as we overtook the boys from the first gun. 'What's the matter with your right hand?'

'Jammed it in the breech-block, sir. They let me do cartridge number,' he answered proudly.

'Bad?' I asked.

'One finger's nearly off, I'm afraid, sir.'

'Tut! tut!' I said. 'You won't be much use for writing, boy, not for some weeks.'

'I'm afraid not, sir—I'm very sorry, sir.'

Dear, dear! If all this got known, I knew I should get into a terrible row at the Admiralty—it was very tiresome.

When I got aboard I sent for my steward.

'How many can I ask to dinner to-night, please, Mobbs?'   [1] Hurrah for the English Navy.

'We might do eight, sir,' he allowed, after a time.

'Give my compliments to Mr. Bostock when he comes aboard, and ask him to give me the pleasure of his company at dinner to-night, the same to Mr. Marchant and the five senior midshipmen when they come aboard.'

'Very good, sir,' he said, much annoyed, 'but it won't be what we call a 'igh-class dinner, sir.'

'Tut! tut! That doesn't matter, Mobbs. We'll not grumble,' I told him, as he went away to consult the cook, scratching his head in despair.

We didn't grumble, and I made the Comfort stand behind young Marchant and cut up his meat for him —it was about the only job he was fit for—and we finished the evening in poor little Navarro's cabin trying to cheer him.

He was very down on his luck—poor little chap.

CHAPTER XII

How We fought the Four Point Sevens

Written by Midshipman Bob Temple

You *must* hear about that lark we had at San Fernando—the day the Santa Cruz fleet steamed up from El Castellar with the transports.

The Angel and I were perched on top of the for'ard fire-control position, watching the ships shelling Cousin Gerald's troops at the entrance, near the fort, but though we could hear the guns plainly enough, and sometimes see their flashes, the ships themselves only looked like black specks under a cloud of smoke.

Mr. Montague, the Gunnery Lieutenant, who was in the control position beneath us, kept on craning his neck round the edge of the sloping iron plate we were squatting on and singing out, 'Don't you two midshipmen fall off! You'd probably kill the Captain and make a nasty mess on the deck, so be careful.'

'Right, sir,' we sang out, and jammed our feet

against one of the foremast backstays, and made ourselves as snug as sparrows on a water-spout.

'I think we should land on the shelter deck and bounce off on top of the for'ard turret, don't you?' I said, as my chum and I looked down.

'Wouldn't old "Bellows" (the Commander) be in a rage if we splodged his best enamel paint!' he said, and we jolly well knew that he'd roar out for Billums, curse him, and tell him he didn't know how to boss the 'Pigstye' (our name for the gun-room) and keep discipline.

'Try one of their caps,' the 'Angel' whispered, 'and see where it falls,' so I crouched over the edge just under which several of the mids. in the control position were crowded together, watching the ships, and whanged off two of their caps, sending them whizzing down on deck.

One fell right at old Bellows's feet.

I hadn't time to scramble back before he spotted who'd done it, and roared for me to come down at once. He was going to make me take them up again when the Captain sang out that we could all go ashore, and you should have seen all those chaps swarming down the mast to get into plain clothes.

Young Marchant wanted awfully badly to stick to the 'Angel' and me when we did get on shore, and we told him he could if he didn't talk. It was jolly kind of us, and he was awfully grateful.

There weren't any of Cousin Gerald's troops left

in the town by this time, we only saw a few frightened-looking old men and women about, and not a horse or a cart was to be had—not even a mule—for love or money, so we had to start footing it, on our flat feet, out along the sea road, towards the fighting. On our way we passed the stable where General Zorilla's black horse—the one Billums had captured —was kept, and popped our heads in to see how he was going on. He hadn't been sent back to Zorilla, because that foot was still too lame to do any work.

But long before we got to Marina and the Casino, where Billums had fought that battle from the top of the roof, we saw the fleet coming along the coast towards us, and some of the insurgents coming back, too, as fast as they could.

We guessed at once what would happen, and that the regulars would be able to land long before enough insurgents gathered to prevent them doing so. We were jolly frightened.

'I wonder what's become of those two 4.7's we helped put together?' the 'Angel' said, and we both wondered, because they were the only guns Cousin Gerald had which might be of any use in driving off the fleet. We were hurrying back to the town with Marchant and a lot more mids., when an Englishman overtook us, so we called out and asked him. He pointed to the ridge behind San Fernando and galloped on.

It was awfully hot, and by the time we did get

into the streets and across the square we were sweating like pigs, the leading ship was hardly a mile behind us, and though we tried to hurry along those lanes leading to the ridge, they were so crowded with women and children carrying things and looking back over their shoulders at the cruisers, that we only pushed our way along very slowly. Then a mule-cart came rattling along, the driver yelling out and driving straight through the crowd as if he were on a fire-engine.

'Come on! Let's run!' we shouted, and doubled along behind the cart. At the top of the ridge it stopped, half-a-dozen chaps, who were waiting there, pounced on it, opened the back, and lugged out some 4.7 shells. Then we knew the guns couldn't be far off.

'Come on!' we shouted. 'Here's a go!' and each got hold of a shell and tramped along after the grinning natives. We found the guns just behind the top of the ridge, dumped down our shells, and doubled back for more, meeting young Marchant staggering along with one under each arm.

We burst out laughing, because he'd shipped such a funny, excited 'death or glory' look on his face. 'Go it, young Inkslinger!' we yelled, and rushed along to the cart. Two fresh wagons had come along with some more shells and cartridge-boxes, more men too, and it was as good as a gun-room 'scrap.' Officers were shouting and yelling, the soldiers were panting and running backwards and forwards, and the *Hector's* gun-room jolly well took a leading part, unlocking the cartridge-boxes, slinging out the brass cylinders of cordite—the beauties—and keeping things humming. Even some of the women chipped in, dropping their bundles and children, and carrying shells to the guns.

The ships were passing the town now—we could just see them by popping our heads over the top of the ridge—and they fired off a few rounds. We heard the shells bursting in the town, not anywhere near us, but the noise was enough for most of the native soldiers, who dropped whatever they were carrying and grovelled on the ground.

The rest of them were more plucky, and carried on unloading the wagons, but by the time they were empty, and all the ammunition had been carried across to the guns, the fleet had anchored two miles below us and past the town. Almost immediately the troops began coming ashore from the transports, and the insurgent officers worked themselves into a tremendous state of excitement, gesticulating and pointing down to the cruisers, and getting their two guns' crews round the guns. We thought that they would open fire in a minute, so climbed up the slope between them, and lay there to watch what would happen. What did happen was that a shell came along and burst in some trees close by, making a most beastly noise, and when we looked round, both

the guns' crews were squirming on their bellies.
'Why the dickens don't you open fire?' we yelled,
and Barton and Sarah Jane jumped down and began
kicking them. They pulled an officer out from under
one of the guns and shook him, singing out, 'Fire!
Fire! Bang! Bang!'

'*Mucho malo! mucho malo!*' was all he could
jolly well say, he was shaking all over, and when
another shell came lolloping along over our heads,
he bolted under the gun again like a rabbit.

'On the word "action," officers hide under their
guns,' the 'Angel' laughed.

The troops were simply pouring ashore all this
time, and though we couldn't actually see them land,
on account of the trees near the sea, we were in an
awful funk, because hardly any of Cousin Gerald's
men had got back to the town yet.

We tried to make those cowardly brutes fire, but
they wouldn't; they were afraid of the ships spotting
them, I suppose, or perhaps they were afraid of the
guns bursting or doing something like that.

'Come on, you chaps,' the 'Angel' sang out, 'let's
show 'em the way.   We'll do it ourselves.'

We tumbled down from the slope, threw off our
coats, Barton rushed away to the second gun, with
Blotchy Smith, Sarah Jane, Young Lawson, and
four more, singing out that he bet us a sardine supper
in the gun-room that his gun made first hit, and
the 'Angel' and I, the Inkslinger and the rest, rolled

© 197

MR. BOSTOCK TAKES COMMAND

up our sleeves, pushed the natives out of the way, and fell in behind the gun.

Oh ! it was a lark if you like.

The 'Angel' stood on the trail and squinted through the telescopic sight, I lugged open the breech, somebody jammed in a shell, the Inkslinger pushed in a brass cylinder after it, I whanged the breech-block back with a bang, hung on to the firing lanyard, and shouted out 'ready !' whilst the rest of them tried to train the gun, the 'Angel' singing out all the time, 'right,' 'right a little,' 'stop, you idiots,' 'left.'

'Do let me fire the first shot,' the Clerk squeaked.

'Get out of it, Inkslinger !' I yelled. 'Get another cylinder.' The 'Angel' sang out, 'stand by !' and then 'Fire !' I gave the lanyard a tug, and off she went, and off went Barton's gun as well. We cheered ; the grass and stuff flew up in front of the muzzle ; the gun jumped back and slid forward again, and we dashed up the slope to see where the shots had gone. We were just in time to see the water shoot up in two great splashes, just short of their biggest ship, and then we dashed at the gun again, slung the breech open, hauled out the smoking cylinder, one of the mids. shoved in another shell, and the Inkslinger, white with excitement, shoved in the cylinder. I shut the breech too quickly, and caught his hand.

'Pull it out,' we yelled, and he did, just giving a yelp, and wrapping his handkerchief round it. Then I locked the breech and we fired again.

'Missed 'em—both of you,' a gruff voice sounded behind us, and there was Mr. Bostock, the Gunner, standing with his hands in his pockets, and looking vexed.

We jolly well thought that we'd have shells coming all round us, but they didn't, though the ships started easing off quickly enough, and their shells banged about all over the town. The native gun-crews had cleared out altogether—they were so terrified.

'You ain't doin' no credit to the Royal Navy,' Mr. Bostock snorted, lighting his old pipe, when we'd fired twice more and not hit anything; 'maybe you never learned the drill.' This of course was meant nastily.

'Come and help,' we sang out, and he did, showing us where we were muddling things. It was the training gear which bothered us, and he showed us that we hadn't slacked it away enough.

'You can't do nothing afore you number off,' he snorted again, and then took his pipe out of his mouth, and roared, 'Gun's crew, fall out!' We jumped back. 'Gun's crew, at'shun!' Then he gave us our proper numbers. 'Gun's crew, number off! 'Ere, fall out, Mr. Marchant. Yer 'and's bleeding; what 'ave yer bin and done with yer 'and?'

'It don't hurt, I can manage all right,' the ass sang out.

'Who closed the breech?' he yelled,

' I did,' I said ; ' I closed it too quickly.'

' Silly ass, don't meddle ; you takes too much on yerself.   Just give Mr. Marchant the firing lanyard, and take on 'is job—and be nippy with 'em cylinders.'

So I had to do the hard work, and wasn't the Ink-slinger proud to do the actual firing !

' Gun's crew, fall in !' Mr. Bostock roared again.

We jumped to the gun and took up our proper stations, and fired twice whilst he watched the result.

' You ain't 'it nothin' yet,' he growled.   ' Cease firin'; you're a disgrace.   Fall out.'

He went for the ' Angel' like anything about his telescopic sight, put it right for him, and then stalked off to Barton's gun, but he'd done everything properly, so back he came.   ' 'Ere! get down off there—I'll take a shot,' and the ' Angel' didn't like it a little bit when he slung him off the trail.   We rather wished he hadn't come and spoilt our fun.

Well, that shot got the biggest cruiser amidships somewhere, and we were so jolly pleased that we didn't mind anything.   The ships had found out now that we were perched on top of the ridge, but I'm certain they never spotted us, because nothing came really close, and most of the shots went over-head, and we heard them bursting amongst the trees in the forest beyond the stream.

You bet your life we were full of buck when the cruisers began to get under way, and then Mr. Bostock told us to aim at the nearest transport, and, after a few misses, we both hit her together and that did the trick—it jolly well saved Cousin Gerald, and San Fernando too—because the troops began embarking again, though the ships went off so quickly that a lot of the boats had to pull after them.

We saw the *Hector's* picket-boat dashing to where the little gunboat sank, and then you know exactly what happened, the whole fleet cleared off, and we followed them as best we could, till they got out of range, or, rather, till we had no more ammunition left. But long before that the proper guns' crews and their officers came doubling back, and wanted to carry on with the job, though we wouldn't let them, and they stood behind us grinning and capering, shouting '*Viva los Inglesas!*' whenever we nearly hit a ship. Mr. Bostock didn't worry his head any more after the transports had begun to move off, coiled up close to Barton's gun and had a snooze.

'It's done me a power of good,' he said—'just like Ladysmith, only them Boers was always firin' back.'

You can guess how dirty we were by this time, and we were sweating like anything—our tongues feeling as if they didn't belong to us, and we would have given anything for a drink.

One of the natives was sucking at a bottle of kola, and it looked so jolly appetising that the 'Angel' bagged it, drank it, and then had a grand idea.

He tapped the bottle—opened his mouth—pointed to all of us (we all opened our mouths)—sang out '*mucho bueno*' — and then pointed down to the town.

The officer whom we had hauled from under the gun—he was brave enough now, and stood with his feet wide apart, twirling his moustaches and scowling fiercely—understood what my chum meant, and sent all his men down to the town, whilst we went on with their job, and in twenty minutes or so, just after we'd fired the last shot, they came back with dozens of bottles of kola and trays of buns and cakes of all sorts.

"'Aving a stand easy?' Mr. Bostock sang out, waking because the guns weren't firing, and he chipped in, and we all had a grand feed.

Wasn't that kola bitters good, that's all! and in the middle of it along came the Captain, the First Lieutenant, the New President and his boss men and fairly nabbed us. What made the Captain so angry was that we'd fired once or twice right across the *Hector*. It was the 'Angel's' fault—he was so excited.

We were jolly frightened, because he glared at us from the eyeglass eye, although he couldn't keep the other from twinkling, and he ordered us back to the ship at once and stopped our leave for ever.

The New President was smiling all over; I don't think he'd smiled very often lately—he didn't look as if he had—and then we tramped back down the lane, giving young 'Inkslinger' a bit of help, because his hand was awfully painful and he was as pale as a ghost. They caught us up in their carriages, and the Captain gave him a lift and took him aboard in his own galley, a very great honour.

'He introduced me to the President—he called me his Secretary,' he told us, full of buck, when we got on board.

The 'Angel' and I rushed off to find Billums and tell him what we'd done.

'That makes up for that silly ass newspaper "business" at Princes' Town,' he said, and was jolly pleased. It made a lot of difference to the gun-room when he was in a good temper, and he'd been beastly ever since that forty-eight hours' leave.

The 'Angel' and I didn't dine with the Captain that night, because we were so junior, and only the five senior mids. and the Inkslinger were asked. We were rather glad because we always felt terrified in his cabin.

Next day we heard that the transports had gone off in such a hurry that more than three hundred troops were left behind, and had, of course, surrendered to Cousin Gerald. The rest were landed down at El Castellar, brought General Zorilla's army up to nearly four thousand men, and in a couple of days he began marching along the coast towards us again, the fleet steaming along with him.

Cousin Gerald had to fall back, because he had very little ammunition left and his men couldn't stand the shells from the ships.

It was fearfully worrying, because every day we saw the cruisers and those two rotten torpedo-boats getting nearer and nearer to Marina and that Casino place which Billums had defended. With our telescopes we could still see the black and green flag on it very clearly if there was any breeze to blow it out.

Then one horrid evening we saw that the ships were shelling the Casino itself, and we were all frightfully worried and afraid that, even now, after all we'd done, General Zorilla would win.

The Captain wouldn't let anybody go on shore, so we got very little news ; but that day two of the Englishmen came off from the Club, and made us more miserable than ever. They told us that Cousin Gerald had hardly any ammunition left at all, and that the New President and the Provisional Government were packing up and standing by, to fly into the forest again. They thought that the town would be captured in a day or two, and wanted to be taken on board of us, if that happened. They'd helped the insurgents too much to stay there in safety when once the Government troops came along. Everything was just as bad as it could be, and we were awfully miserable.

I do believe that the fat little A.D.C. in the Captain's spare cabin was sorry for Cousin Gerald. We often went in to talk to him and cheer him up, and he always had Billums's cigarette case near him, and was awfully grateful for anything we did for him.

'When the revolution finish, you two come and stay with me—at Santa Cruz—I will show you the bull-fight,' he often said, and, you bet, we promised to go.

One morning the cruisers were only four miles away, and a great yellow and green flag hung over the Casino, so we knew that things were pretty black for Cousin Gerald, who, for all that, must have been hanging on like grim death, because all that day and throughout the night rifle firing went on, and in the dark we could see the shells bursting among the trees.

We hardly slept at all, fearing that Cousin Gerald would have to fall back on the town, and feeling horrid because we'd used up all his 4.7 ammunition, and he wouldn't be able to prevent the fleet shelling him out of it.

The 'Angel' and I went up to the bridge before daylight and found Billums there—he hadn't turned in at all.

'There's been a great deal of firing for the last hour,' he said, his face all drawn and tired-looking, 'but it died away all of a sudden. I don't know what to make of it—it didn't seem to get any nearer—I'm very much afraid Gerald has surrendered or taken his chaps inland.'

He groaned, and we waited and waited—not a

sound coming from shore—till it became light enough to see the land.

Our eyes ached with trying to look farther than we could. Still there was no firing. This was strange, because generally at daybreak there'd been any amount of firing, as, in the dark, the people often got very close to each other, or lost themselves, without knowing it, and then fired point-blank at each other when the light showed them up.

'What *has* happened?' Billums groaned again.

Then it was light enough for us to see where Cousin Gerald's men had been last night—but there weren't any ships near there—then presently, as we saw farther and farther along, the Casino showed up under the trees—still no ships near the shore.

'Look, sir! Look!' a Yeoman of Signals, who was using the big telescope, sung out, and pulled Billums across to it.

'Hurrah!' he shouted; 'there's a black and green flag flying over it.' In a minute we could see it with our own telescopes, and knew that Cousin Gerald must have recaptured it during the night. Every one started cheering and shouting, and woke up the Commander, who was furious, but then joined in because the Captain came up with his greatcoat over his pyjamas, and chuckled and cheered too.

Well, we all stood there watching, seeing farther and farther along the shore every minute—not a sign of the ships—till we could actually see the high land at the entrance, near El Castellar, with a great cloud of smoke beyond it, out to sea.

'They've chucked it,' the Captain chuckled, and we all burst out cheering. You should have seen us all there—fat Dr. Watson in his pyjamas, the Forlorn Hope and the Shadow in theirs—the Shadow shivering and his teeth chattering,—Mr. Perkins as red as a lobster, and even the Padré had come up in a nightgown, and had been in such a hurry that he'd forgotten his wig, and stood there as bald as a coot, all except a little tuft of hair that stood up by itself, and made him look like that advertisement of a hair-restorer. Nearly every one was up on the bridge. Then the church bells in San Fernando began ringing like mad, and we could hear the people, ashore, cheering.

Wasn't it grand? though nobody could imagine why the fleet had gone away.

'I expect the Provisional Government are unpacking their bags,' the Captain said to Dr. Watson, as they went below. 'They'll be asking for Recognition again. They ought to get it this time.'

We rushed off and told Billums what we had heard, because we knew that if the Government at home *did* recognise the Insurgent Government, Cousin Gerald wouldn't be punished for chipping in.

We did so hope they would.

CHAPTER XIII

Bad News for Gerald Wilson

Written by Sub-Lieutenant William Wilson

LATER on in the morning, after all those things had happened about which that young ass of a cousin of mine has just told you, and after the Santa Cruz Navy and the transports had disappeared, a boat came pulling off to the ship with a note from old Gerald.

'DEAR BILLUMS—The whole "caboodle" has shoved off home—haven't an idea why, but they were in such a hurry that they left behind them a grand lot of ammunition—the very thing we wanted. Old Zorilla has gone back without his black horse—never mind. There's a report that a white flag is flying over El Castellar. I'm just off to see. GERALD.'

I read it out to the gun-room. Wasn't it grand for old Gerald? He'd just about swept the board.

I thought I'd show the letter to the Skipper, and did so—he was jolly pleased.

'Tut, tut, boy! I'll tell "Old Spats,"' he chuckled, and sent for a signalman, but had hardly spoken before one came tearing in with a 'wireless' message from the *Hercules*—she was still at Princes' Town.

'*La Buena Presidente* put into San Josef two days ago, after carrying out target practice, and, under shelter of Punta Rejos, coaled from a collier. She is flying the insurgent flag.'

'Now we know, lad! That's the reason the Santa Cruz fleet cleared off, lad! They've heard about her. She'll be off the coast any day, and they're flying back under the guns of Los Angelos.'

He sent the signalman back with his message for Captain Roger Hill.

'Tut, tut, boy! I'll be able to ask your brother to dinner in a few days, I hope—that is, if he isn't too big a swell—makes me feel a worm—p'r'aps he won't come—hope he will.'

He pointed his telescope towards the shore. 'Look at those black and green flags flying over the town. The Provisional Government are unpacking their bags again, I expect, and if they demand Official Recognition they'll probably get it.'

'I hope they will, sir,' I said, and went below. You can guess how jolly cheerful I felt, and how I blessed *La Buena Presidente* and the people who'd coaled her.

I knew how awfully happy the news would make them at home, so I got permission to send a telegram to tell them that Gerald was safe. It went to the *Hercules* by 'wireless,' and I jolly well hoped that some one on board her would pay for it to be telegraphed to England. I did so wish that old 'Ginger' and I hadn't parted 'brass rags,' and that I could have asked him to send it.

That afternoon the Captain sent for me ; he'd shipped a sea-boot face, and I knew that something had gone wrong.

'I've just had that signal, lad,' he said, and handed it to me.

'From Captain, *Hercules*, to ditto, *Hector.*—The following signal has been received from the Admiralty : "The cruiser known as *La Buena Presidente*, flying the unrecognised flag of the insurgent Provisional Government, left San Josef on the 22nd. She is to be arrested as soon as possible, and handed over to the Government at Santa Cruz. Force is to be employed if necessary. Steps are to be taken to inform the Government Authorities that she will not be allowed to afford any assistance to the insurgents."

'Identical orders have been received by the Governor of Prince Rupert's Island from the Foreign Office.'

'That's a bit of a knock-out for your brother, I'm afraid,' he said sadly.

I don't know what I answered, I'd never been so miserable in my life ; this simply turned everything upside down again, and whatever Gerald did now, he could never hope to win—things were too hopelessly against him. The possession of *La Buena Presidente*

was the insurgents' only chance of success, and
without her they could do nothing. I knew that
Gerald was too proud to escape from the country,
and he'd probably end by being killed in some rotten
little action or shot against the wall, between those
saluting guns, in San Sebastian. The only bright
thing at all, on that miserable day, was a 'wireless'
from dear old Ginger. 'Have sent your telegram
home.' I wished he was here, I'd have banged him
on the chest, made up that silly row on the spot, and
we'd have talked over things.

The Provisional Government did come aboard,
later on, smiling all over, the New President's un-
healthy face looking happy for the first time, and his
little Secretary bobbing about as if he were on springs.
They came to formally demand Recognition from the
Foreign Powers, and of course the Captain passed on
the demand, by 'wireless,' to the *Hercules* for her to
transmit to London.

Neither the Captain nor any one else had the heart
to tell them the bad news, so they all went ashore
as cheerful as crickets, fully expecting a favourable
reply.

'I'll let you know as soon as the reply comes,' the
Captain sent his coxswain to tell me, and I waited all
the rest of that wretched day, wandering about like a
lost sheep. I couldn't even turn in at night, and
spent most of it on the bridge waiting for the reply
to be telephoned up from the wireless room.

The answer came at last, and it seemed to blotch out the last hope.

'The existence of the Provisional Government cannot be recognised.'

'Don't send it ashore till the morning,' the Skipper muttered; 'bad news will keep. The Government are evidently anxious to make up for their slackness in allowing the insurgents to get hold of that ship in English waters, and I'm afraid no Provisional Government can expect to last long now that we have to hand her over to the Santa Cruz people.'

Next morning we weighed and steamed slowly down the bay of La Laguna, past the Casino where the great fight had been, and anchored under El Castellar. The green and yellow flag was still flying over it, and they had made no attempt to cover up the hole my for'ard 9.2 gun had made in the walls. Every now and then we heard rifle shots, and saw parties of the little insurgents running about among the trees beneath the fort, so knew that Gerald was still investing it.

The Captain sent for me.

'I'm going ashore, boy! going to see the Commandant of that fort and you can come with me. Have to inform him about our Government's decision and about *La Buena Presidente*. I don't like the job, boy, that I don't.'

In half an hour we were alongside a small jetty, built below the fort, and had landed in white uniform, helmets, and swords. An officer and a couple of black soldiers came running down a zigzag path to meet us, the officer saluting and bowing and the two black chaps presenting arms.

' *El Commandante?* ' the Skipper said, shipping his 'tin eye,' and pointing up to the fort.

' He will have much honour,' the officer bowed.

' Thank goodness some one knows a bit of English,' I heard the Skipper mutter as we followed him. My aunt! but it was hot, and the Skipper was sweating like a bull as he walked up that blazing path. The stones under our feet seemed to burn through the soles of our boots, and the withered palm and cactus leaves, stuck in between the rocks, looked as if they'd never known what rain was or a breeze either—they were covered with a thick white dust.

The officer didn't sweat, he looked as dry and shrivelled as the leaves themselves, and as if he hadn't had a drink or a square meal for weeks; his uniform was dirty and torn. Across the flap of his revolver holster there was a long furrow, made, probably, by a bullet, and, to judge by its appearance, within a few hours, but he gave you the impression that he'd never known anything else except war and forest fighting, and that one bullet, more or less, didn't matter.

' Pretty swanky !' the Skipper grunted, taking off his helmet and wiping his forehead.

' I no savvy,' the officer said, and then 'tumbled'

to it and smiled for a second, his yellow leathery face looking as if it would crack.

As we reached the top we passed any number of ox bones and skulls, and the smell was pretty unpleasant.   It looked as if they'd been thrown over the walls.   Then we passed inside the fort, through a small iron door in the thickness of the wall, not that part of the wall which our 9.2 had damaged, but round a corner, and it struck me that we had been purposely taken this way, so as not to see the hole.

As we entered, we found ourselves in a great square red-tiled parade-ground.   There were open thatched sheds all round two sides of it, and a dozen or more soldiers were hurriedly pouring out from under them to form a guard of honour.   A couple of antiquated 'smooth bores' lay on the ground with their trunnions smashed, in the centre was a broken-down well, and the whole place was littered with rubbish, old clothes, bones, and empty ammunition boxes.   We'd hardly had a look round when who should come across, from some buildings on the far side, but old Gerald, a grey-haired, sunburnt, and bent-backed officer talking very fast to him.   For a second I wondered whether he was a prisoner, but then I saw my friend the 'Gnome' and several others of Gerald's officers.   The 'Gnome' recognised me at once, showed his white teeth, smiled, pointed up to a flagstaff where that green and yellow flag hung, and then to a roll of green and black bunting which he

was carrying under his arm, and I knew at once that
Gerald was there to accept the surrender of the place,
and that my bandy-legged chum was going presently
to hoist the insurgent flag.

Poor old Gerald ! He looked so splendidly English,
in his white riding-gear and polo-hat, and so proud,
that I hated to meet him and tell him the awful news.

He introduced the Skipper, and then me, to the
weather-beaten Commandant.

' I no speak the English,' he said, bowing.

' We're just arranging the terms of surrender,'
Gerald told the Skipper.   ' You've come in the nick
of time, because the Commandant won't trust himself
in de Costa's hands.   They are old enemies, and I
cannot persuade him.'

Oh ! Fancy having arrived at this very moment
to spoil all poor old Gerald's hopes.

I saw the Skipper ship his ' sea-boot' face again,
and felt certain that he was wondering whether it was
possible to let things go on as they were, and not tell
the news.

He ' tut-tutted,' screwed in his eyeglass, took off
his helmet, and ran his fingers through his long hair,
as he always did when worried, and then burst out
with, ' Wilson, I've bad news for you—very sorry, lad,
very sorry ; the fleet and the transports cleared out
because that cruiser of yours, *La Buena Presidente,*
may be here at any minute, and, very sorry, lad, but
I've got to capture her and give her up to the people

at Santa Cruz. Our Government won't recognise the insurgent Provisional Government, and I'm ordered to inform the Commandant. That's why I'm here now.'

I could hardly bear to look at Gerald.

He caught his breath for a moment, and his grand jaw tightened the least little bit as he said slowly, 'We shall have to make a fresh start, Captain Grattan.'

'What shall I do?' the Skipper asked him. 'You'd better explain to the Commandant.'

That struck me as being too much to ask of Gerald, but he only tightened his jaws a little more, and began jabbering away in Spanish to the Commandant, whose tired, hungry-looking eyes opened out with pleasure and cunning, so that I knew that my brother had told him everything, and knew perfectly well that there would be no surrender. It wouldn't help old Gerald much now, even if he did get possession of the fort, because that cruiser, whose coming we'd been longing for so much and now so dreaded, would, after we'd handed her over to the Santa Cruz Navy, batter down its walls with the utmost ease.

If I'd been Gerald I'm hanged if I would have told him the truth, and would have taken my chance with the fort. Oh! wasn't it cruel luck?

'The Commandant thanks you for the information,' Gerald said, turning to the Skipper, 'and under the new circumstances will not surrender El Castellar.'

We saw the Commandant speak to the officer
who had met us, and he must have passed the news
round, for, in a minute or two, a couple of hundred
ragged half-starved soldiers surged out from under
those thatched huts, swarmed round us, and began
shouting out, ' *Viva los Inglesas!* ' ' *Viva la Marina
Inglesa!* ' The brutes—they'd have cut our throats,
ten minutes ago, with the greatest pleasure. I saw

the ' Gnome's ' hand go to his revolver, for the
well looked as if they wanted to cut his thro
the other officers'—he was bristling with anger.

' Come along, boy, we've done enough harm
the Skipper said.

' Hadn't we better see my brother safely o
first, sir?' I suggested, for I didn't like the
mandant's eyes or those treacherous-looking so

' Brain wave, lad! Good brain wave!—we w

We did see him out, tramping along throug
main gateway, over a drawbridge, and took

down to where his own little brown men clustered, at the edge of the forest, waiting to see the black and green flag hoisted above the fort they hated so much.

It was the most miserable walk I have ever had, and I could have killed the men shouting ' *Viva los Inglesas!* ' as they lined the wall and crowded through the gateway behind us. I feel certain that, if we hadn't been there, and the *Hector* lying close inshore, they'd have shot Gerald and his officers in the back.

I told Gerald about my having cut the fingers off that little ex-policeman, and implored him not to let him go again, and before we got to the forest we stopped to wish him good-bye. As I was going, he said : ' I know Captain Pelayo, Billums, the Captain of *La Buena Presidente*—he and old Zorilla are about the only types of the old fighting Spaniard left in the country—and he won't surrender his ship without fighting. He's got good men aboard too.'

We left old Gerald there, but I turned to watch him and the 'Gnome' disappear into the gloomy forest among their little men, before I followed the Skipper—a big lump sticking in my throat.

' I'd have asked your brother to come on board, lad,' he said, ' hang the arresting part of it and that warrant, and have taken him out of the country in safety, but I know he wouldn't ; he isn't the kind of chap to leave his fellows in a hole.'

He was about right there.

The same officer who had met us took us back.

and this time we were obliged to pass that hole our
9.2 had made. The pathway was almost hidden by
the blocks of stone and scattered bricks which had
been hurled down by the explosion, and we had to
pick our way very gingerly across them, so that it
was impossible not to notice the huge gap above us.

The officer waved his hands and shrugged his
shoulders, 'We forget — you forget — all *mucho
bueno.*'

'Do you expect that ship to come here, sir?' I
asked him, as we pulled back to the ship.

'Don't know, lad, she *should* make for San
Fernando first, and I'm going to stay here to see
that she doesn't get there, but I've told "Old Spats"
to take the *Hercules* to Los Angelos, in case she
should attempt anything there.'

I told him what Gerald had said to me about
Captain Pelayo, and asked him what he would do if
she did not stop when told to do so.

'Shall we have to fight her, sir?'

'I suppose we shall,' he answered, with a wink.
He looked as though he almost hoped she wouldn't
stop.   So should I have done but for old Gerald.

'She'll be a pretty hard nut to tackle, sir; she's
got eight twelve-inch guns on a broadside.'

'Well, we've got four 9.2's and four 7.5's.   Don't
bother about that, she won't know how to use them.'

Still I couldn't help thinking that, unless we had
the *Hercules* to help us, it would be a pretty hard job.

Most of us on board thought so too, that is, if it did come to a scrap, but the general opinion was that her crew could not possibly be trained, would not be able to fight her guns properly, and, if she couldn't run away, would have to surrender.

Raynor, the Engineer Sub, who knew all about her, pointed out that she was supposed to have three knots more speed than the *Hector*, so might be able to escape.

'Running away won't do her any good,' I said, 'or Gerald's people either.'

However, the possibility of having to fight made every one of us in the gun-room, except myself, extremely cheerful and excited, and when late in the afternoon we began to 'clear ship for action' and 'prepare for battle,' you would have thought by the way we all jumped round and got the ship in fighting trim that we were expecting to pay off old scores on some deadly enemy. It almost made me smile to hear the mids. talking now. At the back of their minds there was a feeling that perhaps the fight might be a bit more even if the *Hercules* came along to help, and they made quite pleasant remarks about her and her hated gun-room.

I know that I myself hoped that if it did come to a 'scrap,' old Ginger Hood would be there to share the fun.

Cousin Bob must tell you what did actually happen.

CHAPTER XIV

La Buena Presidente fights

Written by Midshipman Bob Temple

AFTER we had had that ripping lark with those two 4.7's on shore, the insurgent President sent off a great basket of fruit—oranges, grape-fruit, melons, and bananas — every day whilst we remained off San Fernando, so we were jolly sorry to get up anchor and steam down to El Castellar.

Of course we were very sorry for Cousin Gerald's sake that we had to collar *La Buena Presidente*, but thought it would be splendid fun if she showed fight, and we all hoped that she'd come our way and not give those beastly *Hercules'* mids. a chance. Then we heard what Cousin Gerald had told Billums about her Captain being such a fine chap, and Raynor, the Engineer Sub, told us so much about her, her armour and her big guns, that though we didn't get exactly frightened, we rather felt that we'd like the *Hercules'* mids. to chip in with us after all.

A lot of our chaps thought that she'd simply haul down her flag directly we signalled to her to do so, but Mr. Bostock the Gunner shook his head.

He'd seen a revolution out in these parts, years and
years ago, and said we were wrong: ' She'll not
'aul her flag down whilst she's got men to fight the
guns and shovel coal in the bunkers.'

He told us the story of the fight between the
Shah and the *Huascar*, which was just about the same
kind of show. There had been a revolution and the
Huascar had joined the insurgents down the coast.
She ran short of coal, and not being able to buy any,
took it by force out of an English steamer, so the
Shah—she was our flagship out there then—was
sent after her and they had a stand-up fight. The
Shah was a wooden ship with thin armour-plates
along the side, and the *Huascar* was an iron one
with turrets and very thick armour, so the English
ship found herself up against too big a mouthful and
got the worst of it.

' I was Captain's coxswain aboard 'er,' Mr. Bostock
told us, but we sang out that he couldn't have been
more than twelve years old at the time. ' Believe
me or believe me not, young gen'l'men, I was
Captain's coxswain, and a nice kind gen'l'man he
was too. In the middle of the haction 'e sees a big
round shot from the turret-ship come bobbin' along
towards us—straight as a die. "Full speed astern,"
'e says to me—"Full speed astern, Bostock,"—just
like that—not turnin' a 'air—and full speed astern we
went, and that shot just 'it the water under our bows.
Another time, about 'arf a 'our arterwards, we was

gettin' pretty tired of shootin' against 'er thick sides and seein' our shot bouncing off 'er armour like peas, 'e sees another round shot comin' along. "That'll just about 'it the Admiral's cabin," 'e says, "and aggravate 'im," 'e says, "if we don't 'urry along a bit. Full speed ahead, Bostock."

'Well, 'e was a wonder, was the Captain, but the leadin' seaman, who passed the order down to the engine-room, wasn't very smart about it, and though we did go full speed a-'ead, we didn't do it quick enough, and that shot just took off the life-buoy a-'angin' under our stern. Took it off without even a-damagin' the gilt scroll we' ad there, but that 'ere leadin' seaman 'ad 'is pay stopped till 'e'd paid for it —an' serve 'im right.

'Of course that was in the days of muzzle-loaders, when the shot didn't go along as smartly as they do now ; but that Captain was a smart 'un—'e 'ad judgment, 'e 'ad.'

'They must have been pretty sick of life at your dodging their shots like that,' we said, laughing.

'Believe me or believe me not, but as true as I'm a-sittin' in my cabin 'ere at this moment, they started a-'easin' off two at a time, 'oping to catch us with one of them.'

'What did the Skipper do then?' we asked.

'What d'you think?' he snorted. 'There was those two great black shell comin' racin' along to-wards us, side by side, and 'e turns to me, as quiet

as a babe unborn, and 'e says : "'Ard a starb'ard "—
that's all, and our old tub turns round on 'er 'eel,
just faces them two shell and 'e shoved 'er nose in
between them an' they just splashèd the men in the
batteries a bit. We can't do nothin' like that nowa-
days, young gen'l'men—nothin' like that.'

'We shouldn't think we could,' we shouted, as he
seized his cap and ran up on deck, for the Commander
wanted him.

We cleared for action that afternoon and just before
dark got under way and stood out into the open sea,
past El Castellar.

This clearing for action made it certain that the
Captain was doubtful whether she'd surrender without
fighting, and of course made us all more excited than
ever.

'If she does fight, I hope the *Hercules* will come
and help ; she'll be a bit of a handful to tackle single-
handed,' Barton sang out, and Billums laughed
sarcastically and said, 'I thought you'd rather die
than let them help you,' which made us rather angry.

The 'Angel' and I went in to have a yarn with
the fat little A.D.C. and hear what he thought about
it. He was very excited, and said that Captain
Pelayo would die sooner than surrender—he seemed
to know him very well. That night the Captain had
him taken down below in the 'tiller flat,'[1] so that he

---

[1] A space right aft, below the water-line, where the steering engine and
emergency hand-steering mechanism are situated.

would be out of danger if anything *did* happen, and his being taken down there made us all feel a bit creepy.

Well, nothing happened all night; we simply 'mooned' about, backwards and forwards, near the entrance, and *La Buena Presidente* must have been hovering round, too, waiting till it was light enough to see her way into La Laguna, for, as it grew light enough, she was sighted not five miles away, steaming leisurely in towards the entrance. Although she was painted white she looked enormous.

The Captain was called, and ran up on the fore bridge in a twinkling, and sent 'Blotchy' Smith down with a wireless message to the *Hercules*. He showed it to me as he passed along the upper deck, '*La Buena Presidente* is eight miles off El Castellar steaming towards it. Shall prevent her entering. Come south and prevent her escaping to sea.'

' She'll be here in three hours and a half,' ' Blotchy ' shouted, as he ran aft, and I felt jolly glad, but rather wished it was minutes instead of hours.

Then ' General Quarters ' was sounded, and we all rushed to our stations. Mr. Bigge and I got through the back of our 9.2 turret—the for'ard starboard one just under the projecting end of the fore bridge—and when we'd reported everything 'cleared away' and had filled our 'ready' rack with more shells, we climbed out of the sighting-hood and squatted on top of the turret, whilst they trained it for'ard and aft as far as it would go and raised and lowered the long gun, to test the hydraulic machinery. It was a perfectly lovely morning, the sea like glass, and the *Hector's* bows seemed just to push the water aside, not even breaking the surface. It was so jolly clear that we could see thousands of jelly-fish—all the colours of the rainbow — floating past under our sponson. It really was grand, and we sat there and watched the big ship coming slowly towards us with the sun rising just behind her.

'That's bad for shooting, if it comes to a fight,' Mr. Bigge said; 'it will dazzle the "Gunlayer's" eyes.'

'I don't expect it will; do you, sir?' I asked nervously, because she was so huge, and I knew that she had so much more powerful guns than we had, that, now it came to the pinch, I was in a funk.

'Don't know,' he answered; 'we'll know in ten minutes.'

The signalmen began running about the bridge above us, we heard the Chief Yeoman's voice saying 'Hoist,' and up went three flags and the white international code pendant.

'What's that mean, sir?' I asked, as the halyards were jerked to shake out the flags.

'"Stop engines," I think,' Mr. Bigge said, squinting through his telescope to see if she took any notice.

Something did go fluttering to her masthead—she only had one mast, a tripod one, amidships—but it was the black and green flag, and a huge one at that.

'She's not going to stop,' Mr. Bigge muttered. 'The Sub was right after all. We'll have to fight her.'

I did feel so uncomfortable and horrid 'inside,' and looked to see that the sighting-hood was open so that I could crawl down into the turret again—quickly.

Every one was simply gazing at the big ship, wondering what she would do, and you couldn't hear a sound, except the hissing noise of some steam, escaping from a leaky joint near the syren fog-horn up on the foremost funnel. Just aft of our turret was the first 7.5 turret, and the 'Forlorn Hope'—just a little pale—was leaning against the side of it looking at the ship—I was jolly glad that I wasn't so fat, I felt much too big already—and the 'Shadow' slipped out of the next 7.5 turret to yarn with him and then ran back again and shut the door.

Dr. Clegg came cheerily along from under the fo'c'stle, and stopped near our turret to look at her too.

He sang out asking if we had our 'first aid' bag, and I put my head down the sighting-hood to find out.

'Yes, sir!' I shouted down—it did me good to shout.

'Just seeing that all our things are rigged,' he said, smiling at Mr. Bigge, looking along at the sunrise for a moment with a funny expression in his face before he dived down below.

'He may not see it again,' Mr. Bigge said, and I understood and felt shivery all over.

Inside my turret I could hear the Gunlayer, who had his eye to the telescopic sight, talking to the Sight Setter. ' Now don't you go a-playing none of your tricks, Bill. Tie a bit of spun yarn round your right thumb and you'll know it from your left, and won't be playing the ass with the deflection as you did at the battle practice—a-spoiling the whole ship's shooting.'

Raynor, the Engineer Sub, came along too, and went down into our turret to see if the hydraulic machinery was all right. He climbed out of the sighting-hood in a few minutes, borrowed Mr. Bigge's telescope to have a look at the white ship, told us that everything was working well, and climbed down on deck.

Then, up in the for'ard fire-control position—high up the mast—I heard the ' Angel's ' voice reading off the ranges on the long range finder, ' eight thousand nine fifty—eight thousand nine hundred—eight thousand eight fifty '—and I popped my head down inside to see if *our* range indicator was working properly. It was, and the figures were slipping round all right. I looked up again, but he had his eyes glued to the range finder and didn't see me.

Marchant, the Inkslinger, leaned out of the

'control' position, caught sight of me, and waved his bandaged hand—he was beaming all over.

Mr. Montague, too, looked down and sang out to the fore bridge for some of the signal halyards to be hauled aside as they were fouling the range finder, and I could just see the feet of Pearson, the Assistant Paymaster, who was sitting, straddle-legs, on the top of it, doing 'spotting officer'—to spot whether shots fell short or over. I was jolly glad that I wasn't up there, and that, if it did come to a fight, I had six inches of armour to get behind.

The ship was so close now that we could see her huge guns, but she didn't seem to have cleared for action.

'Fire a port twelve-pounder!' we heard the Captain say; 'they may not have seen the signal.'

Men began running about, the Commander bellowed at them, and the little gun fired almost immediately — to leeward — away from *La Buena Presidente*—and we watched to see if that would have any effect.

It had. A long string of flags went jerking up the tripod mast and the international code pendant was hoisted to her yard-arm. We heard the Chief Yeoman scurrying into the chart-house to find the signal-book, and in a minute the Captain called out to the Commander, 'They refuse to stop. Keep my signal flying and fire the foremost 9.2 across her bows.' Billums was in charge of that turret.

THE EFFECT OF THE SHELL

All this time the 'Angel' had been singing out the range. It had got down to 7250 yards, and we were turning a little in towards the entrance, to prevent the ship closing too rapidly. Then round slewed Billums's long gun over the starboard bow, pointing up in the air.

The Captain sang down to him to fire as soon as he liked, and almost before he'd said it, off went the gun with a roar—back it flew—my cap went flying overboard, and the brown cordite smoke came stinging into my eyes.

'Why the dickens don't you stick your cap on properly?' Mr. Bigge snarled. 'You aren't a blooming infant,' and we watched to see where the shell would fall.

It seemed an awfully long time, and then there was a shout of 'There it is!' all along the ship, and up spouted the water a couple of cables ahead of the white ship.

Mr. Montague shouted down to know what range Billums actually had on his sights, so as to see whether the range finder was working properly or not, and then there was another shout of 'She's turning!' and I was never so relieved in my life as to see her put her helm over and run away.

The Captain roared for the Engineer Commander, and sang out, 'Tell the *Hercules* she's steaming seaward.'

The morning seemed to be quite lovely again, and

we headed after her, smoke pouring out of all our funnels, and that leaky steam joint hissing more and more. Our bows began to break the water now, and the jelly-fish streamed past like a flash.

La Buena Presidente was covered with smoke too, and seemed to be in a jolly hurry to escape.

' She isn't going to fight after all,' I laughed, feeling awfully pleased.

' Don't know—they're getting down her rails and awnings,' Mr. Bigge said, looking through his glass.

So they were. We could see the men swarming on her quarterdeck and the awning coming off her.

I felt all shivery again, and heard the Gunlayer sing out from inside the turret, ' The longer they take about it the farther the sun'll be up, and it won't get in my bloomin' eyes so much.'

' It seems a shame to go killing people a morning like this, doesn't it?' Mr. Bigge muttered to himself, and I jolly well agreed with him.

We were buzzing along finely now, and could feel the ship shaking and throbbing.

The 'Angel' was still at the range finder, and our indicator showed 6250, when suddenly the big ship turned again—she was going at a tremendous speed —and—oh, it made my backbone feel cold—made straight for the entrance and El Castellar.

We still had our signal ' Stop Engines ' flying, but there wasn't the least doubt now that she was simply going to rush past us. Clatter, clatter, came the signalmen down from the fore bridge to take shelter, everybody disappeared into their turrets, popping down the sighting-hoods like rabbits, the Captain and the Navigator came down and clambered through the top of the conning-tower, the 'Forlorn Hope,' with a grimace at me, squeezed

himself into his turret and closed the armoured door, and, with my heart in my mouth, I wriggled down into mine.

'Aren't you coming, sir?' I asked Mr. Bigge, but he shook his head. I felt a little safer inside there, and stood watching the range indicator. It was simply altering every few seconds—5400—5300—5200 —there was no time to show the fifties.

Mr. Bigge sang out for me—he wanted to know something—and I popped my head out again and couldn't see the ship—she had slanted away a little, to pass along our port side—but I just caught sight of Billums sitting on the back part of the top of his turret, on the fo'c'stle, with his knees drawn up to his chin, resting his field-glasses on them.

You couldn't hear a sound anywhere—except that escaping steam—and then the gong inside the turret began sounding the 'stand by'—the next time it sounded it would mean we had to fire. The able seaman at the telephone sang out, 'The port battery's just got the order to fire, sir,' I almost fell down inside the turret again, and then the whole of our guns that could bear on the port beam fired, and some of them had time to fire again before we heard the roaring 'clap' and the crash of the shells bursting against the big ship's side. The range indicator showed 3200 yards, and we couldn't miss her very easily at so short a distance.

She was passing down our port side and going in the opposite direction, so that we had to circle round to follow her, and I knew that the starboard turrets would then come into action.

Mr. Bigge shouted down that we were turning to starboard, the bell at the telephone from the conning-tower rang, the able seaman jammed his ear against it, sang out, 'Starboard guns, stand by, sir!' and the gun's crew jumped to their proper stations.

'Remember your right hand, Bill!' the Gunlayer called out, and wedged his eye into the indiarubber sleeve of the telescopic sight.

'Train aft,' Mr. Bigge shouted down through the sighting-hood, and round we slewed.

The gun's crew was ready, the gun loaded, and the next shell lying in the loading tray, so I had nothing to do except to see that the Sight Setter kept the same range on his sights as the indicator showed, and that everything was done properly.

'We're coming "on,"' Mr. Bigge sang down. 'Stand by!'

The Gunlayer jerked out, 'I've got her, sir'—he'd spotted her through his telescope—and I just had the pluck to pop my head out for a second and caught sight of the big white ship tearing across our stern as we swung round, and then the fire-gong clanged loudly and I slipped back again.

There was a roar and a shake, men jumped about, banging and clattering—I heard the ammunition hoist rattle-rattle up to the gun, and the breech-block snap 'to,' and off she went again.

'We're hitting her!' Mr. Bigge sang out. 'Aim under her mast and bridge.'

'She's going to fire,' he shouted, a second later, and almost before he'd said it, there was a most awful roar, like a thunder-clap, and then the most appalling noise and hot glare—the whole ship shook and seemed to be tearing in pieces. The Gunlayer was cursing that he couldn't see out of his telescope, and wedged his arm along it to wipe the glass.

' That's better,' he growled, and fired again.

The range indicator, all this time, had been showing bigger ranges, and it had just showed—3650—when that same awful thunder-clap sounded a second time, and then the noise and the hot glare ; the ship seemed to be breaking in pieces again, things came crashing down on deck, and she trembled as if she'd run aground.   Something had struck her, somewhere close below us ; a huge flame shot up just in front of the gun port, I was banged against the side, the Gunlayer came tumbling down from his sighting platform, and we could hardly breathe.   I felt quite silly too.

The Gunlayer scrambled up again and fired, but we didn't know whether he was hitting her, because she was covered with smoke and almost hidden by the spray and the smoke of shells which burst short. I began to get my breath back.

' The range indicator ain't working, sir !' the Sight Setter called out.   ' It ain't altered for the last three minutes.'

I jumped across.   It still showed—3650—and I tapped it to see if it had jammed, but it didn't move. Just as I was going to tell Mr. Bigge, *La Buena Presidente* fired again, there were those awful noises, and something came crashing down on top of our turret, bulging in the roof.

'Can't move her, sir, the turret's jammed,' the Gunlayer yelled. He sprang up through the sighting-hood—something red and slippery was dripping down through the holes in the top of the turret—and I followed him. Mr. Bigge wasn't there, but the top was covered with the twisted rails and smoking burning planks of the projecting end of the bridge—I knew it was the bridge because the stump of the semaphore was still fixed to a rail.

I didn't really realise anything or know quite what I was doing. I burnt my hands trying to pull the wreckage away, but we couldn't move it, and I had to keep my eyes down so as not to see the big ship firing—I couldn't have stayed there if I had. I knew that Mr. Bigge must have been killed, and that I was now in charge.

Then that awful thunder-clap sounded again, there was a terrific crash behind us, a huge mass of iron crashed down on the deck, and one of the men said quite calmly, 'The foremost funnel's gone, sir,' but I dare not look—I was too terrified.

We couldn't move that wreckage off the fore bridge, so I ordered the men inside the turret, and then tried to ring up the conning-tower, but couldn't make the telephone work. I tried the telephone to the transmitting station, the room below the water-line, at the foot of the foremast, which passed all messages to us from the fire-control position, on the mast above it, and I heard the Fleet Paymaster's

voice at the other end. 'Please tell the Captain——
I'd just got as far as that when the ship shook and
trembled again, and we could feel something crashing
and bursting inside her.

I tried the telephone once more, but it wouldn't
work at all. I knew that I ought to tell the Captain
and ask what should be done, so I bit my lips and
crept out of the turret, down the rails at the back,
and jumped down on deck, but it was all covered
with burning bits of wood and twisted and torn,
almost red-hot, iron plates. Smoke and steam was
pouring up from where the foremost funnel had been,
and flames from the boiler furnaces were licking the
grey paint off, but the rest of our guns, on the starboard side, were still firing very fast.

I kept my eyes down and dashed through the
smoke to try and get under the fo'c'stle and nearly
fell through a hole in the deck. The gangway was
blocked up with wreckage. Several bodies lay
underneath it, and I saw one arm sticking out, a
signalman's badge on the sleeve. I ran back and
had to crawl under the fallen funnel, through a gap
where it had crumpled up, wondering when that
next thunder-clap would come and kill me. I crawled
under it, noticed that the 7.5 turret next to ours
seemed out of place and the deck very uneven, saw
the Shadow's face in the sighting-hood of the second
7.5 turret just as his gun fired, and darted between
the funnel casings to the port side. I had to go

quickly because the paint was burning on the iron plates on each side of me. That thunder-clap seemed to be awfully long in coming, and I thought that perhaps, after all, we'd beaten the huge ship and scrambled for'ard, over more smoking wreckage, towards the fo'c'stle, 'Blotchy' Smith looking out from the port for'ard 9.2 turret, very white in the face, and yelling to know how things were going.

I couldn't stop to speak to him because of the smoke pouring up from the foremost funnel hatchway, and I just put my sleeve in front of my eyes and my mouth and darted through it, under the fo'c'stle. Even then I couldn't get to the conning-tower, where the Captain was, because the whole of the shelter deck was crumpled up like paper, but the port door leading on to the fo'c'stle had been blown off, and just as I looked through it, the for'ard 9.2 fo'c'stle gun fired. I heard Billums shout, 'Hit!' and there he was still perched on top of the turret, his head bare, and his yellow hair showing.

'We're jammed! Mr. Bigge's killed! I want to tell the Captain,' I shouted, but he couldn't hear what I'd said, and only pointed over the starboard quarter. He put his hands to his mouth and shouted, 'The *Hercules*!'

Oh! wasn't I glad, and was just going to try and climb up to the conning-tower, when I saw O'Leary put his head out of the sighting-hood and speak to Billums. I heard Billums shout, 'Cease fire.' Then the Commander came scrambling along past me with some men, a bugler sounded 'Collision Quarters,' and I noticed, for the first time, that we had a tremendous list to starboard. The Commander bellowed at me to make myself useful, and sent me down below with a message to the First Lieutenant, so I hadn't time to ask any one what was the matter.

I could hardly find my way along the lower deck. Everything was wrecked, the mess tables and lockers were burning furiously, and I could hardly see for smoke, which poured out through great gaps in the port side. I managed to find one of the hatchways open—the cover must have been blown off—and got down into the 'bag flats,'[1] but it was worse here, pitch-dark, and water, up to my knees, was rolling from side to side. There was a sickening smell there too. As I groped my way along to try and find the for'ard hatchway leading down to the ammunition passages, where the First Lieutenant was, I saw a light and heard the Fleet Paymaster's voice. He was looking out of the fore transmitting room, and some candles were burning inside it. 'We haven't been able to make any one hear for the last quarter of an hour,' he said. 'What's gone wrong?'

'I don't know, sir. The ship has escaped, I think; Mr. Bigge's killed.' Mr. Perkins came along, splashing through the water, so I gave him the message

---

[1] Narrow spaces, below the water-line and behind the upper coal-bunkers, where the men's bags are stowed.

and climbed up on deck again.   I met Billums under the shelter deck—or rather what had been the shelter deck—and he told me that some armour-plates had been smashed in below the water-line—that was why we were heeling over so badly.

'Two shell struck almost together, drove a plate clean through the side, and killed every one in the after bag flats—Dr. Clegg, the Padré, and the whole of the 'stretcher party' aft there.'   He was very sad.

'Is the "Angel" all right?' I asked, feeling perfectly miserable.   He put his hand on my shoulder and led me back out on the fo'c'stle again.   I knew at once that my chum was killed.

'Be brave, Bob; look up!' he said.

I looked; oh! it was awful, the topmast and the control-position had disappeared, and there wasn't anything left there, except a few bits of wire hanging down, and a copper voice-pipe sticking out by itself.

'One shell in that second broadside burst against it, Bob,' and Billums put his hand on my shoulder, very gently, to steady me; 'it must have been all over in a second.   They felt no pain.'

I simply buried my face in his monkey-jacket and sobbed and sobbed.

'Pull yourself together, Bob,' he whispered, 'remember that you are an officer.   They felt no pain.'

I heard the Commander bellow at Billums; he

roared my name too and cursed me, sending me
down to the Engineer Commander for as many
stokers as he could spare.

I was too absolutely frozen to care about anything,
and when I met 'Blotchy' Smith, half blubbing, and
he told me that Barton had been killed in the after
turret and the Forlorn Hope in his, I hardly heard
what he said—I felt quite silly and 'wobbly' in my
head.

I really could not tell you what happened for the
next five hours—I was so dazed and numbed—but I
found myself going down into a boat with a lot more
of our mids., and we crawled up a ladder on board the
Hercules. We huddled up in a corner of her gun-
room, and they brought us something to eat, but
it nearly made me sick to look at it. The *Hercules*
mids. let us alone and didn't ask any questions, and
for hours we sat there, covered with dirt and smoke,
till some one led us away and made us clean ourselves.
Some one lent me a pair of pyjamas, and I crawled
into a hammock, but daren't shut my eyes, and had
to get out and sit close to a light. I don't know how
long I sat there, but one of the *Hercules*' doctors
found me, and lifted me back into my hammock. He
injected something into my arm, and was going away,
but I clutched his sleeve—I couldn't be left alone—
and then cried till I thought I should die.

CHAPTER XV

The Santa Cruz Fleet again

Written by Sub-Lieutenant William Wilson, R.N.

FOR days after that awful morning we seemed half stunned. We had left El Castellar the night before, as smart a ship and as cheery a lot of officers and men as there were in the Navy, and fifteen minutes after *La Buena Presidente* fired her first broadside the *Hector* was a complete wreck above the water-line, and was so badly holed beneath it that she only managed with difficulty to keep herself afloat and crawl back into shallow water. Fortunately one anchor and cable had not been destroyed, and we anchored under El Castellar, the *Hercules* anchoring as close as possible in case it should become necessary for us to abandon the ship.

She sent working parties aboard at once, and we eventually managed to make the *Hector* fairly water-tight, pump her dry, and get her on an even keel again. But that was not until the third day, and those three days and nights have always been like a horrible nightmare.

We could not get away from things—the stump

of the foretopmast and that single copper voice-pipe, sticking out where the fore control had been, to remind us that Montague, Pearson the A.P., Marchant the cheery little Clerk, and the 'Angel' had simply disappeared—blown to pieces ; the stump of the after 9.2, inside the turret of which Barton had been killed, and the wreckage of the bridge, on top of the starboard foremost turret, which had crushed poor Bigge.

It was two days before it was possible to cut a way into the wreck of the Forlorn Hope's turret and get out what remained of him and his crew, and really I don't know what we should have done had we not had to work, hour after hour, day after day, trying to make the *Hector* seaworthy, and ready to tackle *La Buena Presidente* again.

Practically everything above the level of the armour had been either completely destroyed, or so crumpled and twisted, as to be almost unrecognisable. We had not one single boat left, and the *Hercules* had to lend us two of theirs. The foremost funnel had fallen during the action, and the next one was so damaged that it fell overboard that same night. The fo'c'stle mess-decks, the sick-bay, the whole of the lower deck, the ward-room, and nearly all the upper cabins were now simply great blackened spaces, filled with tangled and crumpled iron bulkheads, deck plates and beams, from which every vestige of paint had been burnt off.

Our galleys had been completely destroyed, and it was impossible to do any cooking, so the *Hercules* cooked food for us and sent it on board till we could rig up temporary fittings.

Of Dr. Clegg and the poor little Padré, or of their stretcher party, not a trace remained. We did find a foot in the wreckage of the after magazine cooling-room, but we could not tell to whom it belonged, and it was buried at sea by the *Hercules* with the remains of Barton, the Forlorn Hope, and what we thought were thirty-two bodies.

Twenty-four men were missing besides these, and we sent forty-one wounded on board the *Hercules* to be treated there.

To think that—— No! It's no use thinking.

Strangely enough the Captain's quarters had not been damaged, nor had the gun-room and the gun-room flat; and when I first went below from that scene of desolation above to where the midshipmen's chests stood in four rows, their hammocks slung above them, and their blankets hanging down untidily, just as they had been left when 'General Quarters' had sounded, and the gun-room clock was still ticking cheerfully, I almost imagined that I *had* woke from some horrible dream.

I am thankful to say that the mids. were all sent on board the *Hercules* to get them away from the ship, and also to let the ward-room officers come down into the gun-room. Their chests were sent after them the following day, and it was the saddest thing in the world to see the four belonging to Barton, the 'Angel,' the Assistant Paymaster, and Marchant standing alone by themselves. We could not stand the sight of them, and Mr. Perkins had them taken away somewhere.

The only bright spot in those dreary days was that Ginger and I told each other that we were silly fools, and made up our stupid quarrel. His mids., too, had behaved so jolly well to mine that there was every chance of them also making friends.

The fact that *La Buena Presidente* had escaped did not even give me any pleasure, for Gerald's sake, because the Skipper was determined to sink her as soon as he could steam to San Fernando, off which she had anchored, and whatever she did, and however she damaged us above the water-line, she could not, in the narrow Laguna, escape our torpedoes.

I had a long yarn with my chum Navarro, the fat little A.D.C. Strangely enough he seemed quite pleased that the insurgent ship had escaped.

'It was a great fight,' he said, his eyes glistening, 'for Santa Cruz—the Santa Cruz Navy have much honour to beat the great English ship.'

'But if we'd captured or sunk her the Santa Cruz fleet would have been safe,' I said, wondering why he was not sorry that she had got away.

He shrugged his shoulders: 'Captain Pelayo is the best officer in the Navy of Santa Cruz—all men on board her belong to Santa Cruz Navy—it has much honour to Santa Cruz.'

Nobody was allowed ashore, and no boats came off to the ship, so I never heard from Gerald ; but the green and black flag now flew over El Castellar, and we knew that the Commandant had at last surrendered. I thought of the ' Gnome' marching across that dirty red parade-ground with the black and green bundle under his arm, and hoped that Gerald had allowed him to hoist it himself.

In a week there was no danger of our sinking, and the *Hercules* went across to Princes' Town to land the wounded at the Colonial Hospital, and to telegraph home news of the engagement and request orders. I got Ginger to send a telegram to the pater to tell him that Bob and I were all right, although, as a matter of fact, I was very worried about my cousin. He had not ' bucked up' in the least. Ginger told me that he hardly spoke a word to any one, and moped all day, so I very much hoped that the change to Princes' Town, and getting away from the sight of the *Hector* and of that broken mast, would do him good.

Whilst the *Hercules* was away the Skipper got out a kedge-anchor astern, to keep us ' broadside on ' to the narrow entrance, in case *La Buena Presidente* tried to put to sea, and each night we swept ' La Laguna ' with our searchlights, and stood ready to fire our torpedoes.   However, nothing happened, and when the *Hercules* returned with orders that *La Buena Presidente* was to be sunk at all costs, if she would not surrender, we almost immediately weighed anchor and steamed towards San Fernando.

Captain Roger Hill wanted to lead the way in the *Hercules*—as we were crippled—but the Skipper would not hear of this at any price, so with our mutilated foremast, wrecked bridge and upper works, and our two remaining funnels we started up the bay.

All our big guns, except the after 9.2 and two of the 7.5's, were fit for action, Mr. Perkins took charge in the after fire-control position, and I do not think we cared what happened to us so long as we sunk the insurgent ship, and avenged our defeat.

The Skipper did not mean to stand off and plug at *La Buena Presidente*, but to steer straight at her and torpedo her. In fact, if he found her still at anchor, he intended to send everybody, even the guns' crews, down below the water-line, only himself and enough people to transmit orders and fire the submerged torpedo-tubes remaining above in the conning-tower.

We went to 'General Quarters' before we were abreast Marina and the Casino, and I sat on the top of my turret with the long 9.2 cocked up in the air in front of me.

I soon spotted *La Buena Presidente's* tripod mast, and as we gradually drew nearer expected her to open fire any minute, but she didn't, and we crept along for another ten minutes or so. She seemed to be very low in the water, and I was wondering whether that would be due to the mirage, when a signalman, perched on the wreck of the fore bridge, shouted that she was sunk, and, sure enough, as we drew still nearer, we saw that her upper deck was all awash, and only her tripod mast, funnels, and upper works showed above water—the black and green flag hanging from her gaff.

We were too astonished to feel relieved, and anchored within a couple of cables of her.

Almost immediately the Provisional Government came off to make the most abject apologies for what had happened—they wouldn't have come, I suppose, if their ship had not sunk—and with them came Captain Don Martin de Pelayo—just such another as General Zorilla, as Gerald had told me. He wore eyeglasses, talked English, was awfully polite, and genuinely sorry for the damage he had done.

'I had my orders—you had yours,' I heard him tell the Skipper, after they had shaken hands very heartily. 'I am very sorry. We are not enemies of the English. I try to run past you without firing, but—*voila!*' (and he shrugged his shoulders) 'you shoot so fast and you damage my ship so much, I fear that I shall never arrive at San Fernando. Fifty times you fire—I do nothing—but then I had to fire—it was necessaire, and my guns—*voila!* they are very big.'

'Why did you sink her?' the Skipper asked.

He shrugged his shoulders. ' Treachery—the night after that we come in—we land our wounded—they are many—and many killed—some traitor open our valves, and in the middle of the night we sink in the mud.'

' We should have sunk you with our torpedoes, so it doesn't make any difference,' the Skipper said.

Well, that was the end of *La Buena Presidente* and the end to all the hopes of the insurgents. The Santa Cruz fleet could come and go where and when it pleased, land another army, and drive Gerald and the Provisional Government into the forest again, beyond the reach of their guns, and there was not the slightest chance either, whilst the fleet controlled the coast, of joining forces with the insurgents in the north and of attacking Santa Cruz itself.

That same evening our young red marine sub-altern, the ' Shadow,' went mad.

He'd been very peculiar ever since that awful morning when his chum, the Forlorn Hope, had been killed, and the strain of the next few days, followed by the prospect of fighting the insurgent ship again, was too much for his brain. He went raving mad, and had to be shut up in his cabin and his marine servant shut in with him, to see that he did not hurt himself. For three days and nights, although the Fleet Surgeon tried everything to make him sleep, he did not stop shouting and knocking on the cabin bulkhead, and as his cabin was in the gun-room flat we couldn't get away from his shouting, and it got on our nerves most terribly, so much so that we were all beginning to feel jumpy ourselves. On the fourth morning he was quiet, and the Fleet Surgeon hoped he would recover, but he died early in the afternoon without having ever regained intelligence.

This had a most awfully depressing effect on us all, and, in addition, Cousin Bob was giving Ginger and me a lot of worry. Several times I had been across to the *Hercules* to see him, and I didn't like the look of him at all. He could talk of nothing else but that awful fifteen minutes, and of his poor little chum the 'Angel,' so that I feared that his brain, too, might be affected.

'He's young,' the Fleet Surgeon said, 'he'll get over it;' and I only prayed that he was right.

Gerald, I heard, was all this time busy mounting some of *La Buena Presidente*'s small guns on the walls of El Castellar and on that ridge behind San Fernando, hoping to drive off the Santa Cruz fleet if it came again and brought old Zorilla with another army. Still, even if he did drive the fleet away, he had no possible chance of bringing the revolution to a successful termination till he had destroyed it, and there was not the slightest chance of his doing that.

There had been a good deal of trouble ashore since we left San Fernando, because, as soon as the insurgent troops learnt that *La Buena Presidente* was to be captured by us and handed over to President

Canilla at Santa Cruz, and heard of the part we had
played in delaying the surrender of El Castellar, they
were so bitter against the English that they burnt the
Club, and would have killed the Englishmen if the
Provisional Government had not, with much difficulty,
prevented them doing so.   Now, however, that the
big ship had been sunk by treachery and El Castellar
had surrendered, they, in some way or another,
thought that we would again help them, and were
just as keen on us as ever.   The Provisional Government simply loaded us with fruit and fresh food whilst
we remained at San Fernando busy trying to make
the poor old wrecked and gutted *Hector* seaworthy.
No leave was given because of the trouble ashore, so
that I could not go and see Gerald, and of course,
with that warrant for his arrest still lying in the
Skipper's knee-hole table, he could not come and
see me.

We heard that General Zorilla and the fleet were
preparing for another attack on San Fernando—now
that *La Buena Presidente* no longer could prevent
them—and every day we expected to hear the guns
firing from El Castellar and to see the ships steaming
past it.

And one afternoon they did come ; they were half-
way between us and the entrance before they were
sighted, and we rushed on deck to see them, very
glad of any excitement to make us forget our own
troubles, but we couldn't understand why we hadn't

heard any firing, and how it was that Gerald had allowed the ships to slip by him without making an effort to stop them. Poor old Gerald, he'd had a good many 'ups' and 'downs,' but now it seemed to be all 'downs.'

I ran below to tell Navarro, and he was as puzzled as I was, shrugging his shoulders as he always did when he couldn't understand, or didn't care to tell what he thought.

I ran up on deck again, and on shore we could see the people running about in a scared kind of way, and the small guns on that ridge being manned. I only wished that our mids. could have fought them again.

The flagship was already abreast of El Casino, the three remaining ships, the two torpedo-boats and one wretched transport, following her.

Why only one transport, we wondered!

As we watched and waited for the small guns to fire, the torpedo-boats suddenly increased speed and came steaming quickly towards us.

'What can be their game?' we were all thinking, when there were shouts from all over the ship, 'Look at their flags! Look at their flags! The stripes are horizontal! It's the black and green flag! It's flying on the flagship as well! Look!'

There wasn't a doubt about it. Each torpedo-boat had a huge black and green flag at her masthead, and in ten minutes we could see the colour and the horizontal stripes with the naked eye, as they dashed along close to the shore. We heard hurrahing, and saw hundreds of the little brown forest-men crowding down on the beach as they passed, jumping about on the sand, wading into the sea up to their waists towards them, and waving their rifles. The shouting and the hurrahs spread along the road till the town itself was full of voices, all the bells in the place began ringing, and hundreds of black and green flags were hoisted.

'I'm blowed if they haven't become insurgents themselves,' the Skipper muttered, dropping his eyeglass in his surprise ; and there couldn't be the least doubt of it, for now we could see the crews of the torpedo-boats waving their caps to the troops on the beach, and could hear the crews of the ships cheering.

Well, that pretty nearly knocked us all ' flat aback,' and we realised at once that now Gerald, with the Santa Cruz fleet to help him, would be master at sea and could do anything he liked, join forces with the insurgents in the northern province, and attack Santa Cruz itself whenever he was ready. It was so grand and so jolly unexpected that I hardly know what I felt, only awfully thankful that the revolution would be over soon, and that Gerald wouldn't be worrying them all at home.

The two torpedo-boats slowed down as they came towards us. '*Viva los Inglesas! Viva la Marina*

Inglesa!' their crews shouted, and then they were past and abreast the poor old *La Buena Presidente*, with the water running through her upper works and the top of her foremost turret just showing above the surface like the back of a whale.

They stopped, their crews stood to attention along their rails and saluted the flag that drooped over her, and suddenly burst into cheers, shouting, '*Viva El Capitaine Pelayo! Viva Pelayo! Viva la Marina Santa Cruz! Viva Presidente de Costa! Viva los Horizontales! Viva Don Geraldio!*'

The last shout made me warm up all over. Good old Gerald! they hadn't forgotten him, didn't bear him any ill-will, and were proud of him too.

'I'll be able to ask him to dinner after all,' the Skipper said, twinkling and rubbing his hands. 'The Government is almost certain to recognise the Provisional Government now. Don't expect he'd come, though—wouldn't care to dine with the poor Skipper of a beaten ship.'

The ships themselves came along now, and this time they *did* notice us, their crews crowding behind the hammock nettings and in the gun ports to see the awful destruction *La Buena Presidente* had done to us. The flagship had only 'Presidente' on her stern—the 'Canilla' part had been knocked off—and she slowed down and fired seventeen guns to salute the sunken ship.

For the first time since that awful morning I felt

happy, and rushed down below to tell Navarro what
had happened.

He did not seem in the least depressed, and
shrugged his shoulders. 'I make the guess. When
you tell me El Castellar no fire guns when they
pass, I had the suspic—ion. De Costa will now be
Presidente—Canilla will fly.'

'What will become of General Zorilla?' I asked
him. I didn't want to see the old chap go to the
wall.

He raised his eyebrows. ' He never change. If
Canilla tell him " fight," he will fight till he killed ;
but when de Costa is *Presidente* and tell him to fight,
he also fight till he killed.'

I knew what Navarro meant, and it was just what
I thought the grand old chap would do.

Well, that is what happened and how everything
was changed in a single hour ; the Santa Cruz
Admiral came to call on the Skipper and explain
matters, and the Provisional Government came off
to renew their claims for Recognition. It was just
as Navarro had thought. The news that their old
comrades in *La Buena Presidente* had beaten one of
the finest cruisers in the English Navy had come
to the ships huddled under the breakwater at Los
Angelos, expecting every hour that she'd come along
and sink them, and they were so proud of her and
her people, and so enraged when they heard that
she'd been treacherously sunk after her glorious fight,

that they hoisted the black and green flag and came along to throw in their lot with the insurgents.

The Provisional Government, as a reward for his great services, made the Admiral Vice-President and gave his job to Captain Pelayo.

This pleased the fleet even if it did not please the Admiral, who must have known that it was only done so that there'd be no chance of his altering his mind again. Gerald told me, long afterwards, that he'd been given the choice either of becoming Vice-President or of being shot.

The *Hercules* went off to Princes' Town to renew the Provisional Government's demand for Recognition, and came back again, two days afterwards, with the welcome news that both the British and United States Governments had granted it. This was like a weight off my chest, because Gerald now could come and go wherever he liked without fear of arrest.

The Skipper sent a private note to de Costa telling him the news, and let me go with him when he and Captain Roger Hill went ashore to communicate it officially. We could hardly get through the crowds that blocked the streets and filled the square in front of the *Alcade's*[1] offices, where the Provisional Government were installed; thousands of the insurgent troops surged round us cheering for all they were worth, but we got through them eventually and I spotted Gerald.

[1] Mayor.

'It's all splendid,' he said; 'won't the mater be glad? D'you know that that transport they brought is "chock-a-block" with ammunition and stores from Los Angelos?'

'I expect you'll be back at the rubber plantation soon,' I laughed, I felt so jolly happy; but Gerald only smiled and shook his head, 'Not exciting enough.'

'How about that little beast?' I asked. 'Is he safe in hospital?'

'You cruel brute!' he answered; 'you maimed him for life. He's cleared out somewhere—they let him go—no one knew him.'

I felt awfully vexed and angry about that, and implored Gerald to be careful, but he only smiled and knocked the ashes out of his pipe. He was looking as fit as a fiddle, he'd done away with the sling for his arm, and it did please me so to see him, in the same smart white riding things and polo helmet, 'bossing' it among all the other fellows, who'd put on their most gorgeous uniforms for the occasion, and were covered with huge green and black sashes.

The Skipper came up to congratulate him, and I went off to shake hands with the 'Gnome'—he hadn't put on any rotten sashes—and with José, who was squatting outside, on the steps, holding Gerald's horse. Then we went back to the *Hector*.

'Couldn't get your brother to dine with me,' the

Skipper said, looking as if he'd been snubbed, 'he's too busy and has no clothes.'

I was very sorry, because I had so looked forward to showing him off to every one on board.

Next day we crawled across to Prince Rupert's Island, the *Hercules* close by, in case we wanted assistance, and people came swarming off to see us and the wreck we were. Navarro was sent ashore to the Colonial Hospital, the mids. were still kept aboard the *Hercules*, and the local ship-repairing yard commenced to patch us up and make it safe to find our way to Bermuda for a more thorough repair.

The black 'washer' ladies came crowding aboard, as before, and were struck all of a heap when they saw the mess we were in.

Arabella Montmorency had brought back some of the 'Angel's' washing—it had been left behind—and when I told her that he'd been killed, she burst out crying, sobbing out, 'De Good Lo'd take de pretty little boy ; why He no spare him for Arabella to vash his clo's. Oh, de pretty boy, de pretty boy !' She was terribly upset about Perkins's washing too. A shell had entirely destroyed his cabin and everything in it, so that he had absolutely nothing to wear except what he stood up in.

She burst out into fresh sobs. 'Poor Massa Perkins ! poor Massa Perkins !—no clo's—no vash clo's—Arabella more sooner vash for him for noddings than Massa Perkins have no clo's for Arabella to vash.'

For five weeks we remained anchored off Princes' Town, and everybody began gradually to brighten 'up' as the memory of that awful fifteen minutes and the next week of woe became less vivid, though we still had not the heart to arrange any matches with the *Hercules* or with Princes' Town. At first the shore people were always saying, 'Couldn't you arrange a cricket-match for this day or that?' and we'd answer, 'Ask our doctor, ask Clegg. He runs the cricket,' and then remember that he had disappeared, and that Bigge, our best bat and bowler, and Montague and Pearson, two others of our team, had also been killed. It was very difficult to forget about them.

We had plenty of news, all this time, from San Fernando, because those local steamers, which had been lying idle for the last few months, resumed their work and ran regularly up to La Laguna. Gerald even found time to write a letter and let me know that preparations were being made for the final attack on Los Angelos and Santa Cruz, but he wrote that there would be some delay as the insurgents in the northern province were not yet ready. They were exhausted, temporarily, by the effort of driving Canilla's army into the mountains and wanted rest. I knew that if Gerald was there they wouldn't get much rest, but he couldn't be in two places at once.

He didn't mention the ex-policeman, so I hoped that the little brute had disappeared for good.

From Santa Cruz we heard very contradictory reports, but there was no doubt that President Canilla was making desperate efforts to defend the city, and that the batteries above Los Angelos were practising almost daily. He was issuing fiery proclamations to encourage his troops, but, in spite of them, and in spite of General Zorilla's popularity, his men were deserting in great numbers.

It was known that directly the insurgents commenced to make their final attack on the city, the *Hercules* was to go across to Los Angelos, to be there in case any trouble arose and she might be wanted to back up the authority of the British Minister. As the *Hector* was to go to Bermuda you can imagine that every one on board her was rather sorry not to be able to see the end of the revolution. Of course I was especially sorry because of Gerald. You can therefore guess how jolly pleased I was when the Skipper sent for me one morning and told me that he was transferring me to the *Hercules*. One of her lieutenants had been invalided home and I was to take his place.

'Tut, tut, boy!' he said; 'I chose you because I knew you'd like to keep an eye on that haughty brother of yours.'

It was jolly good of him, and when the local repairs had been completed, and the *Hector* was fit to steam

to Bermuda, I packed my gear, was taken across to
the *Hercules*, and, with Ginger and Cousin Bob,
watched her slowly crawl past us, out through the
northern entrance.   The band struck up 'Rolling
Home' and 'Auld Lang Syne,' and I felt rather mourn-
ful to see my old ship steaming away without me,
looking, even now, very desolate and dreary with her
jerry foretopmast, patched bridge and upperworks,
and only her two after funnels.

I had a very jolly time aboard the *Hercules* with
Ginger, found Cousin Bob much brighter, and Ginger
and I often chuckled to see how his mids. and mine
had become as thick as thieves.

CHAPTER XVI

The Attack on Santa Cruz

Written by Sub-Lieutenant William Wilson, R.N.

TEN days after the crippled old *Hector* had crawled away from Princes' Town, we heard of her arrival at Bermuda, and very glad we all were to know that she had reached there safely.

I heard from Gerald once or twice, and he wrote that the departure of his expedition from San Fernando was still delayed, owing to the difficulty of obtaining transports for the troops, but the Provisional Government now had an Agent at Princes' Town, who was chartering any steamer which would take the risks—a pretty penny they were charging—and he hoped to be ready in a fortnight or so to put to sea and effect a junction with the troops from the northern province in front of Los Angelos.

It was rather monotonous waiting, all this time; but at last one of the local steamers came in from San Fernando with the news that the expedition was on the point of departure, and we immediately weighed anchor and steamed across to Los Angelos, anchoring once more off the white breakwater and lighthouse at the foot of the gloomy mountains of Santa Cruz.

On shore they must have known of the imminent approach of the insurgents, because we could see them working like ants on the breakwater and wharves, piling up sand-bags to form breastworks for rifle-fire and emplacements for field-guns. Once I felt sure that I recognised Zorilla, tramping among the men and encouraging them.

That night half-a-dozen steamers, of sorts, came down the coast from the northern province of San Juan, and anchored outside us, and outside the range of the guns in the forts. How President Canilla must have raged when he saw them, and cursed his Navy for having deserted him !

They waited there till morning, then got up their anchors and stood out to sea. We guessed that they were waiting for Gerald, and, sure enough, by mid-day, the four insurgent men-of-war and the two torpedo-boats appeared from the south, escorting seven steamers ; they joined forces with the other transports and steamed towards us.

'There, lad !' the Skipper said, chuckling and pointing his telescope at them. 'There's an illustration for you of the value of sea power. If those four miserable cruisers still flew the yellow and green flag, not one single transport could have moved.'

It really was a very striking example of how the possession of the cruisers and the 'Command of the

Sea' had entirely altered the chances of the two sides.

If *La Buena Presidente* had been allowed to destroy those cruisers, whilst they flew the green and yellow flag, the same thing would, of course, have happened, but if, after she had been sunk, they had not revolted, Gerald would still be wandering about the forests, and the insurgents from the northern province would still be confined to their plains, and San Fernando and every town along the coast would still be liable at any moment to bombardment or capture by any expedition President Canilla chose to land there.

The transports anchored before they came within range of the guns above Los Angelos, but the men-of-war and the two torpedo-boats stood boldly inshore, and immediately came under a very heavy fire. We had to 'weigh' and steam off, so as not to interfere with it, but you can imagine that we stayed as close as we could, in order to see all that was going on.

The firing was very rapid, and very badly directed, the shells striking the water anywhere but near the ships, and what we noticed chiefly was the peculiar noise the long dynamite shells made—there were two dynamite guns in the forts, you remember—hissing through the air like enormous rockets, though they did not make much more noise when they struck the water than the ordinary shells. I and the rest of my mids. aboard the *Hercules* were, of course, authorities on shell-fire now, and most of them gave themselves tremendous airs, although Bob and one or two others changed colour, and got very white every time a shell burst anywhere near the ships—that wasn't often—and I knew pretty well that they were still suffering from nerves, and hadn't recovered from those fifteen minutes which wrecked the *Hector*.

The cruisers never took the trouble to reply ; they knew the weak spot in the defences of Los Angelos ; steamed right inshore, where the big guns in the forts, high up above their decks, couldn't touch them, and began blowing the sand-bags about in fine style.

The torpedo-boats darted in along the wharves and inside the breakwater, firing their machine guns, at point-blank range, into the crowds of troops there, and the amount of ammunition expended was enormous.

A good many rifle-bullets and a few shells from field-guns came our way, but no one was touched.

Late in the afternoon, when the firing was slacking down, one of the torpedo-boats came buzzing along quite close to us. She was on her way to the transports, and as she passed us, we saw that her funnel and some boiler-plates she'd built up on deck, round her machine gun, were pitted with bullet-marks. They looked, for all the world, like the inside of a nutmeg grater. Two bodies were lying close to the machine gun, but the rest of the crew were coiled down, resting, and not taking the least notice of them.

She went alongside one of the transports and came hurrying back. Standing just for'ard of the funnel was old Gerald, smoking his pipe. He was still in the same rig—brown boots and gaiters, white duck riding breeches, white duck Norfolk jacket, and white polo helmet—and José, with his scarlet sash, was squatting on the deck at his feet. He looked up as he went by, and nodded cheerfully as I waved to him, and he saw who I was. He was then taken alongside the flagship.

Firing did not cease till dark, but none of us thought that the green and yellow flags would be flying in the morning, and we were quite right. Los Angelos itself was deserted, and white flags as big as table-cloths were hoisted above the forts up the mountain-side.

The transports immediately went alongside the wharves and began to disgorge their ragged little brown troops; the cruisers and gunboats took up their old moorings behind the breakwater, and we anchored again outside it and just clear of the lighthouse.

You can imagine how keen we were to go ashore and see what was happening; but Captain Roger Hill was as strict as he was prim, and refused to give any leave whatever.

'If we had your Skipper—"Old Tin Eye"—here, Billums, I bet every soul would be ashore by now,' Ginger said; but I don't know, he had had a bit of a

fright when our mids. fought those 4.7's, and had
been much stricter ever since.

We could only hang about on deck with our
telescopes and watch the little insurgents pouring out
of Los Angelos, and crowding along that road, up
the mountain-side, towards Santa Cruz. A long way
up, at a place where it curved sharply, the yellow and
green flag was still flying, and we could make out
trenches and could see the wheels of some field-guns
half hidden among the trees. The trenches were continued up the mountain-side, and it looked, from
where we were, as if a hundred brave men, behind
them, could stop a thousand.

Before nightfall Gerald's people were swarming
below this line of trenches, and during the middle
watch desultory firing went on continuously, but in
the morning the yellow and green flag still flew there,
and when we could see the little white-shirted insurgents dodging in and out among the trees, they
hadn't got any nearer to the guns. Next night there
was still more firing; the field-guns were booming
every few minutes, their shells bursting, with a vivid
glare, lower down on the mountain-side. It was
most fascinating to watch, but, as Bob said, gave us
a 'crick in the neck' looking up all the time.

The flags and the field-guns were still there in the
morning.

'Your brother will find that a pretty awkward road
to Santa Cruz,' Captain Roger Hill said, speaking to

me, off duty, for the first time since I joined the ship. I bridled up and got angry at once, for he said it in such a tone as to imply, 'What the dickens can a mere rubber-planter know about war?'

'He's beaten General Zorilla once, sir; I expect he'll manage it again somehow,' I answered, as he stalked away, smiling in his superior way. I'd jolly well like Gerald to meet him and take him down a peg. He'd sized up Captain Grattan, my own Skipper ('Old Tin Eye'), and put him in his place quick enough—good chap though he was—and he'd have an easy job with Captain Roger Hill.

The Captain went over to the insurgent flagship that afternoon to see about some complaint which our Consul at Los Angelos had made, and I slipped a note for Gerald into his coxswain's hands, hoping it would get to him.

'Hope things are going all right. For goodness' sake, get Bob and myself ashore—I'm sick of this ship. Get my chum, Hood, ashore, too, if you can.—BILLUMS.'

By a bit of luck he actually was aboard, and sent me back an answer scribbled on the envelope.

'Will do my best — things are humming.— GERALD.'

The coxswain brought it back when the Captain returned, and I'd hardly read it when I was sent for.

'Ha! Hum! Mr. Wilson, I met your brother on

board the flagship. He seems to be the head of the revolutionary army, and will—Hum! Ha!—be a very important man in the country if it is successful. He's asked me to let you accompany him in the advance. Ha! Hum! I've no objection. If you want to get killed, you can.'

'Thank you very much, sir,' I answered, though I jolly well wanted to kick him.

'Did he ask for Hood or my cousin, Bob Temple?' I asked, putting in a word for them.

'Ha! Hum! he did, but Mr. Hood is a *valuable* officer, and Mr. Temple too young.   Good-morning!'

He *was* an irritating chap, if you like, and the amusing part of it was that he thought every one was fearfully impressed with his importance.

And Gerald sent for me too—sent the same little harbour launch which had brought me on board the *Hector*, after I'd been released from San Sebastian— sent it fussing out from behind the breakwater, and it waited alongside whilst I shifted into plain clothes.

'I've done my best for you both,' I said, as Ginger and Bob watched me 'change,' 'but it can't be done —very sorry—the Captain says your a valuable officer—meaning that I'm not—and that Bob is too young.'

I filled my baccy pouch, shoved the mater's last letter into my pocket to show Gerald, and went ashore, feeling as happy as a bird and jolly important.

How the chaps did envy me !

José was waiting for me on the wharf, smiling all over his honest ugly face, and took me along with him, though it was pretty awkward 'going' because of the sand-bags scattered everywhere. The shops and warehouses along the front were simply riddled with bullets and shell marks, and some men, with a mule-cart, were searching round for bodies and dumping them into it.

We tramped along—it was so hot that the place was like an oven—and found Gerald inside an office kind of place with the black and green flag flying over it, and I knew he was happy by the way he puffed his pipe. There were a great number of officers there, many of whom I had seen before at San Fernando, and they bowed and smiled in the most friendly way ; I almost felt one of them.

'Hullo, Billums! Just in time! Go inside and get some grub—you'll get no more till to-morrow,' Gerald sang out, looking up from some papers.

'Your next meal will be in Santa Cruz—with luck,' he said, coming in when I'd got through a 'fid' of tinned meat.

'Not in San Sebastian, I hope!' I answered, stuffing down the last bit.

'Don't be an ass!'

'You're not making much headway along the road, are you?' I asked presently.

'No, we aren't, and we don't mean to. That's not the main attack. I'm going over the mountain

to-night—hope to be above Santa Cruz at daylight—
you've got a pretty stiff climb before you.'

'But won't all the paths be defended?' I asked,
jolly excited to think of what was going to happen.
'Surely old Zorilla would do that?'

'He's left one open,' Gerald winked, 'one that
chap you call the 'Gnome' knows. He's going to
lead us, but you'll have to wait here till it's dark.'

'What became of that black horse?' I asked him,
as he was going out of the room.

'Brought it round from San Fernando, and sent
it up to Zorilla yesterday. He's awfully grateful.
I can't stop any longer ; I must go up that road and
show myself, below those trenches, before it gets too
dark, or Zorilla will begin to imagine we're not in-
tending to attack that way.'

Then I had to tramp up and down and wait for
the sun to set, thinking of Gerald riding up the
mountain road towards Santa Cruz, till he was close
enough to those trenches we had seen to be
recognised and be potted at.

At last it was dark—rather too dark, because a
tremendously black thunder-cloud came sweeping
in from seawards—and José came for me and took
me away through narrow steep streets which were
almost pitch-dark because the electric light from
Santa Cruz had been cut off. There were bonfires
at the street corners, but they only seemed to make
the darkness greater.

We got up past the houses, well above the town, and came to a flatter piece of ground, and although it was pitch-dark, and I couldn't see anything, I knew, by the smell and the murmur of voices and rattling of rifles, that there were thousands of the little brown men all round me. We found Gerald at last, the 'Gnome,' in a great state of excitement, with him.

'We're just going on. We've a five-hour climb before us,' Gerald said—he didn't seem excited.

'It's going to be a beastly night,' I whispered—I could not help whispering, because I was so excited.

'So much the better,' he said cheerfully. 'We shan't be heard.'

Then he gave some orders very quietly, said, 'Come along;' and we four, the 'Gnome' leading the way, began climbing. I was in pretty good training, but it was all I could do to keep up with them; I hadn't nails in my boots, either, which made climbing all the more difficult.

'Hold up, old chap; you can't afford to slip,' Gerald said, clutching me as I stumbled, a few minutes after we had started, 'it's a long way to the bottom.'

I told him about my boots.

'Boots are a nuisance,' he answered; 'those little chaps of mine looted an army boot-store yesterday; they think boots make them look more like real soldiers. They've never worn boots before, and will be footsore in an hour, but they *will* wear them. I can't prevent them.'

I could hear them slipping and sliding behind me in the darkness. To make matters worse, after we'd been climbing for a couple of hours, the rain came down in bucketsful, drenched us to the skin, and made everything more slippery than ever.

'I'm going to take mine off,' I told Gerald when I had slipped badly again, and so I did, hanging my boots round my neck, and stuffing my socks inside them.

Presently we heard a sliding noise behind us, a rifle went bounding and clattering down, a man gave a scream, and then, far below, we heard a crash, as if the body had fallen into dry bushes.

'That's one gone over the edge,' Gerald said, quite coolly, 'I wish the others would do as you've done and take off their boots. Keep well to the right.'

I didn't like it at all, and you bet I put each foot down jolly carefully before I trusted my weight to it.

We were walking, or scrambling, up a rock path, and I knew that on our left the mountain-side sloped down very precipitously, and far below, under my feet, could hear the noise of a rushing stream; it sounded thousands of feet below.

Noise! Why, it didn't much matter what noise

we made ! For, although the rain had ceased nearly as quickly as it had commenced, the night and blackness was full of the noises of mountain torrents, splashing down the rocks above and below us—all round us, in fact—sluicing stones along with them, and making a great rattle.

We knew that the 'Gnome' was still plodding on ahead, for he kept calling softly back every few seconds. Then a great black gap seemed to open right out at our feet—it looked like the end of the world for blackness. My nerves were pretty jumpy —they hadn't yet recovered from that fight with *La Buena Presidente*—and I clutched at a rock and shivered in my wet things. We had stopped, and the 'Gnome' was taking off his boots.

'You'll have to be careful here,' Gerald said. 'Lean well to the right and get a good grip before you put your weight on your feet. Come on !'

I heard the 'Gnome' scrambling round something, sending stones flying down into space, Gerald disappeared, and I followed with my heart in my mouth.

'Dig your toes in and get a good grip,' he sang out, and I stuck them into a ledge and a little crack I felt, skinning them, I know, and worked my way along. My shoulders were hanging over that black pit below, and I had that awful feeling that I wanted to let go and fall down. I dare not move hand or foot, but just as I was beginning to sweat with fear, Gerald caught me by one hand and pulled me round.

'That's the worst bit, Billums; we shall lose some of them here.'

I couldn't answer—my jaws were chattering so much. I was trembling all over.

No! I certainly hadn't quite got over that terrible fifteen minutes while the poor old *Hector* was being shattered.

I followed him in a second or two, but we had barely gone twenty paces before we heard some one slipping at that corner we had just passed; there was a scream—it sounded again hundreds of feet below us—then absolute silence, while I waited, with my ears tingling, for the crash.

At last it came up to us out of the darkness, just like the noise a plum would make if you threw it on the ground. I dug my bare heel among the stones and clutched some bushes.

'Come along!' Gerald whispered nervously, but stopped again because there were more screams from that awful corner. He groped his way back. 'I'll make them join their belts together and form a line round there,' he said, as the 'Gnome,' José, and I waited shivering for him.

'*Don Geraldio, mucho bueno,*' the 'Gnome' muttered under his breath.

My brother's voice sounded again after what seemed like half an hour, 'I had to go round that blessed corner place, Billums, but I've got a dozen belts fixed together and men holding them on each side, so it's pretty safe now.'

I myself wouldn't have gone round that corner, or whatever it was, for anything in the world.

We scrambled on, and the rain came tumbling down; in five minutes the path we were in was a raging torrent, and my naked feet slipped back one step for every three I made. They were getting tender now—very tender.

'We're past the worst part, put your boots on again,' Gerald sang out, and I tried to do so, but they were so wet and my feet so swollen that they wouldn't go on, so I had to do without them.

'What's the time?' I asked Gerald presently, when we'd halted to let the column close up. 'Is it safe to light a match?'

'My goodness, no! Zorilla's people would see us for miles; he has watchers all over the hills. Whatever time it is I'm afraid we shall be late.'

We *were* late too, and by the time it was light enough to see my wretched feet—and wasn't I jolly glad to begin to see anything—it was half-past two, and we still had a long climb before us. But we went much faster now, and began edging away to the right, bearing round a tremendous mountain shoulder that loomed up over our heads.

'On the other side is Santa Cruz,' Gerald whispered. That was exciting enough, if you like.

He was busy hurrying on his men, who now began slipping past us, going on ahead. They looked pretty well exhausted, and most of them had done as I had done—hung their boots round their necks; but in spite of their being soaked to the skin, and in spite of their tremendous climb, they were cheerful enough, and their eyes were flashing all right—at the prospect of sacking Santa Cruz, I expect. The officers looked much more weather-beaten than they did.

Then we went on again, and I asked Gerald whether we had lost many men during the night, but he didn't know. We were walking through coarse grass that cut my feet and made them smart like the mischief, so I stuck my socks on. That eased things a little.

'We can see Santa Cruz from here—in daylight,' Gerald whispered presently, as we reached the top, and I knew by the waver in his voice that he was—at last—excited; I know that the blood went tingling to *my* ears at the mere thought of being so near the city.

The men were thrown out in a single line; we stopped to get them into something like order, and as they marched into position they threw themselves down on the wet ground, clutching their beloved rifles feverishly, and looking down through the gloom and the mist to where Santa Cruz lay at our feet. That long line of little crouching men with their glittering eyes all trying to pierce the dim light

c 197

SCRAMBLING DOWN THE MOUNTAIN SIDE

and see the city they'd heard so much about and come so many miles to capture, was the most extraordinary sight.

As I looked at them I couldn't help thinking what an awful fate was waiting for Santa Cruz if they should get out of hand and sack it. They were more than half-savages, and their officers, standing there among them, didn't look as if they could control them once they began to see 'red.'

'Is everything all right?' I asked Gerald, who had come back out of the mist from where the far end of the line extended, out of sight, and he nodded cheerfully, so I didn't mind being wet through and hungry, and longed for him to give the signal to rush down to the city below us. Poor old Zorilla! I couldn't help feeling sorry for him.

Presently he did give a sign, the officers drew their swords, and the whole crouching mob sprang to its feet, and we began scrambling and sliding downhill. It was a jolly sight easier work than scrambling up, but we made the dickens of a noise.

In a quarter of an hour we could smell the city, and then the faint outlines of the old cathedral tower showed up, the fierce little men drawing in their breath with a hissing sound as they pointed it out to each other. Suddenly, right under our feet, I recognised San Sebastian—we were looking down on top of it and on those short saluting guns along the parapet.

As I pointed it out to Gerald there was the crack of a rifle and then another, then hundreds of bullets came flying past, hitting the ground in front of us and whizzing overhead. Gerald's men sank to the ground behind us, and I could hardly see them among the brown rocks.

The 'Gnome' came waddling along—out of breath—Gerald told me to lie down, and he and the 'Gnome' and about a hundred men crept forward to reconnoitre. I crawled after them, and caught up with my brother just as he was looking round a big boulder.

'Look there!' he whispered, 'down to the left!'

I peered through the dim light, and there, drawn up between us and San Sebastian, on some level ground, I saw several regiments of regulars. A few companies, already extended, were lying down and firing up at us, some were deploying as rapidly as they could, and others were crowding into San Sebastian and lining the walls. Four field-guns came bumping along out of the mist and began unlimbering and a little group of horsemen galloped up behind them.

'There's old Zorilla!' we both sang out. You couldn't possibly mistake him and his black horse.

'He's too late,' Gerald whispered excitedly. 'We'll rush 'em.'

He got up and back we climbed to where we'd left our men. Bullets were spluttering and splashing all

round us, but no one was hit. Gerald collected some
of the officers and jabbered away to them in Spanish.
I saw their tired eyes begin flaming.

'Look here, Billums!' he said, turning to me.
'Would you mind hurrying down in front of those
chaps on the left? I'm going to take the right of the
mob—I'm going straight for the guns—but you cut
along to the left and try and get into San Sebastian.
Shout, wave your arms, but keep going, and they'll
follow all right. Here, take my polo helmet, that'll
make you all the more like me. It's all right;
Zorilla won't get his chaps to stand when they see
we mean things.'

Off he ran to his part of the line.

My aunt! that was fun, if you like. I went across
to the left and began halloaing; the officers began
shouting, '*Viva los Horizontales!*' and before I could
say 'Jack Robinson' the whole of those little brown
chaps and I were scrambling down the mountain-
side straight for San Sebastian, yelling blue murder.

My old boots were knocking up against each other
and against my back, but I jammed Gerald's polo hat
firmly on and slid and scrambled, and ran and slid
again. The field-guns fired once or twice, there was
an appalling triumphant shrieking noise behind me—
you couldn't call it a cheer, it was much too savage
for that—and Gerald was right. Zorilla's infantry
could *not* stand the torrent of brown forest-men
dashing down the mountain-side on top of them, and,

just as I was wishing that I had a stick or a stone
—anything, in fact—in my hand, they fired a volley
and began running and racing back to the town and
behind the walls of San Sebastian.

The mule-drivers unhitched the mules from the
guns and galloped madly along after them—helter-
skelter—dodging behind the walls, and then streaming along the road towards the city itself.

We were after them like smoke, and just as some
of them dashed across the drawbridge and tried to
close the heavy iron doors, we rushed in.

They didn't show fight, I should think they didn't;
it was only the backs of them we saw as they tumbled
over themselves to escape, throwing away their rifles
and clambering through the embrasures of those
saluting guns.

Well, that was how I paid my second visit to San
Sebastian—a bit of a change from my first visit,
wasn't it?

I dashed out again to help Gerald and, as I turned
round the walls, along he came and old Zorilla with
him. The poor old chap was mopping some blood
off his forehead, and though he did look so forlorn
he bowed to me in quite a friendly way. I gave his
hand a jolly good hard grip.

It turned out that only a very few of his men
round those guns had made any stand, and that
Gerald had simply swept through them, driven them
back under the walls of the fort, and the old man had

surrendered.   The little brown men were rushing
like a pack of hounds after the retreating regulars,
and Gerald's officers were trying to stop them.   They
did manage to bring some back, but couldn't stop
the rest, who went careering along towards Santa
Cruz, till fifty or sixty regulars, braver than the
others, or perhaps unable to run any farther, faced
round, formed up across the road, and began firing
at them, when back they came grinning and smiling
like spaniels who have been ranging too far ahead
and know they deserve a hiding.   A lot of them
scrambled up the mountain-side to fetch their beloved
boots, which they had dropped before they began
charging down.

'The revolution is finished,' Gerald said quite
quietly, and began loading his pipe; but his fingers
shook a little, and I knew that he was fearfully excited,
although he did his best to conceal the fact.   He had
the field-guns brought into the fort, and stuck them
through some vacant embrasures, where they could
command the road leading down to the city.   Then
he began to get his chaps into some kind of order
again.

'Would you like to hoist the flag, Billums?   You
can if you like,' he said; and you bet I would.
Some one—the 'Gnome' it was—brought along a roll
of black and green bunting; we climbed up to the
flagstaff on top of the walls, and hitching it to the
halyards I hauled it up, hand over hand.   You

should have seen Gerald's chaps yelling and dancing about, and heard them shouting, '*Viva de Costa!*' '*Viva los Horizontales!*' and '*Viva Don Geraldio!*' I need hardly tell you which were the loudest shouts, but old Gerald never moved a muscle, and took them all as a matter of course.

I stood on top of the wall and smiled down on them, and never had had a jollier spree. It was quite light now—a most beautiful calm morning, the air crisp and fresh—and the top edge of the ridge we'd just climbed down was a rosy red.

Whatever the weather had been it wouldn't have made much difference to me ; I felt simply glorious, and thought of old Ginger, down aboard the *Hercules*, keeping his morning watch and trying to prevent the men from making too much noise over the Captain's head and waking him.

It was grand to be alive ! I managed to get on my boots, though they wouldn't go on over my socks, then I took my coat off and shook some of the water out of it, for I was still as wet as a rat. Any number of weird noises were coming up from the city.

'They'll come and attack us, I suppose ; won't they ?' I asked Gerald, but he only smiled and said something to General Zorilla, who smiled too, rather sadly, and shook his head.

Then I thought of that room place with the barred iron door where I'd been shut up, and took Gerald over to have a good look at it, but he'd had it opened already, and quite a number of 'plain clothes' people were standing about, not quite knowing what to do, but highly delighted with themselves. They had just been released. I showed him those three graves, although they were not very distinct now as grass had already grown over them. It *was* a happy time if you like, and I was getting more hungry every second.

Half an hour later a carriage came driving furiously up the road towards San Sebastian, and two civilians and an officer jumped down. They came up very humbly to Gerald and spoke to him. I knew their news was good, because Gerald's face twitched so much, and directly he called out something in Spanish, every one inside and outside the fort began shouting and yelling with delight.

'Canilla has vanished,' he told me; 'the place is empty, and they're going to hoist the black and green flag over the cathedral tower as soon as they've sewn one together.'

'Then it's all over,' I said, just a little disappointed that there was to be no more excitement.

'Yes! we can march in now, but——'

'But what?' I asked, seeing Gerald look a little anxious, and he swept his hand round to where the little half-savage men were cheering and shouting, dancing about like children.

'——but if I took them in now, Santa Cruz would be in flames in an hour,'

I rather guessed that that was the trouble.

The carriage drove back again, and General Zorilla went in it, little José went as well, sitting up with the driver and looking very important.

Gerald told me that he'd appointed old Zorilla Commandant of the city, and that he'd sent him in to get together as many regular troops as he could find to guard the streets and keep order. Funnily enough, it never even occurred to me that old Zorilla could not be trusted ; nobody who'd seen the old man could possibly doubt his honour.

'D'you know what the troops will be doing for the next half-hour?' Gerald smiled.

'No ! what?'

'Twisting round the yellow and green badges in their hats till the stripes are *horizontal*, and blacking out the "yellow" part.'

'What's José gone for?' I asked him.

'He says that I left a clean pair of riding breeches and a new helmet at the Club, and he's going to see if they are still there.'

I must say that old Gerald wanted them badly ; we both looked pretty disreputable. Just then the bells in the cathedral began ringing, and the great cracked bell banged out with its jarring clang. Bells began ringing, from one end of the city to the other, till the whole place seemed nothing but bells, and in half an hour a big black and green flag was hanging down over the old tower,

'If they don't send food out pretty soon for my chaps, there'll be no holding them,' Gerald said presently, and looked worried again; but old Zorilla must have hurried up the townspeople considerably, because very soon carts came out with bread and fruit and rice cakes, and the fierce little fellows were soon filling their stomachs.

José came back from the city, his eyes glittering with pride; he'd found Gerald's room at the Club quite undisturbed, and brought him a complete change of clothes and some shaving tackle. We went into one of the living rooms in the fort and made ourselves look more respectable, José coming with us and polishing Gerald's boots and gaiters till you could see your face in them.

All this time the men were round those carts stuffing themselves contentedly; but don't think that old Zorilla had forgotten us, rather not, he had sent us out some breakfast, and you may guess we were ready for it by the time we had cleaned.

'First meal in San Sebastian! I *said* so!' and I laughed.

'So it is! Well, here's luck to it!' Gerald answered; 'and thanks very much, Billums, for coming along with me.'

'My dear chap, don't be an ass!' was the only thing I could think to say.

'I wish I could make my little chaps give up their rifles,' he said, 'but I can't; they're too proud of them.'

'But surely if you disarmed them the regulars might attack them?' I asked, but Gerald only smiled.

'Of course not! My dear Billums, didn't I tell you that they are busy blacking out the yellow stripes; they'll obey my orders now as cheerfully as they'd have shot me an hour ago. Now Canilla has vanished Zorilla only takes orders from the New President—and that means me.'

'Oh!' I said, and, like the sailor's parrot, thought a good deal.

Then I gave him the mater's last letter, and, after he'd lighted his pipe, he sat back in a chair and read it, stretching his legs out in front of him whilst José knelt down buttoning up his gaiters and giving them a final polish. I did wish that the mater could have seen him.

Officers with green and black badges in their caps and helmets came backwards and forwards from the city for orders, and some of them, I saw, had done just as Gerald had said, simply turned the badges round and inked out the yellow stripe. It made *me* laugh, but he kept a face as sober as a judge, and sent them flying here, there, and everywhere, and they clicked their heels, saluted, and rushed off, as if he had always been their Commanding Officer. I don't expect they would have dared come among our little chaps without blacking out the yellow stripe, although now, with their stomachs full, they were quite peaceful and contented, and went to sleep on the slope below the fort or sat drying themselves in the sun, and forgot, for a time, about looting the city.

Mr. Arnstein, the German Minister, came out during the morning to arrange for the safety of European property, and as he was an old friend of my brother, was jolly pleasant. Whilst they were yarning together de Costa's Secretary drove hurriedly across the drawbridge, to say very excitedly that the New President and the Provisional Government were coming up the mountain road from Los Angelos, and wanted to see Gerald. Gerald sent him back again as quickly as he'd come.

'I'm hanged if I'm going down there,' he told me. 'For one thing, I daren't leave these chaps of mine. I've told him that it's simply impossible for me to leave San Sebastian, and told him to warn de Costa to bring along as many regulars as he can get hold of—as soon as they've shifted their badges.

'We shall have them here as soon as they can come,' he added, smiling. 'They'll be so frightened lest I seize the palace and become Dictator before they can get hold of it, that they'll come along like "one o'clock."'

He was right too. An hour later de Costa and the whole of the Provisional Government came rattling across the drawbridge, and simply threw themselves on old Gerald; they would have kissed him if he'd only taken his pipe out of his mouth, but as they'd got hold of both his hands he couldn't. They shook

my hands, too, till they ached, and then went away
to take up their quarters in the palace, feeling more
easy in their minds, I expect, about that Dictatorship.

I wished that they had never come, for one of
them had a note for me from the Commander of the
Hercules, ordering me back on board as soon as
possible.

I showed it to Gerald. 'Confound the ship, I'll
have to go back at once.'

He got me a horse, and sent the 'Gnome' down
with me in case there was any trouble on the road,
shouting out, 'Good-bye! Hope to see you up again
before long,' as we clattered out of San Sebastian. I
shouted '*Buenos! Buenos!*' to the little brown chaps,
a great number of them jumping up and giving me a
fine 'send off' as we cantered down to the city.

Regular troops were at every corner—their badges
twisted round and blackened—and it really was
ludicrous to see the attempts the townspeople had
made to show their loyalty to the New President; for
at nearly every window there was some kind of an
attempt at a black and green flag with the stripes
horizontal.

A great number of people thought I was Gerald
himself, so I came in for quite a royal reception, but
we cantered rapidly through the square, field batteries
at every corner, past the front of the cathedral, with
that huge bell still jarring overhead, and as we passed
the Hotel de l'Europe I looked up at the window from

which Bob and I and the poor little 'Angel' had
seen the funeral procession and tried to escape that
beastly little ex-policeman. I wondered what had
become of him, and whether the stumps of his fingers
had healed.

It was a long and tedious journey down the road
to Los Angelos, because at many places barricades,
thrown up to prevent Gerald's troops advancing,
were being lazily pulled down, and the litter on the
road made it impossible to get along quickly.

However, I did not want to be caught in the dark,
so we made our horses hurry whenever the road made
it possible, and we managed to reach Los Angelos in
two hours and a half. One of the boats belonging
to the Santa Cruz flagship happened to be waiting
alongside the wharf; the 'Gnome' said something
to the coxswain, and off I went in her, in great style,
to the *Hercules*.   Good little 'Gnome,' he was pretty
well worn out by the time I wished him good-bye,
and he went away with our two horses.

CHAPTER XVII

The Ex-policeman

Written by Sub-Lieutenant William Wilson, R.N.

As you can imagine, I wasn't half pleased to get back to the *Hercules*, and there I had to wait, not a soul being allowed ashore, for a whole week. We heard that order was being maintained in Santa Cruz, and as this was the chief thing Gerald worried about, I was very glad indeed. I never told you that, directly the English and United States Governments had recognised the insurgents, Canilla had sent every foreign Minister, except Mr. Arnstein, and every European merchant, out of the country. Now, however, they all came back from Princes' Town, and things seemed to be settling down peaceably, just as peaceably, indeed, as after a General Election and a change of Government at home. Canilla and a very small number of officials, who'd made themselves too obnoxious to stay, simply disappeared, finding their way down to some village farther along the coast, and taking refuge on board a Colombian gunboat which happened to be there. No one seemed to worry about him or them—not in the least.

Then came a formal invitation for the Captain and
Officers of H.M.S. *Hercules* to attend the inauguration
of the new Government.   There was to be a triumphal
entry of the former insurgent army into Santa Cruz,
a full dress ceremony in the old cathedral, and a
banquet afterwards at the palace.   What made me so
pleased was that they'd sent me a separate invitation,
in recognition of my 'services to the Republic of
Santa Cruz.'   Just think of that !   I've got the card
now with a great spidery signature—Alvarez de Costa
—across the bottom of it.

Captain Roger Hill couldn't possibly refuse to let
me go, although I'm certain he would have done so
if he could.

Gerald sent me a note telling me to meet him at
the Club, and Mr. Macdonald, who had turned up
again from Princes' Town, drove Ginger and Cousin
Bob and myself up to Santa Cruz, just as he had done
before.

We had to go in uniform, 'whites' with swords,
and as mine was an old-fashioned helmet, which came
down well over my eyes and the back of my neck, it
hid my hair.   The result was that hardly any one
noticed me or mistook me for Gerald, though, wherever we went, there were shouts of ' *Viva los Inglesas!* '
from the crowds in the streets and at the windows.
The English were tremendously popular, chiefly on
account of Gerald, so Mr. Macdonald told us.   'Look
up there !' he called out, as we came in sight of

San Sebastian, and we saw that the slopes of the mountains, below and above it, were simply swarming with Gerald's little brown men in their white shirts.

It was just such another scorching hot day as the first time we'd been in Santa Cruz, and the whole place was a flutter of green and black, green and black flags in front of every house, green and black rosettes in every one's coats, and of course the regular troops were plastered with green and black badges.

Troops! Why, there were more regular troops than ever, cavalry, infantry, and artillery, and not a sign of the fierce little brown men in the streets or big square, except in front of the cathedral steps, where about two hundred of them formed a guard of honour, their ragged shirts and cotton drawers washed for the occasion, new cartridge-belts round their waists, and brown boots on their feet, but not looking particularly happy in their finery, although there was a great crowd watching them curiously. There was a funny feeling of tension in the air, and every one had the same worried expectant look on his face, just as I had noticed on that first day we drove through the city.

'Aren't there any women in the place?' Ginger asked. 'We never seem to see any,' and Mr. Macdonald shook his head. 'They know when there's danger. It's always a bad sign when they stay indoors. They're afraid of the insurgent troops from the forests down south and the plains away to the north. There's no knowing what they'll do when they enter the city. Every one's nervous about them.'

We drove to the Club, and there we found any number of fellows from the *Hercules*, and most of the European residents too. They had the same anxious look about them as we'd noticed outside, and one of them, turning to me, said that practically everything depended on my brother and his personal influence and popularity with the ragged armed mob who were going to march into Santa Cruz. He told me that Gerald had just gone up to his room, so Ginger and Bob and I went up and found him changing into clean things, José, with a huge black and green rosette in his coat, helping him. I introduced Ginger, and unbuckling our sword-belts we sat on his bed and yarned to him.

'How are your chaps going to behave?' I asked him.

'So long as I can keep my eye on them they'll be all right,' he said, 'but I don't like the idea of leaving them outside when I have to go into the cathedral, or to that banquet they talk so much about. I wish to goodness I hadn't to go through this tomfoolery; I have to ride immediately behind the President's carriage. (How the dickens can he expect to be popular if he don't ride a horse?) He won't let me off the job either, although he's jealous of me, and hates hearing people singing out my name, but he

knows he can't keep my little brown chaps in hand
himself, so he's going to keep me as close to him as
possible.'

'But *must* they come in?' Ginger asked.

'Yes!' he said; 'they must. They must have
their triumphal entry. I've had bother enough keeping them out as long as this, but they won't go home
till they can say that they've marched through Santa
Cruz as victors. Thank goodness, they've hardly got
a cartridge among them.'

'How many are there?' Ginger began to ask, when
there was a gentle tap on the door, and one of the
Club servants came in, handed Gerald a visiting card,
and went out again.

'I don't know who the chap is,' Gerald said, looking at it; 'I wish people wouldn't bother me now.'

There was another tap at the door, and in came a
man, dressed in a black frock-coat and grey trousers,
holding a tall silk hat with the thumb and the stumps
of the fingers of his right hand. For a second I
seemed to feel frozen with fear, for it was the ex-
policeman, the man whose fingers I'd cut off on the
beach at San Fernando, and as I sprang at him, he
drew a revolver from his breast with his left hand,
dodged round me, and fired point-blank at Gerald.
I heard Gerald catch his breath, and I'd caught the
revolver, hurled it away, and got the brute by the
neck in a second, José, with a scream, rushing across
to help me. He reeled over the foot of Gerald's bed,

and whether José choked him, or I broke his back in my rage, I don't know, but he gave a shudder, slipped out of our hands, and flopped down on the floor —dead. Oh! that I had killed him that day at San Fernando!

I turned to Gerald, who was standing where he'd been shot, with his hand over his stomach, Ginger and Bob holding his arms.

'He got me in the stomach, Billums,' he said quietly.

'Don't move a muscle,' I yelled, 'we'll lift you on the bed.'

As we laid him down very carefully, people came rushing up from down below to know what had happened.

'Get a doctor,' I shouted, and I know that I was blubbing like a child.

Dr. Robson of the *Hercules* came rushing up, and I shall never forget how we three watched his face as he pulled down Gerald's riding breeches, very carefully, to examine the wound.

'When did you have food last?' he said, and when Gerald answered, 'Six hours ago,' he muttered, 'Thank God!'

'What size bullet was it? Show me the revolver.'

Bob brought it. It was a Mauser automatic pistol.

'Well, what's the verdict?' Gerald asked quite calmly.

'I can't say, must get some one else. Don't move

till I come back—not a muscle,' and Dr. Robson went away.

Ginger went away too, some one dragged the body out of the room, and only Bob, white and trembling, with tears running down his face, José, crouching dumb with grief on the floor, and myself stayed with him.

Oh! that I'd killed the brute when I'd had that chance at San Fernando!

I saw that Gerald was thinking and worrying about something. Presently he said : 'Billums, old chap, you've often asked me why I left the rubber job; I wanted excitement, and I wanted to see how I could run a revolution. Well, I've run it; I'm the Commander-in-Chief, or whatever they call it, of the Republic, and this is a great day for Englishmen out here; we were rather going "under" before the revolution, but now our chaps are "top of the tree," and an Englishman must be behind de Costa's carriage to-day. It's up to you now, you must take my place.'

' I can't, Gerald ; I can't really—I can't leave you,' I stuttered, half choking.

He thought a moment, and then went on. ' You must, Billums. You know the reason. They're afraid of my men. Once they get into the city with arms in their hands they may get out of hand at the least thing, they are so wild and excitable. I am the only one who can control them, and for them to sack

Santa Cruz would spoil all I have done. In my rig,
you will be as like me as two peas, and so long as
they think I'm there, giving all the orders, they'll
obey their officers. They won't otherwise.'

Just then there were some firm footsteps outside
the door, and General Zorilla came gently in, in full
uniform, covered with medals, his old war-worn face
looking very sad, his thin lips very tightly pressed
together. He smiled at me, and then gripped Gerald's
hand, his stern old face working strangely. They
talked together for a minute or two, and I knew somehow or other that they were not talking of Gerald
himself.

'Yes, Billums! it's up to you now. You must
get into my ordinary rig out. Zorilla wants you to
do so, too—says it's the only thing that can save
Santa Cruz.'

'But a great many people will know me!' I cried.

'Many more won't; the people of the city won't,
and most of my men will think you are I. You've
only got to ride behind that carriage and return
salutes, and you've done it. You must do it, Billums;
my horse is as quiet as a lamb, he doesn't even mind
their atrocious bands or the guns firing.'

I'd never felt so utterly wretched in my life. 'All
right, I'll try,' I said.

Zorilla bowed to me and went out, though, first
of all, looking very sad, he clicked his heels and
saluted poor old Gerald as he lay on the bed. José,

with red eyes and trembling fingers, began un-
buttoning Gerald's gaiters, while Bob and I held
his legs above the knee to prevent any shaking.
The only clean riding breeches Gerald had were the
ones he was wearing, so he made us take them off.
I stripped and got into them ; I could not have felt
more miserable if I was going to be hanged, and to
make things more wretched, just below the inner left
braces button was the small hole made by the bullet
and a tiny stain of blood.

I dragged them on, José laced them at the knees,
then I put on Gerald's brown boots, and José fastened
on his gaiters, rubbing off his tear-marks with his
sleeve.   He helped me into one of Gerald's white
duck ' Norfolk' jackets and handed me his newest
polo helmet.

' You're the very thing,' Gerald said, looking at
me, and even José appeared astonished, so I suppose
I must have looked very much like my brother.

Then Dr. Robson came back with the Fleet
Surgeon of the *Hercules* and the swagger Santa
Cruz surgeon, an extraordinarily fat man with fat,
greasy, tobacco-stained fingers covered with rings.
They examined the wound again, and the fat man
shrugged his shoulders and I saw him draw one
finger across the other hand and look at Robson
very suggestively.

I knew he meant to cut Gerald open.

The Fleet Surgeon and he talked French to each

other for some minutes, and I could see that our
doctor didn't like the idea of an operation, but the fat
chap was evidently talking him round to his own
way of thinking.

'Well, what's the verdict?' Gerald asked, looking
from one to the other rather anxiously, and the Fleet
Surgeon said, in a low voice, 'We must give you
a little ether and have a look at you.'

'All right, doctor, I'm ready,' Gerald answered
quite quietly; thank goodness, he was in hardly any
pain.

Then the 'Gnome' came in to fetch Gerald for the
procession, thought for a second that I, in his things,
was he, but then saw him lying on the bed. He
nearly broke down when Gerald spoke to him.

'You go with him, Billums,' Gerald said.

Dr. Robson followed us out of the room. 'We're
going to operate almost immediately; that fat chap
thinks it necessary, and as he's the best surgeon anywhere here, we must take his advice.'

I darted back, 'Good-bye, old chap! good luck!
—there won't be any pain.' I tried to say it cheerfully, but I had to dart out again, for there was a lump
in my throat and I was afraid it would burst.

'Good-bye, Billums!' Gerald sang out after me.
'Don't be conceited when they cheer you. I'm thankful you're to be in my place.'

Well, I don't mind saying, honestly, that, if I
could, I would have changed places with him then,

because old Gerald was such a splendid chap and had done such grand things and I was only a rotter.

The 'Gnome' led me down through the Club, but I seemed half dazed and didn't notice a soul there; one of Gerald's horses was waiting for me outside the arched gateway where I had first seen that little beast, I got on his back, and then heard Ginger's voice singing out, 'Buck up, old Billums! Bob and I will hang round till you come back.'

Buck up? I could have blubbed more easily as I rode after the 'Gnome' with a couple of nigger orderlies trotting behind me.

'Señor! Señor!' I heard the 'Gnome' mutter imploringly, and saw him pushing up his own chin with his finger and then pointing to mine, so I sat more upright and held my head higher.

Directly we got into the main street, the place was one seething mass of waving arms and flags, people pressed round my horse and even kissed my gaiters, and the whole air was alive with shouts of ' *Viva Don Geraldio!*' I tried to do what Gerald would have done and smiled, and by the time we'd managed to force a way through into the great square, the shouting was really extraordinary. The people stopped my horse, and if a very officious young cavalry officer had not brought up a half-squadron of his men, I do believe they would have pulled me off my saddle in their excitement.

However, we got through them all right and cantered up the road to San Sebastian, round which the little brown forest-men were camped.

My aunt! miserable as I was, it made my blood dance to hear their shouts and to know how keen they were on my brother.

As I entered the fort across the drawbridge, General Zorilla was waiting for me, clicked his heels and saluted gravely as I dismounted. Then he took me by the arm and led me away to an upper part of the wall, where it was just broad enough for two to walk abreast, and talked all the time—in Spanish, of course—and, though I could not understand a word, I guessed quickly that he'd taken me up there, where no one else could come and try to talk to me, and where all the people, both inside and outside the fort, could see me.

I thought that probably a rumour of Gerald's having been shot by an assassin had spread, and that old Zorilla feared what the forest-men would do if they believed it.

We walked solemnly up and down for, I should think, quite twenty minutes, and then the President drove up in a carriage, drawn by six white horses, and it was time for the procession to start.

General Zorilla gave some orders, and immediately there was a stir among the little brown chaps. A great column of them, quite two thousand I should imagine by the time they took to pass beneath us, wound round the fort and began marching down into the town.

They had cleaned themselves for the occasion, looking quite spruce as they surged along that road, their officers trying to make them keep some military formation—with very little success. A few were wearing those brown boots which they'd looted, but most of them were barefooted, so made very little noise on the hard ground, but, for all their lack of uniform and discipline, their eyes were flashing under their white hats and they bore themselves very bravely. After them came another mob—men only armed with *machetes*—the terrible little *machetos*, immediately in front of the six white horses and the President's carriage. Behind it was a space of about fifty yards, where I was to go, and then came more carriages with the Provisional Government, another mob of wild *machetos*, two companies of sailors from the ships, and those two hundred regulars who'd helped me bring little Navarro and those guns into San Fernando. I didn't know that they had come along, and was jolly glad to see them.

They had been given the honour of dragging the two pom-poms through the city—those two pom-poms we had landed at San Fernando with the rest of the 'hydraulic machinery'—and seemed very proud of the privilege.

To me, of course, they were the most interesting part of the procession, and I wondered what they would think if they knew that it was I who had untied their arms that morning and brought them along through the forest ; but every one took it for granted that I was Gerald, so it was no use wondering or pretending to be myself.

Behind them another huge column of riflemen began to defile down into the road, but by this time we had climbed down from the top of the wall, Zorilla had mounted his black horse, I had got on to mine, and we waited in the shade of the weather-beaten walls of San Sebastian, with the muzzles of their saluting guns sticking out above our heads, till the last of Gerald's army had marched past, doing their best to look like real soldiers whether they had brown boots on or not, their eyes flashing fiercely, and their shoulders well thrown back.

Thank God! they had hardly a cartridge among them.

Zorilla motioned for me to ride on, so I cantered away to my place behind the President's carriage, the 'Gnome' close to me, and the two orderlies coming after.

We got into the city just as the saluting guns began firing, and the great cracked bell in the cathedral began to set my nerves on edge—I hated the sound of it. We got through the first appallingly hot streets comfortably enough, but I scarcely noticed anything, because I was thinking all the time of poor old Gerald and how I could possibly write home to tell the mater. I was getting intensely miserable, wondering how the operation was going on, and imagining those fat tobacco-stained fingers, with the gold rings on them, cutting up old Gerald, when the 'Gnome' startled me by riding up alongside, saluting, and pointing to his chin, so I tried to buck up and look like a victorious General. The 'Gnome' smiled and dropped back again. I wonder what the people thought he had said to me.

As we got nearer the square, the massed bands were making a terrific noise, and what with that and the cheering, my little horse began to play the ass— *he* knew I wasn't Gerald if no one else did and took liberties. I got him in hand quickly enough, but I must say that the cheering was sufficient to make any animal lose his head.

The people were rather quiet when they saw the little forest-men leading the procession, they rather feared them and their terrible *machetes*, but began cheering loudly when the President's carriage rolled along, and then, as I passed, it was one continuous roar of '*Viva Don Geraldio!*' from the dense sea of heads and waving arms, on both sides of the streets, behind the lines of regular troops, and from the windows and even the roofs of the houses.

I saw the President shift rather uneasily in his seat as the shouting of Gerald's name drowned his altogether, but he kept raising his hat and bowing to left and right as if he was still the popular hero, doing it so vigorously that I saw his collar getting limp and the perspiration rolling down his neck.

The little Secretary's face was a picture. I don't know whether he knew whom I was, but I'm certain that, even now, he was worrying lest I should suddenly call on Gerald's army, seize the palace, and become Dictator, and I'm perfectly sure that I could have done it, or rather that Gerald could have done it, without the least trouble.

Almost before I knew it, we were passing the Hotel de l'Europe, and I looked up at that window again. It was full of Europeans, and one of them sang out, 'Three cheers for Gerald Wilson!' and they waved their hats and gave three grand cheers— a jolly homely sound it was, and I did wish that dear old Gerald could have heard it. Then—well, I did sit upright and tingled right down to Gerald's boots, because one of them yelled, 'One more for his brother!' that was for me, and they shouted, 'The two Wilsons!' and gave three grand cheers. I wonder how the President enjoyed them!

I took Gerald's polo helmet off, waved it to them, and saw them look puzzled, stretching their necks over the balcony to have another look.

The 'Gnome' darted to my side, touching his hat and shaking his head.

I knew well enough what he meant. My face and hair showed just sufficiently under the polo helmet, but I wasn't so much like Gerald without it.

Still, it was grand to be myself for half a second and hear those cheers.

The carriage had stopped in front of the cathedral, with its guard of insurgents, so I dismounted and followed the President up the steps, at the top of which the old Archbishop was waiting to receive him—with uplifted hands, just as he had stood when the coffin, with *La Buena Presidente* in it, had been borne up those steps three months before. By his side stood General Zorilla, grim and fierce-looking, and I did so wish that I knew enough Spanish to ask him, as a joke, whether he had any more of those blue warrants knocking about him. I wondered if he would have smiled.

In we all went, the Provisional Government trooping after us, and jolly glad I was to take off Gerald's polo helmet and get into the cool for a few minutes.

The cathedral was crowded with people, who stood up as we entered and turned their faces towards us. I saw some of them look surprised, and heard a murmur of '*No! Don Geraldio!*' when they saw me, and just as I was thinking what I ought to do, old Zorilla put his hand on my shoulder, whispered something in Spanish, and beckoned me out again.

I guessed what was wrong, and clapped the helmet on, but that wasn't it—Gerald's people were already giving trouble. They were to have marched out to some barracks, on the other side of the town, where a huge meal had been prepared for them, but they

were still pouring into the square, pushing the
regulars and the people back against the railings
on the other side, and didn't show any inclination
to leave it, although I could see their officers, going
in among them, pointing away to where they should
have marched. They were calling out for Gerald;
all over the square I could hear his name being
called—it was most extraordinary; I could *feel* that
trouble was brewing; they looked like wild cattle
driven into a strange place, very nervous and suspicious and liable at the least thing to stampede, and
I knew what would happen if they once got into a
panic. The regulars, too, looked 'jumpy,' uncertain
what they should do, and I saw some artillery men
stealthily opening an ammunition limber. The
townspeople were streaming out of the square as fast
as they could, and I knew that if a single shot was
fired, there'd be an awful massacre.

Zorilla made me get on my horse and we rode in
among them.

Immediately they saw me they broke out into
wild huzzahs, and a fierce roar of ' *Don Geraldio!
Don Geraldio! Viva Don Geraldio!* ' simply filled
the square. Zorilla, smiling grimly, rode away,
evidently thinking that he was better out of it.

I knew what I was expected to do, the 'Gnome'
was at my side looking anxiously at me, so I nodded
to him, pointed across the square, and began forcing
my way among them in the direction they ought to

go. The 'Gnome' sang out half-a-dozen orders in a stentorian voice, and the whole, huge, half-terrified, half fierce-looking mob came along after us, as good as gold.

Well, that was simply another triumphal procession for Gerald ; the little *machetos* were all round me, they fought for the honour of leading my horse, and, thank goodness, I got them out of the square and the city without anything going wrong.

Old Zorilla had evidently gone ahead of me and hidden away all the regulars, for there wasn't one to be seen. We marched through absolutely deserted streets, and though the little brown men hesitated a moment, and began to look troubled and suspicious, when, at last, we came to the barracks, the smell of the food was so tempting that they poured in after me. It was a huge rambling barracks, with an enormous parade-ground, crowded with tables, and an army of timid-looking people was waiting to serve food. I stayed there half an hour till the little brown chaps had forgotten all their grievances and suspicions, and then I bolted back to the palace, where the official banquet was to be held, and got through that all right, being placed among the foreign Ministers, who, of course, knew whom I was, and had heard of Gerald having been shot.

Mr. Arnstein, in his gorgeous uniform, bent over to tell me that he'd heard that the operation was going on all right, so that I was quite happy.

Every one was awfully nice to me about Gerald, and about my having taken his place successfully, but after lunch I wanted to get away, though I could not do so, for some time, because of every one wanting to congratulate me. Captain Roger Hill actually came up, too, but I'd been Gerald all the morning, I still had his clothes on, and, somehow or other, I felt like him and was very 'stand off the grass' when he tried to patronise me.

Fortunately, old Zorilla came to the rescue, his eyes gleaming very curiously, and he led me away to where a closed carriage was waiting.

We drove away from the palace, and when we'd got some distance off, he put his hand inside his tunic and pulled out—what do you think?—a blue packet—another of those warrants—and handed it to me.

It was the exact counterpart of the one which I had torn up that day in the Hotel de l'Europe, with Gerald's name written in among the printing, only this had Alvarez de Costa scrawled across the bottom instead of José Canilla.

Phew! my heart began thumping and I caught my breath for a moment, but Zorilla took it out of my hands, shrugged his shoulders, and began tearing it into little bits and throwing them out of the carriage window, one by one.

I simply hugged his thin old hand.

What a beastly cad de Costa was. Riding behind

him, two hours ago, I thought he meant mischief, and now I knew that he'd only been waiting till Gerald's men were safely outside the city again. I really don't know whether he had heard of Gerald's wound, and knew that I was only his brother or not, but if he had heard of it, I hated him all the more— the miserable ungrateful coward !

Presently the carriage stopped outside a big house, and Zorilla took me in through the courtyard. It turned out to be his own house, and Dr. Robson, Ginger, and Bob were there.

'How's Gerald?' I sang out, and gave a whoop of joy when Dr. Robson said, 'We found several holes to stitch up, I don't think we missed any, so I hope he'll do well.'

He stopped me making an ass of myself, 'Your brother is upstairs, you can't see him yet.'

Fancy Zorilla having taken him to his own house ! Wasn't that just what you'd have expected of the dear old man?

I was so brimming over with anger about the warrant that, for a second or two, I had an insane idea of riding off to those barracks and bringing back Gerald's men, seizing the palace and the President, and proclaiming Gerald Dictator. I'm certain that if only I'd known a few words of Spanish I could have done it.

I don't know whether Zorilla guessed what I was thinking about, but I caught him watching my face, smiling very grimly, and then he said, 'Inglese Minister com',' and took me away in his carriage.

We found him, and Zorilla evidently explained what had happened, for he said, 'Don't bother your head about your brother; if Zorilla won't execute the warrant, no one else will, and no one will dare to disturb him while he's in the General's house.'

He drove back with us, and then the two of them went away to the palace and had a pretty stormy interview with the President, leaving me to potter about with Bob and Ginger till it was possible to see old Gerald. They came back again before I was allowed to go into his room.

'We reduced him to pulp,' the British Minister said; 'he caved in immediately, and apologised to both of us. Zorilla threatened to bring in the insurgent troops and his own regulars and make him a prisoner if he didn't immediately cancel the warrant and re-appoint your brother Commander-in-Chief. He was petrified with funk and wriggled out of it like the ungainly toad he is.'

Then Dr. Robson called out that Gerald was asking for me, so I went softly upstairs into a big bedroom, where he lay, his face very puffy, with a nun on each side of his bed, looking after him. They dropped their eyes as I bowed. José was crouched in a corner gleaming at me like a faithful dog.

'I *am* so glad,' was all I could say, as I gripped Gerald's hand under the clothes.

'Everything go off well?' he asked.

'Yes, grand! the cheers for you made more noise than anything else.'

'De Costa will be getting jealous,' he smiled feebly. 'How did my chaps behave?'

'Had a little trouble getting them out of the city again,' I told him; 'but I went with them, and as soon as they smelt the grub in the barracks, they bolted for it.'

He smiled again, 'Good little chaps!'

Of course I did not tell him of that warrant.

'If he gets over the first three or four days safely he'll be all right,' Dr. Robson told me; and before the British Minister went away, I implored him to try and get leave for me to stay in Santa Cruz till then. He was awfully decent, drove straight away to the Club, found Captain Roger Hill, got leave not only for me but for Cousin Bob, and made us stay at his house too—which was jolly kind of him. As it was not far from General Zorilla's house we could very often run in to see Gerald for a few minutes at a time.

They sent our clothes up from the ship, and as Gerald went on very well indeed, we had quite a good time; but on the second day after he'd been shot, I had to get into my brother's things and lead his little brown chaps down to Los Angelos. They wouldn't go without him, were getting troublesome again, and the city was in deadly fear lest they should still take it into their heads to sack the place. The little chaps still took me for Gerald whilst I was on horseback, with his polo helmet jammed down over my head, but I don't imagine that most of the officers did so. They pretended that I was Gerald in order to keep their men under control, and were much too anxious to get back to their homes and plantations in the provinces to give the show away.

The 'Gnome' and José both came with me to help the deception, and I heard the 'Gnome' give a great sigh of relief when, eventually, the last of Gerald's men were put aboard those transports inside the breakwater. As each transport steamed out of the harbour, the little Santa Cruz ships cheered wildly and the men cheered back, ' *Viva los Horizontales!* ' ' *Viva de Costa!* ' ' *Viva Don Geraldio!* ' and as the last one steamed slowly round the lighthouse and passed the *Hercules*, I could still hear cries of ' *Viva Don Geraldio!* ' ' *Viva los Inglesas!* '

I stood on the wharf for some time, watching the transports steaming along the coast, some northwards, the others to the south, and I really felt very sorry to see the last of the little chaps with whom I had gone through so many exciting days. I could see that the 'Gnome,' however relieved he was for them to go away, felt as I did, and they seemed to have had so little reward for all they'd done in the last three months that you couldn't help feeling that, after all their pluck and hardships, they hadn't gained much for themselves.

We rode slowly up the mountain to Santa Cruz, and at that sharp turning, where we had seen the yellow and green flag last flying, we stopped and for a minute watched the transports, little smoky dots on the glistening sea, a thousand feet below us, as they carried the brave little chaps to their homes.

On the fifth morning after the operation, Bob and I had to wish Gerald good-bye, and go back to the *Hercules*. He was going on grandly.

'You'll have a pretty big job as Commander-in-Chief when you get well,' I said jokingly, but he shook his head. 'No, Billums! I shall chuck it and try and make some money on the estate again. I'm rather bored with revolutions and fighting just at present, and want to get away from here. I'll get that little chap you call the "Gnome" to come with me, and I'll see if I can't pay off some of my debts.'

No one had told Gerald about the warrant, so it wasn't funk which made him think of leaving Santa Cruz, and you can guess how pleased I was to hear him say this, and how jolly pleased the mater would be too.

'We've had an exciting three months of it, old chap, haven't we? but I'm going to take a rest. We've done all this fighting and killing, marching and starving, and we've only turned out one bad

President to put another, just as bad, in his place.
The game's not worth the candle.'

At the back of my mind I really thought the same,
and I only hoped that he would still stick to his
determination when he did get strong again. I had
to leave him there, in Zorilla's house—with the two
nuns and José to look after him—and Bob and I
rode, for the last time, through that square.

Dear old Zorilla had lent us horses, and he and
the 'Gnome' came with us along the road past San
Sebastian and beyond the spot where Bob, the 'Angel,'
and I had knocked over the carriage with the *Hercules'*
midshipmen, right along till the road began to drop
down towards Los Angelos.

I shook the old man's hand—I felt that Gerald
would be safe with him—and I gripped the 'Gnome's'
hand too ; it was all I could do, for we could not speak
each other's languages, and we rode away. At the
next turning we looked back and they were still there,
watching us, the General on his big black horse and
the 'Gnome' on a little white one—showing up against
the sky. We waved our hats, they gravely waved
theirs, and that was the last we saw of them. We
both felt intensely miserable, and didn't say a word
for quite half an hour, when Bob at last said, 'Do
you know what those two remind me of?—the picture
of Don Quixote and Sancho Panza.'

I smiled at him. No knight of old could have
been a grander chap than was old Zorilla, and I

thought of what the British Minister had told me just before we left him. 'The first time in his life that old Zorilla has ever been known to disobey an order was when he tore your brother's warrant into pieces.'

Funnily enough, the one thing that always makes me feel so glad, when I now think of this three months, was that I rescued his black horse, and was the means of him getting it back again.

CHAPTER XVIII

The *Hector* goes Home

Written by Sub-Lieutenant William Wilson, R.N

I HAVE not much more to tell you.

The *Hercules* went off to Bermuda the morning after Bob and I had come back from Santa Cruz, and we waited on deck till the long lines of towering black mountains were lost to sight. I couldn't bear to leave Gerald up among them, although he was in Zorilla's house, and practically out of danger, as far as the wound was concerned, but I'd learnt enough about politics, and the way they were 'run' in the Republic, to feel sure that his greatest danger lay in the jealousy of the New President, and that he would never be safe in the country—not even if he did resign the Command of the forces.

We ran through the 'Narrows' five days later and anchored in Grassy Bay, off the naval dockyard of Ireland Island, Bermuda. It was rather a shock to see the poor old *Hector's* two funnels and damaged foremast sticking up behind the dockyard wall, and I noticed that Bob and one or two of the others looked very white when they saw them.

As soon as the repairs to her ward-room had been completed the officers moved out of the gun-room, and I and my mids. were sent aboard her again. It didn't make much difference to me, but a good many of the mids. did not like going back a little bit. The still half-dismantled ship had too many sad memories for them, and I am sorry to say that Cousin Bob began to mope again—everything reminded him too much of his poor little chum.

Every morning, before breakfast, I made them all run round the dockyard to Moresby Plain, for a hockey practice, below the little Naval Club, and whilst we remained here we had two very pleasant games against the *Hercules'* gun-room, but as we had none to fill, properly, the 'Angel's' place at 'centre-half,' or Barton's at 'outside-right,' were beaten both times.

'What a difference, Ginger, old chap,' I said, as we watched them scrambling into the tea-house together, after the match, just as chummy as they could be.

'Difference!' Perkins, who was standing near us, said, smiling, 'I should think it was a difference. They won't leave a thimbleful of tea or a bun in the place, and I shall have to go without any, I suppose.'

'It's taken a good deal to make 'em friends, hasn't it?' Ginger said sadly.

A fortnight later Gerald sent me a telegram, as he had promised, to say that he was allowed out of bed, and I knew that he had sent the same message home to the mater, and felt awfully glad.

Nothing more happened at Bermuda worth telling about; we had to work very hard indeed; in six weeks' time the ship was seaworthy enough to steam home, and one beautiful Sunday morning in May, the *Hercules* and ourselves anchored behind Plymouth breakwater.

As you can imagine, the poor old *Hector* was a great object of curiosity, and paddle-boats were bringing people off from shore, and steaming round her, all day long.

Next morning two dockyard tugs made fast alongside us, we slipped our moorings, and as their paddles began churning the water and we commenced to move up harbour, Captain Roger Hill unbent, for the first time in his life, and 'cheered ship.'

'Three cheers for the *Hector*,' we heard his Commander shout, and the whole crew swarmed on the upperworks and sent us three great cheers.

'Tut, tut, lad!' our Skipper stuttered, dropping his eyeglass, '"Old Spats" has forgotten himself. Look at him! He's actually waving his cap.'

He nodded to the Commander, whose great roaring voice bellowed out, 'Three cheers for Captain Roger Hill and the *Hercules*,' and we all shouted.

We were taken up harbour and put into dry dock immediately, and we heard that we should probably stay there for several months.

As soon as it could be arranged, we got up a subscription for a tablet to the memory of all our people who'd been killed in that fight with *La Buena Presidente*, and got permission to place it in Portsmouth Dockyard Chapel, where you can see it now.

There were, unfortunately, a great number of names to go on it—Montague, Clegg, Bigge, Pearson, the 'Forlorn Hope' and his chum the 'Shadow' (whose name was put there because he died as a result of the fight), Barton, the 'Angel,' Marchant (the Inkslinger), the cheery, good-tempered, little Captain's Clerk, and below these the names of fifty-four men—several had died of their wounds at Princes' Town Colonial Hospital.

Cousin Bob still moped and slept badly, often waking the whole of the gun-room flat by shrieking in his sleep, so that I worried very much about him.

I told the Captain.

'Well, boy! What d'you want me to do? The Fleet Surgeon has been speaking about him too.'

'I think it would be best to send him home for as long as you can, sir,' I said.

'Right oh, lad! Tell him to leave his address and I'll wire for him when I want him. Have a bit of lunch?'

I stayed to lunch with him, and we talked about Gerald.

'Grand chap! grand chap! a little too haughty

for me. Grand chap though—never thanked me for taking him that hydraulic machinery.'

'But he never thought you knew about it, sir,' I said, surprised.

He polished his eyeglass very carefully, screwed it into his eye, and then very deliberately winked at me.

I shipped Cousin Bob off home that very day and was jolly glad to get him away from the ship, although, as a matter of fact, I need not have been in such a hurry, because all the mids. were sent to other ships a few days later. Still he managed to get a little longer leave than the others, and I had a very grateful letter from his sister Daisy.

I had a long letter, too, from Gerald some time afterwards. He had gone back to the rubber plantation with José and the 'Gnome,' and *said* that he was jolly glad to get back there again, start rebuilding the house and planting more trees, but I feared that he was of much too restless a disposition to remain there for long.

Old Zorilla had taken on his job as Commander-in-Chief, and Gerald said that things were going on swimmingly, though what actual difference the change of President had made, he was hanged if he could tell. Little Navarro was limping about Santa Cruz as cheerful as ever, and every one wanted to be remembered to me.

Well, however long I live, I shall never forget them.

formation can be obtained at www.ICGtesting.com
the USA
1534200116

BV00003B/63/P

9 781633 910362

CPSIA in
Printed in
BVOW08
433634